· CLASSIC ·
FRENCH COOKING
FOR TODAY

· CLASSIC · FRENCH COOKING FOR TODAY

A Practical Guide to Healthy French Cuisine

· *Christophe Buey* ·

JUNIPER

Dedication

To Sabine and Patrick Brassart who supported me and treated me like a son. Thank you for these eight years of trust, may this continue throughout our lives.

First published in Great Britain in 1987
by Sidgwick & Jackson Limited
1 Tavistock Chambers, Bloomsbury Way
London WC1A 2SG

This edition published in 1991
by Juniper Books London, an
Imprint of Swallow Publishing Limited
260 Pentonville Road
London N1 9JY

Editors: Susan Fleming and Anne Yelland
Art director: Elaine Partington
Designers: Judith Robertson and Su Martin
Photographer: Tim Imrie
Home economist: Mandy Wagstaff
Assistant editor: Catherine Tilley
Studio: Del & Co

ISBN 1-85-605-0971

Printed in Hong Kong by Imago Publishing

Title page The vegetable garden at at Clapham House, home of l'École de Cuisine Française Sabine de Mirbeck. Page 1 Clapham House. Page 30 *Gougère* and *Pissaladière à la Niçoise*. Page 46 *Peperonata, Terrine de Foies de Volaille, Tourte aux Épinards* and *Potage Crècy*. Page 80 *Bar Farci en Chemise, Huîtres au Gratin* and *Filets de Sole Pochés au Vin Blanc*. Page 104 *Ballotine de Faisan, Poulet Sauté à l'Estragon* and *Escalope de Veau Woronoff*. Page 150 *Salade de Champignons de Sabine, Salade Niçoise* and *Salade d'Endives*. Page 164 *Tarte aux Fraises*

CONTENTS

FOREWORD

CHRISTOPHE BUEY AND SABINE DE MIRBECK-BRASSART

All art evolves constantly, and the art of French cooking would be lost if French chefs did not move with the times. Cooking methods must be adapted to suit changes in lifestyle, and that means finding a way to accommodate today's stressful and sedentary habits. In short, modern food must be lighter and healthier than before.

So the concept of cooking traditional French food with health and nutrition in mind was developed in our school, not as a break with traditional French cuisine, but as a continuation of it, modified to today's tastes and demands. We teach both traditional French recipes and their modern counterparts at our cookery school as part of our courses, and comparisons between the two have fascinated both staff and students.

Although the concept of modern recipes is not the invention of a single person, its development owes considerably to our head chef, Christophe Buey. When my husband Patrick Brassart (who was a member of the board of the Cordon Bleu de Paris) decided to open a cookery school in England, I was happy to become *directrice*, but I was faced with the important and delicate task of appointing a teacher. Should I, as they did at the Cordon Bleu de Paris, appoint a well-known chef with an international reputation, such as Monsieur Pellaprat, or should I choose a more academic sort of person who would lack the knowledge and experience of a great chef but have the communicative flair of a teacher?

Despite his youth – he was twenty-six at the time – we decided to give this opportunity to Christophe, who had earned the Diplôme de l'École Hotelière de Lausanne, and allow him to create his own methods of teaching our students the classic techniques and skills. We felt that his original approach would open the doors of the French culinary arts to competent amateurs as well as to those who wanted to become professional chefs.

At the time, this choice was very much a gamble, but one we have never regretted, as Christophe has made an invaluable contribution to the formation of what we hope is a truly professional cookery school. Not the least of it is his role in the development of a new form of cookery which we hope will affirm the flexibility and continuing supremacy of French cuisine.

To him, to the rest of the excellent staff at our school, and to everyone else involved in the production of this book, I should like to say, '*Merci beaucoup, et bonne santé!*'

Sabine de Mirbeck Brassart

SABINE DE MIRBECK-BRASSART

INTRODUCTION

Everyone involved in and concerned with food has long been aware of a major shift in dietary habits – a shift towards food that not only tastes good but which is also good for the health of the body. The bourgeoise and haute traditions of classic French cuisine have been the first to fall from grace because of their use of ingredients which contain saturated animal fats, salt, sugar, and a lot of alcohol – all now disapproved of by the medical establishment – and too little dietary fibre. Nouvelle and other related cuisines have attempted to redress the balance by limiting or entirely omitting potentially harmful ingredients, but in so doing have been criticized for concentrating on appearance at the cost of quantity – and, occasionally, even of flavour.

Our modern classic cuisine which has been evolved to satisfy the concerns of the most health-conscious gourmet, is an alternative to all of these – while, at the same time, it retains many of the principles, techniques and flavours which have for so long characterized the very best of French cooking. It provides a well-balanced cuisine that favours the use of fresh fruit, fresh vegetables, the very best of white meat, fish and wholefoods, and avoids foods that have been artificially flavoured, processed and refined. Fats too are avoided where possible: oils high in polyunsaturates are used in place of the butter of traditional French cuisine; low-fat strained yoghurt is used instead of cream – and if cream *is* called for, we use the lighter whipping or single rather than double cream. Herbs are important for their wonderful aroma, delicious flavours and their general beneficial effects, and many of them reduce the need for salt – another potentially harmful ingredient which we over-use these days. Desserts rely more on fruit, thus they contain more fibre, and much less flour, sugar and cream in general.

Many of the recipes in this book are versions of the traditional classic cuisines, redesigned so that they are healthier without sacrificing flavour. The favoured cooking methods are also those which retain the maximum freshness and nutritional value of foods – poaching, steaming, sweating, braising and casseroling.

This is not a dieting book. It does not involve calorie counting, but examines every recipe for its fat, sugar, salt and fibre content. To show more clearly what the concept does and what it can achieve, we have in fact compared our recipes with those from which they were adapted: the comparison of ingredients, and the calorie, and protein, carbohydrate and fat contents (in grams), will illustrate much more vividly than can even the most enthusiastic words, just how 'derivative' in one way, but 'revolutionary' in another, our cuisine is.

CUISINE BOURGEOISE

Cuisine bourgeoise is family cuisine of good, satisfying, honest – and substantial – home cooking. Our version can also be good, satisfying and honest – but without the calorie-rich substance of many bourgeoise dishes, as below. The original recipe for *Potage Orge Perlé Brunoise* contained butter and flour, as well as the barley to thicken. A lot of double cream was also added; in our version we are quite happy with a little single cream mixed with Greek yoghurt.

POTAGE ORGE PERLÉ BRUNOISE

Cuisine Bourgeoise original	Our version
25 g (1 oz) butter	*1 dsp grapeseed oil*
100 g (4 oz) onions	*100 g (4 oz) onions*
100 g (4 oz) leeks	*100 g (4 oz) leeks*
100 g (4 oz) carrots	*100 g (4 oz) carrots*
100 g (4 oz) celery	*100 g (4 oz) celery*
100 g (4 oz) pearl barley	*50 g (2 oz) wholemeal barley*
1.5 litres (2½ pt) stock	*1.5 litres (2½ pt) stock*
salt	*salt*
freshly ground black pepper	*freshly ground black pepper*
150 ml (5 fl oz) double cream	*50 ml (2 fl oz) single cream*
1 egg yolk	*50 g (2 oz) Greek yoghurt*

Proteins	= 39.12	Proteins	= 39.41
Fats	= 103.34	Fats	= 26.38
Carbohydrates	= 182.82	Carbohydrates	= 122.10
TOTAL CALORIES	2055.69	TOTAL CALORIES	1831.25
CALORIES PER PERSON	513.92	CALORIES PER PERSON	457.81

HAUTE CUISINE

Haute cuisine was the cuisine of the city restaurants – the cuisine of the chef with his kitchen brigade of *sous*-chefs and their individual specialities. Most of the ingredients used were expensive and rich – truffles, *foie gras*, etc. – and the presentation was elaborate and time-consuming, often to the detriment of the food itself. Our adaptation has absorbed the techniques and skills of haute cuisine but has cut out the rich ingredients and concentrated on healthier methods of cooking.

BALLOTINE DE FAISAN

Haute Cuisine original		Our version	
1 pheasant, about 750 g (a good 1½ lb)		*1 pheasant, about 750 g (a good 1½ lb)*	
125 g (4½ oz) pork fat (to wrap only)		*1½ tsp grapeseed oil*	
salt		*salt*	
freshly ground black pepper		*freshly ground black pepper*	
250 ml (8 fl oz) Madeira		*250 ml (8 fl oz) Madeira*	
MIREPOIX		MIREPOIX	
1 thyme sprig		*1 thyme sprig*	
1 bayleaf		*1 bayleaf*	
100 ml (3½ fl oz) stock		*100 ml (3½ fl oz) stock*	
20 g (¾ oz) butter		–	
20 g (¾ oz) flour		–	
STUFFING		STUFFING	
30 g (1¼ oz) pork fat		–	
1 shallot		*2 shallots*	
60 g (2¼ oz) foie gras		*pheasant liver*	
20 g (¾ oz) mushrooms		*100 g (4 oz) mushrooms*	
110 g (4½ oz) veal		*150 g (5 oz) veal*	
100 g (4 oz) pork		*100 g (4 oz) pork*	
5 egg yolks		*1 egg*	
100 g (4 oz) white sauce		*50 g (2 oz) Greek yoghurt*	
		a pinch of ground allspice	
Proteins	= 229	Proteins	= 216
Fats	= 181	Fats	= 37
Carbohydrates	= 52	Carbohydrates	= 18
TOTAL CALORIES	2684	TOTAL CALORIES	1546
CALORIES PER PERSON	671.11	CALORIES PER PERSON	386

NOUVELLE CUISINE

Nouvelle cuisine was the response of chefs to demands – from businessmen and regular restaurant eaters in the main – for lighter, less rich food. Technically speaking, it is not a '*nouvelle*' (new) cuisine, as it is soundly based on classic French cuisine, but it places more emphasis on healthier methods of cooking and preparation, and uses unusual and fashionable ingredients which did not have a place in traditional French cuisine. It has also led to the emergence of the chef as artist, arranging foods to make a feast for the eye as well as the palate. However, many chefs and restaurant proprietors have taken advantage of the new cuisine's popularity, serving ridiculously small portions at astronomical prices, and breaking the sensible balance of ingredients. Our cuisine, however, has embraced all the original precepts of the nouvelle cuisine, while giving decent portions and concentrating on the highly important matter of correct and sensible balances of flavours and nutrients.

FILETS MIGNON DE PORC À LA NORMANDE

Nouvelle Cuisine original		Our version	
400 g (14 oz) pork tenderloin		*750 g (a good 1½ lb) pork tenderloin*	
salt		*salt*	
freshly ground black pepper		*freshly ground black pepper*	
1 tbsp oil		*grapeseed oil*	
25 g (1 oz) butter		–	
40 g (1½ oz) each of carrot, turnip, leek and celery		*200 g (7 oz) each of carrot, turnip, leek and celery*	
–		*1 cooking apple*	
1 shallot		*1 shallot*	
25 ml (1 fl oz) Calvados		*25 ml (1 fl oz) Calvados*	
150 ml (5 fl oz) cider		*150 ml (5 fl oz) cider*	
500 ml (18 fl oz) stock		*500 ml (18 fl oz) stock*	
500 ml (18 fl oz) double cream		*100 ml (3½ fl oz) whipping cream*	
Proteins	= 107.77	Proteins	= 178
Fats	= 315.07	Fats	= 107.05
Carbohydrates	= 293.12	Carbohydrates	= 183
TOTAL CALORIES	3239	TOTAL CALORIES	2425
CALORIES PER PERSON	810	CALORIES PER PERSON	606

To conclude, this is no passing or dictatorial culinary fad – abolishing certain ingredients, insisting on the use of others. It is a sensible, highly professional and affectionate rethinking of the best cuisine in the world – and is probably the next great movement in culinary history.

CHRISTOPHE BUEY

HOW TO USE THIS BOOK

This section is designed to help you – the cook – to use this book as efficiently as possible. Even though the recipes are not difficult, there are certain 'lessons' to be learned before they should be attempted. On the contrary, they have been especially evolved so they can be easily understood and followed – even the ones which require up to three days and three stages of preparation (don't panic, each day's work only takes up to an hour at most). But these lessons are necessary because we have used a form of shorthand in describing certain ingredients, techniques, pieces of equipment, and so on. You need to know, for instance, what is special about Greek yoghurt (and how to 'manufacture' an alternative if that is unavailable); you need to know the constituents of *fines herbes*, a *bouquet garni* or a *mirepoix*; and once you know that 'cut into *chiffonade*' means simply 'cut into thin strips', you can cook with the ease of a professional!

There are four essential elements in cooking, all four as important as one another, and they are closely interlinked.

The first element is *the cook*, with his or her interest in and love of palatable, good and healthy food.

Equipment is the second element, through which the cook can apply his or her knowledge with confidence. This equipment should be the very best you can afford, and we have prepared a list of what we consider vital for good cooking. A fat-separator, for instance (see page 13), is a necessity for all our fat-free dishes.

The ingredients, the third element, are obviously highly important. All foods – meats, fish, fruit, vegetables and oils, flours, etc. – should be the very freshest and best possible to produce the highest quality and healthiest dish or meal. 'Choose the best or refuse' would be our motto, except that compromise might occasionally be necessary – when, say, you have to use dried herbs because fresh ones are not available. The more often we, as consumers, insist on the best, the more suppliers will be forced to supply just that!

We have prepared a brief list of the majority of ingredients used in this book, which will help you to understand the particular ingredient and how best to use it. It also contains tips on what to look for when shopping. Do read this list – it shouldn't be a chore – before attempting any of the recipes.

The techniques are the final element – the cooking techniques favoured by us, and the cutting, chopping, preparation and garnishing techniques which are basic to French cuisine in general. Many of these we have illustrated as well as described in words so that you can fully understand what the recipe means and demands.

Finally, it should be understood that this is not a dogmatic cuisine – nothing could ever be exact or final in a recipe. We have found at the school that although every student receives exactly the same tuition and uses exactly the same basic ingredients, the results always taste slightly different. Each student will have added to his or her dish their own individual attention, interest and love – with perhaps a pinch more of this or that – and this is what we should like you to do too. Add your own 'signature' to our basic recipes – and live and cook happily, wisely and healthily!

You do not have to be an expert gardener to grow your own herbs. In fact, you can produce a good selection in a single pot, as I have done here. This contains a basic selection: parsley, sage, rosemary, thyme, sweet marjoram, chives, mint and fennel.

INGREDIENTS

Allspice The dried berry of a tropical plant, used with cloves to give a strong and spicy taste to a stock, sauce, or stew. Use sparingly.
Apple juice Buy sugar-free juices with no additives or preservatives.
Asparagus Look for freshness. Stale or old asparagus spears appear dry and have droopy, soggy tips. Rich in vitamins A, B, B_2 and C.
Aubergine Look for medium heavy ones with bright, shiny, unblemished skins. When cooking in oil be careful, as they can absorb vast quantities!

Baking powder A mixture of acid and alkaline substances which, when heated and/or moistened, produce carbon dioxide gas which helps cakes rise.
Barley Whole barley is high in vitamin B and full of protein. It is the oldest of the cereal crops and has a slightly nutty taste.
Basil A very important herb used mostly in dishes from the Mediterranean where it grows well. Available in more northerly climates in the spring and summer. It grows well in a sheltered south-facing spot. Preserve it for the winter in jars of olive oil. The oil, in small quantity, can also be used to prepare salad dressings. Basil is a natural tranquillizer, and is good for stomach troubles.
Bass, sea As with all fish, look for bright eyes, shiny and firmly attached scales, firm flesh and a pleasant smell. Sea bass is costly, but has a lovely flavour. Eat as fresh as possible.
Bayleaf The Romans used it as a symbol of peace, victory and triumph, thus the 'laurels' of success, the wreaths of leaves with which they crowned the heads of caesars. However, it is most efficient used in cooking: its strong aroma flavours, and it is also antiseptic and digestive. Used mostly in stocks, sauces and stews, and in a *bouquet garni.*
Beans French beans or dwarf green beans. Simply top and tail, and de-string if tough. Cook very quickly. Buy small, crisp regular-sized beans which break easily when raw. Rich in vitamin C, potassium, calcium and iron.
Broccoli Look for bright compact tight buds; yellowing buds indicate poor quality. Cook in very little salted boiling water for minimum time to retain colour. Contains vitamins A, B and C.
Butter We always use the unsalted kind.

Cabbage, red Available all year around. Rich source of vitamins B and C. Like all cabbage, it loses a lot of its nourishment during cooking, so cut finely to keep cooking time short.
Cabbage, savoy Rich in vitamins A and C. Buy tight, firm heavy ones. The winter variety has wrinkled leaves. Remove outer leaves and stem before using.
Calvados Apple brandy from Normandy.
Capers Small immature flower buds of a tree which grows all around the Mediterranean, which are pickled. Look for large soft capers which are grey-green in colour. Always keep in liquid as, uncovered, they develop a nasty taste.
Caraway A very strongly flavoured seed used as an aromatic in a *court-bouillon.* Cooked with cabbage, it helps certain disorders.
Carrots Buy young, small ones which are best washed and cooked unpeeled. Used in *mirepoix* as well as stocks, vegetable garnishes, etc. Carrots contain iron, phosphorus, vitamins A, B and C, and the carotene content strengthens the eyes!
Cauliflower Buy ones with good white/cream colour with little foliage, and which are heavy for their size. Cook with care as they are easily ruined if overcooked.
Celeriac (celery root) Same family as celery, has similar taste. Knobbly root vegetable, best peeled with a knife. Discolours when exposed to air, so rub with lemon to stop oxidation. Excellent puréed as a vegetable, or grated and marinated for salads.
Celery Choose crisp, tight heads. At its best after frosts have started.
Champagne Sparkling wine from the Champagne region of France, the area around Reims and Epernay. Only wine made in this area and using grapes from this region can be called 'champagne'. Other so-called champagnes are made by the 'méthode champenoise', and are often very good substitutes, especially in cooking.
Chard Popular in Mediterranean countries as it continues to produce during winter and spring. Similar to spinach, which is a good alternative. Difficult to find in UK and USA.
Chervil A constituent of *fines herbes.* Delicate taste of aniseed. Stimulating, diuretic, good for blood circulation and weak livers. Use always fresh as cooking destroys its virtues.
Chicken If you don't eat the skin, chicken, like all white meats, is much better for health than dark red meats. Try to buy a whole chicken with giblets – useful for sauces, etc. Clean well before cooking.
Chicken livers A very rich source of iron. Can now be bought frozen in supermarkets. Remove the tubes and membranes before cooking.
Chicory A slightly bitter vegetable. Can be eaten raw or cooked. Look for white, firm, crisp plants. Often confused with endive because that's its name in the USA.
Chives A member of the onion family: this perennial plant which grows well in temperate climates. Leave a few flowers to grow and bloom, but remove most to produce more leaves – herbs. Cut often to obtain a regular supply. A constituent of *fines herbes.*
Cider Apple-fermented drink. Like wine it can be dry or sweet, still or sparkling.
Cinnamon A good antiseptic as well as natural preservative, it is best fresh in sticks of bark. Cut a piece off and cook with it. Remove after cooking. Mostly used in sweet dishes but can also be used to give an unusual flavour to a savoury sauce.
Cloves The flower buds of an Asian tree dried in the sun. Extremely strong. A very good antiseptic and a well-known natural preservative. Use in casseroles, soups and stocks as well as in pickles, chutneys and preserves. For stews, prick into a small onion so they are easier to retrieve after cooking.
Cognac A brandy distilled from wine, made around the town of Cognac. Use a relatively cheap French brandy for cooking – a 3-star for instance.
Coriander Used either as a fresh herb like parsley for its unusual flavour, or as seeds mixed in with peppercorns and ground as a flavouring, seasoning agent. Sometimes used in *fines herbes.*
Courgettes Low in calories, 90 per cent water, rich in vitamin C. Often need to be sprinkled with a little salt to remove some of this water so they cook properly. Do not forget to rinse well before using.
Cream We use only whipping or, occasionally, single – both lower in fat than double – and we use very little.
Crème de riz (rice flour) Ground rice, useful thickening agent. Gluten-free.
Cucumber A very refreshing vegetable because of its high water content. Always buy young ones. Cooked cucumber is an interesting alternative to courgettes or marrow.

Dijon mustard Pale-coloured, prepared mustard with vinegar and spices. A speciality of Dijon in the heart of France. The whole grain version is delicious too!
Dill Sweet aniseed-flavoured herb which is antiseptic and helps digestion. Excellent with fish but delicious, too, added on its own to a sauce. The seeds can be crushed like pepper to season a dish.
Dover sole Best of the flat fish. Its flesh is

white, firm, delicate and easily digestible. Sole, along with skate, is the exception to eating fish as fresh as possible. The flavour can be enhanced by keeping the fish for a couple of days after landing.

Eggs We cook with size 3.
Emmenthal A hard, cooked Swiss cheese, with a mild flavour, distinctive because of its holes.
Endive A lettuce with curled leaves and a bitter taste, often blanched.

Fennel The bulb fennel – Florence fennel – is delicious raw or cooked. The herb fennel, like dill, has a strong aniseed flavour; it also has the same antiseptic and digestive qualities as dill. Fennel seeds are also used in cooking.
Fines herbes A mixture of parsley, chervil, tarragon, chives and coriander in equal proportion, which adds iron, calcium and vitamins (especially C). Best used raw and chopped at the last moment on to any savoury dish or sauce. The combination depends on the availability of the herbs, but each addition makes its own flavour contribution.
Flour We always use plain 75% wholemeal flour or strong white flour for bread making.

Garlic Strong flavour, and size of cloves vary, so use to taste. An easy way to peel them is to crush cloves gently with the hand or flat of a knife. Has disinfectant properties and thus is good for cleaning the blood, as well as for a lot of ailments.
Gelatine Protein substance which sets liquids. We use the leaf kind: simply soak it in cold water until soft, then add to the warm mixture so that it melts, and then leave to cool and set. If unobtainable, use powdered gelatine and follow manufacturers' instructions. Vegetarians should use agar-agar, made from seaweed – and tasteless, fortunately!
Gherkins These are not necessarily baby cucumbers, but a special variety of cucumber found in the Caribbean. Pickled in vinegar, and used as a condiment or garnish, or in sauces.
Grand marnier Orange-flavoured liqueur.
Grapeseed oil A very pure oil, light in polyunsaturated fats.
Greek yoghurt This is the thick, smooth type which normally has some whey running out. It also contains more fat than ordinary yoghurt, so use as we do instead of cream and not instead of yoghurt! If none is available use ordinary live yoghurt and leave overnight in a sieve lined with muslin on top of a bowl.
Gruyère A hard, cooked Swiss cheese, with strong flavour, with holes like Emmenthal.

Haddock fillets, smoked Look for fillets that are pale yellow in colour; a bright yellow means dyes have been used. Also known as Finnan haddock, after the village of Findon, near Aberdeen.
Hake A member of the cod family, easily boned. Best from May to September.
Herbes de Provence A blend of dried Mediterranean herbs such as thyme, bay, oregano, rosemary and savory. Add sparingly to meat, fish and vegetable dishes, as it is very strong. Its wonderful aroma will evoke the evening smells of Provençal wild herb fields!
Herbs, fresh Now available in supermarkets – but it is easy to grow your own! Use dried if necessary, rehydrating them first, or allowing time for them to do so in a sauce. Use half quantities of dried which are stronger than fresh.
Honey Different honeys have slightly different tastes. Clear or runny honey is easier to use.

Lamb Do not buy muddy looking meat. Look for bright, firm textured meat which does not smell and has a deep, even, rose colour.
Leek Member of onion family, often called the 'asparagus of the poor'. Rich in vitamin C, iron and fibre. It needs very careful washing to remove dirt and grit trapped between layers. Buy fresh young, small leeks with a large proportion of white. The 'wrapping' of a *bouquet garni.*
Lettuce Rich in vitamins A and C, iron and minerals. Many varieties are available. Wash and dry well, and keep in the fridge to crisp. Low in calories, less than 20 per 100 g (4 oz).

Madeira A fortified wine. Buy either Sercial (slightly nutty, dry, light blend) or Verdelho (sweeter, and better with cakes or soup). Use sherry or port as an alternative.
Mangetout A variety of pea. The pods are topped and tailed and eaten whole when young. Buy bright green, young, crisp ones.
Milk A range of milk is available, from full fat to skimmed. A general good balance is semi-skimmed which has half the fat of whole milk.
Mint A deliciously aromatic herb, refreshing, antiseptic, and digestive (thought to be aphrodisiac too!) Makes a good tea.
Mushrooms Buy small, tight button mushrooms, often called 'Paris mushrooms'. Cultivated mushrooms never have the flavour of wild ones. The large open cap mushrooms have a better flavour but don't look as good for a garnish.

Nutmeg A tropical 'nut' or 'kernel', best grated fresh. Use sparingly in soufflés and stews as it is very strong. (It's also said to be soporific and digestive.)

Olives We use the black, ripe ones (green are unripened olives that are pickled, having been split and soaked to remove bitterness). Drain and wash well to remove brine or vinegar flavours. The best are those from the South of France, Italy or Greece, marinated in olive oil. Add a little *herbes de Provence* and leave to marinate for a couple of weeks before eating or using!
Olive oil Buy the cold press, first pressing, virgin oil. It is expensive to buy, but only a little is needed. Complement it with grapeseed oil.
Onion One of the most basic ingredients in all cooking. A useful tip if they make you cry is to wash your hands and knife under running cold water.
Oregano This herb is more widely available dried. Widely used in Italian cuisine where the fresh sun-cultivated herb is very strong. Delicious in sauces and stews and on our *Pissaladière.*

Parsley Rich in iron, calcium and vitamins. Use raw for best results. The stalks are used in a *bouquet garni* and to flavour stocks and sauces, and the leaves or sprigs chopped or whole, are added at the last moment to the dish. A constituent of *fines herbes.*
Partridge When buying, choose plump birds with supple skin and smooth, firmly attached feathers. Avoid badly shot birds and ones which have an unpleasant smell.
Passion fruit juice If not available use the 'tropical' blend available in supermarkets.
Peppers, sweet Peppers change as they ripen from green through yellow to red. They have little food value, and are more prized for their flavour, although those grown under glass are rather insipid.
Pernod French aniseed-flavoured liquor.
Petits Pois (baby peas) Frozen ones are easier to come by and in fact are often better than old peas bought in the market. However, fresh garden peas have an inimitable flavour.
Petit-Suisse Soft unripened cheese, available now in supermarkets.
Pheasant Most common game bird, normally sold in a brace (hen and cock). The hen is the better eating bird. Always hang a bird unplucked, for 2-3 days maximum. Young birds have pliable beaks and the wing tip feather is pointed.
Pine nuts or kernels From the Stone pine, a Mediterranean tree. They have a slightly buttery taste, especially when roasted.
Pistachio nuts Edible and expensive green nuts easily removed from the shell. They have a mild, sweet, nutty taste.
Pork The tenderloin or fillet has the lowest fat content.

Port A full-bodied red wine fermented with brandy.
Potato Many different varieties. Buy potatoes that are heavy for their size. When fresh they are rich in vitamin C and potassium. Steaming helps retain these. Peel very thinly if at all. Potatoes are easily frost- and light-damaged, so be careful about storage.
Potato starch Non-wheat flours are richer in protein and are good in gluten-free diets as a substitute for flour. Useful thickening agent.

Rabbit A white meat, now becoming fashionable again. Unlike hare, it ought to be eaten within days of being caught or shot. It is a cheaper and healthier alternative to other meats.
Ricotta A very good Italian low-fat soft cheese. Push through a sieve to eliminate lumps.
Roquefort Blue cheese made from sheep's milk. Strong, sharp taste, but creamy texture.
Rosemary A constituent of the *herbes de Provence* mix, this is a strongly flavoured evergreen herb. It is antiseptic and a stimulant. Especially good with meat dishes like lamb. It can be used also as part of a *bouquet garni*.
Rum A spirit distilled from sugar cane residues. Use the darker varieties, they have a better flavour.

Sage Coming from the Latin word 'salvere', to save or heal. It has an aromatic, slightly bitter and very powerful flavour. Dries very well. A pinch of sage infused in boiling milk helps prevent the start of a cold. It helps the digestion of fatty meats. Do not use with parsley or chervil as they do not combine well.
Salmon, smoked Buy the wild kind, it is worth the extra expense. If buying to use as a flavouring, as for a soufflé or quiche, try to buy trimmings, often a lot cheaper. When buying, look for firm flesh which is moist and has a true smoked colour, not bright and artificial.
Salt Use 'Lo-Salt', or raw grey sea salt – and very little of it.
Savory A constituent of the *herbes de Provence* mix, excellent for the digestion (it is thought to be an aphrodisiac too!) Its taste is very similar to that of thyme, and it can be used similarly.
Shallot A variety of onion with red-brown papery skins, about the size of pickling onions. They have a lovely flavour and are particularly good in sauces.
Skate Flat, cartilaginous fish which is kite shaped, hence the use of the wings only. The taste is improved by hanging for a couple of days. Very gelatinous.
Sorrel A vegetable, but usually thought of as a herb. Its acidity adds flavour, but use only a little as it can affect those with rheumatism or gout. It is delicious in combination with spinach, or stuffed inside a fish.
Spinach Rich in vitamins and iron, and contains more calcium than most vegetables. Buy young, glossy, green leaves. Wash thoroughly. Best cooked by dry steaming; place in pan with *nothing* else – the moisture from the washing makes the steam.
Spring onions Can in fact be bought all year round. Mild onion flavour.
Star anise A very pretty star-shaped spice, widely used in Chinese cooking (and available in Chinese shops). A strong aniseed flavour for stocks, sauces and stews.
Sugar For general use we caster sugar, which is very fine and dissolves quickly. We also use golden granulated sugar, icing sugar (for cake decoration and in some desserts) and Muscovado which is very dark, almost treacle-like in taste from the added molasses.
Swede A swede is generally yellow, larger than a turnip and totally smooth. They are also sweeter and drier than turnips. Make sure not to choose spongy ones when buying.
Sweet marjoram Similar to oregano but a milder, slightly sweet and spicy flavour. Helps digestion.

Tarragon A constituent of *fines herbes*. It has an aniseed flavour. A perennial plant, the French variety is better than the Russian, which differs in flavour and is not as strong. A good substitute for salt in a recipe as well as vinegar because of its acidity.
Thyme Best used in dishes that involve long, slow cooking. Major ingredient in the *bouquet garni*. Thyme is a strong antiseptic, stimulating good breathing and helping blood circulation and digestion.
Tomato Buy firm, smooth-skinned tomatoes, sun-ripened, if possible.
Tomato concentrate One of the few canned products we use. A great standby that adds good flavour to stocks, sauces, etc.
Trout Buy as Bass.
Turbot An expensive flat fish because it is difficult to catch. Large with lean, white, firm flesh and a good flavour.
Turnips Not such a popular vegetable in Britain, and largely grown as cattle feed. However, small baby turnips have a lovely flavour. Buy small, unbruised ones.

Vanilla The pod of a tropical climbing orchid. It is very aromatic, and is used mostly in sweet dishes, split in half. It can be used more than once: rinse the pod well after use and store in a tightly closed jar of sugar. The pod imparts its flavour to the sugar.
Veal The best veal comes from animals several months old, which have been milk fed. May be difficult to obtain in Britain – most veal seems to go to France, where the demand is high.
Verbena A lemon-flavoured herb. As an alternative, use a little lemon rind.
Vermouth Slightly fortified wine infused with herbs, spices, etc. Many different flavours and sweetnesses.
Vinegar Always try to use wine vinegar. A good-quality vinegar, like oil, makes all the difference, particularly in dressings and sauces. Tarragon vinegar is particularly flavourful.
Vinegar, raspberry is simply a raspberry-flavoured wine vinegar.
Vine leaves If fresh ones are not available, don't bother. The leaves cured in brine are not as good.

Watercress Use in soups, salads or garnishes. It's best raw, though, as like chervil it loses its goodness during cooking. It contains iron, copper, calcium, potassium, and iodine.
Wine Use a good table wine for general cooking. A better wine gives better results for sauces.

EQUIPMENT

SMALL EQUIPMENT

1 set of saucepans, either cast-iron enamelled or copper – 14, 16, 18, 20 and 22 cm (approx. 5½, 6½, 7, 8 and 9 in) – complete with lids.

1 cocotte/casserole, 25 cm (10 in) cast-iron enamelled, complete with lid. Some come with a concave lid in which water can be placed to give extra moisture inside the dish (the hot steam inside the dish comes in contact with cold and creates extra moisture).

1 set of skillets, cast-iron – 16, 20 and 26 cm (approx. 6½, 8 and 10 in) – enamelled or not. Essential when braising/wet roasting meats or vegetables using both top of cooker heat and the oven.

1 × 20 cm (8 in) heat reducer, either a cast-iron plaque, or a specially made one. When fitted between a low flame/hot plate and a saucepan/casserole, this will considerably reduce the amount of heat permeating through to the food, and make the cooking more succulent, while avoiding any burning or sticking at the bottom.

1 wok about 40 cm (16 in) in diameter. Those in carbon steel with a wooden handle diffuse the heat very evenly, but require special care to avoid rusting, or a lighter weight one, Teflon-coated with a flat bottom.

1 steamer, if not a component of the wok, either stainless steel or wood. The base should be large enough to contain at least 2 litres (3½ pt) water/liquid. A *couscoussier* is ideal as it has a large top and a narrow base, or invest in a steamer basket which fits inside a saucepan.

1 set of mixing bowls – 8, 10, 15, 20 and 25 cm (approx. 3, 4, 6, 8 and 10 in) in diameter. Earthenware ones can be used at the table as well as in the kitchen, and can be fitted on to a saucepan of water to use as a bain-marie. Stainless steel are good too, but don't look as attractive on the table!

1 flat sieve (passoire) made of stainless steel is essential for straining vegetables and running them under the tap.

1 chinois sieve – essential for puréeing or sieving those sauces full of skin and pips into a thin stream. I use this a lot, as you will see!

1 hand food mill – still the best piece of equipment ever invented! It is versatile (except for chopping) and does the job of a food processor, liquidizer and round strainer combined. Very useful for fruit with pips and pits, for vegetables with skins and pips.

1 salad/herb spinner – essential for cleaning and drying salads and herbs, as well as vegetables. A small easy-to-use version is available for herbs.

1 scale – preferably graduated from 10 to 450 g (roughly ½ oz to 1 lb) in 10 g (½ oz) graduations. Look for one of the new electronic scales which are designed for dieters (the graduations are lower and more accurate).

1 fat separator, which is a jug with the spout starting at its base. When liquid is poured into it, the fat rises to the surface, leaving the useful – and healthy – part of the liquid at the bottom of the jug. Stop pouring when the fat reaches the spout. This is *vital* for Cuisine Santé!

1 measuring jug which will accommodate a chinois sieve, through which sauces can be strained.

Miscellaneous:

- **2 balloon whisks**, one 20 cm (8 in) high, the other 40 cm (16 in) for use only in combination with the copper bowl.
- **2 wooden spoons.**
- **2 wooden spatulas.**
- **1 rubber spatula.**
- **1 plastic dough scraper (corne)** – useful for making pastry using the flat edge, and as a bowl cleaner using the rounded edge (like a rubber spatula).
- **1 slotted spoon.**
- **1 ladle.**
- **1 cheese slicer** to slice cheese very thinly and make *Lichettes de Légumes* (see page 24).
- **2 peppermills**, one containing a combination of white and black peppercorns and coriander seeds, the other containing *herbes de Provence*.
- **1 rock salt mill.**
- **1 salt box** with loose cooking salt.

ELECTRICAL EQUIPMENT

1 electric hand whisk is useful but not essential for beating egg whites; making salad dressings; mayonnaises, etc. Choose one with variable speeds.

1 food processor is very useful for chopping a *mirepoix* quickly and finely. Remember to run it only for a few seconds at a time, and do not allow to run with food in for a long time.

1 liquidizer – better than a food processor for soups.

1 mini chopper/coffee mill – very useful for chopping herbs and grinding coffee beans.

1 plunger mill — combines well with a food processor and liquidizer (choose either as both might be extravagant!)

1 ice-cream machine – a good investment for easily prepared granités, sorbets, and ice-creams. I could not be without it!

PASTRY MAKING EQUIPMENT

1 rolling pin, 50 cm (20 in) long, without handles. Do not leave in water or it will warp and roll pastry unevenly.

3 tart tins, loose bottomed – 20, 24, 28 cm (8, 9½, 11 in). All are not essential, and the 24 cm (9½ in) one is most versatile.

6 tartlet tins of 7 cm (3 in), and **6 oblong barquette tins** of 10 cm (4 in).

1 pie tin, loose bottomed, straight edges, 18 cm (7 in) in diameter and 3 cm (1¼ in) deep.

1 timbale tin, loose bottomed, 20 cm (8 in) in diameter and 5 cm (2 in) deep.

1 cake tin (génoise), Teflon coated, 18 cm (7 in) in diameter, 5 cm (2 in) deep.

1 marquise tin (useful also as roasting tin) Teflon coated, tin or stainless steel, 30 × 24 cm (6 × 9½ in) and 6 cm (2¼ in) deep.

1 long cake/terrine pyrex mould, 10 × 20 cm (4 × 8 in) and 6 cm (2¼ in) deep, and another 12 × 25 cm (5 × 10 in) and 7 cm (2½-3 in) deep.

1 savarin mould, pyrex, 23 cm (9 in) in diameter.

12 ramekin dishes, pyrex or china, 8 cm (3¼ in) in diameter.

2 cooling racks, one rectangular, 25 × 40 cm (10 × 16 in), and one round, 28 cm (11 in) in diameter.

1 set of pastry cutters.

1 set of tit-bit cutters, for cutting aspic and pastry in all shapes.

1 pastry brush, flat, 1 cm (½ in).

CUTTING EQUIPMENT

1 set of knives: carbon steel is the best, and easy to sharpen, but they need attention or they rust – don't put them in the dishwasher! Or buy stainless steel with a good sharpening tool. You'll need 1 each of 10, 15, 20 and 25 cm (4, 6, 8 and 10 in) filleting knives, 1 × 15 cm (6 in) boning knife, 1 zester and 1 decorator (or 1 'decozest' combining the two tools in one), 1 peeler, 1 × 15 cm (6 in) palette knife, 1 apple corer, 1 × 15 cm (6 in) trussing needle, 1 × 15 cm (6 in) larding needle. If using all carbon steel, buy a 10 cm (4 in) stainless steel knife to use on acid food like citrus fruits.

Techniques

In the following pages are illustrated and described many of the more complicated or characteristic techniques for preparation, cooking, mixing and garnishing, which recur throughout the book. Specific references to the individual techniques are given as necessary in the recipes.

Baking Blind

This is the best way to avoid a soggy tart or quiche base. Line the tin with the rolled dough and prick lightly all over the base with a fork (to prevent the dough from rising). Cover the base with a circle of greaseproof paper (see page 29) and rest in the fridge for 10 minutes. Cover the paper with baking beans (any dried pulse can be used for this) and bake for 10 minutes at the recommended temperature. Remove the beans and paper and continue baking until the base is well dried, and starts to colour. Egg wash (see below) to fill in the holes in the pricked pastry, and cook for 2 minutes. Repeat this once or twice more until the pastry is well glazed.

Egg Washing

Egg wash is a versatile and edible kitchen glue! Mix a whole egg with 1 teaspoon of water in a ramekin with a fork. For a glossier look, add another yolk or use yolks only. Follow the instructions for brushing it on (with a pastry brush) in each recipe. Glazing a blind-baked pastry case is essential to prevent liquid added later from seeping through and making the pastry soggy.

Feuilletés

BUTTERFLY CASES

These are wonderful presentation cases for a variety of fillings (see Feuilletés aux Champignons, *page 72).*

1 Roll out the *Pâte Feuilletée*, trim to a 40 cm (16 in) square, and cut into sixteen 10 cm (4 in) squares.

2 Fold each square in half diagonally and cut through the two layers from the outer edges to the point. Leave the point uncut on both sides.

3 Open out the square and egg wash the edges lightly. Lift the two cut corners and bring together.

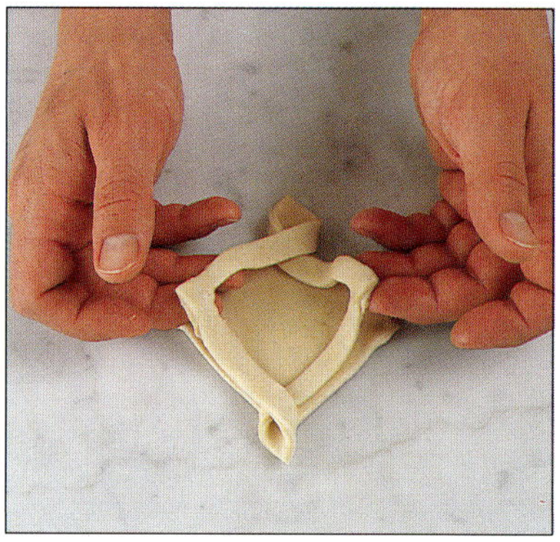

4 Take one corner under the other to meet the opposite corner, and press the layers together to seal. Knock up the outside edges with the back of a knife.

Poaching Eggs

Bring a pan of water to the boil, adding about 75 ml (3 fl oz) white vinegar (distilled malt vinegar) per 600 ml (1 pt) water. Break an egg into a small cup, then drop the egg slowly into the gently simmering water. Repeat the operation, but increase the heat each time another egg is added (the more eggs, the more heat is absorbed). The water should be simmering all the time. If the white does not cling immediately to the yolk, help it along with a wooden spoon and increase the heat. Cook the eggs for 3 minutes, then lift out with a slotted spoon. Check that the egg is sufficiently cooked by pressing it with your finger: it should be soft for a runny yolk, and fairly firm for a semi-hard yolk. Transfer to a bowl of cold water to stop the cooking or serve immediately. Poached eggs will keep in the water, in the fridge, for up to 3 days. To reheat, trim off excess white and plunge into a bowl of hot water for 2-3 minutes, then drain and serve. Poached eggs can be used in various ways with different sauces – as starters or light supper dishes (see *Oeufs Pochés à la Chantilly*, page 63, and *Oeufs Pochés Colombo*, page 55).

Boning a Round Fish

Round fish include cod, mullet, trout (pictured here) and salmon.

1 Slit open the belly from the head to rear vent. Remove the viscera and any blood and rinse the fish well.

2 Using a knife, ease all the bones away from the fillets on each side, working from backbone to belly.

3 Using scissors, snip open the flesh from vent to tail, and snip *through* the backbone at the tail. Pull this up gently and pull towards the head. Snip at the end and remove the backbone.

4 Cut through the skin in between the two fillets to remove the dorsal fins from the fish, then trim off all other fins with scissors and discard.

5 Finally, feel for any missed small bones with your fingers, and remove with tweezers.

Dégorger

This is a term used in French cookery, and means to soak a food in cold water to remove impurities. Sweetbreads, for instance, are soaked to remove blood and to whiten them. Fish bones, too, are cleaned in this way before being used for a *fumet*: put them in a bowl and run cold water from the tap over them for 20 minutes.

Skinning and Filleting a Flat Fish

Flat fish include plaice, turbot, halibut, flounder, and Dover sole (as here).

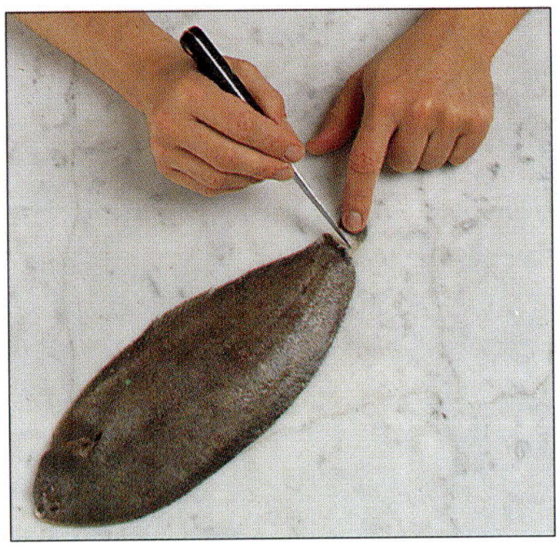

1 Lay the fish white side down on your work surface. Using a sharp filleting knife with a flexible blade, cut through the dark skin at the tail, and then starting from the tail, carefully scrape the skin off the flesh, working towards the head. Ensure that the whole of the tail skin is lifted.

2 Holding the tail with a cloth in your left hand, grab the flap of skin with your right (using the cloth) and pull the skin off towards the head.

3 When the skin reaches the head, continue pulling (taking care around the mouth) and down the other side of the fish, thus removing the skin in one go.

4 To fillet, cut along the backbone from head to tail and insert the tip of the filleting knife between the bones and flesh on one side of the fish at the head end (see step 1 below). Slowly work the knife down towards the tail, keeping it as close to the bones as possible. Turn the fish round and remove the second fillet, then turn the fish over and remove the remaining two fillets.

Stuffing a Flat Fish

If stuffing a whole flat fish as in Sole Farcie Soufflée *(see page 86), do not remove the fillets.*

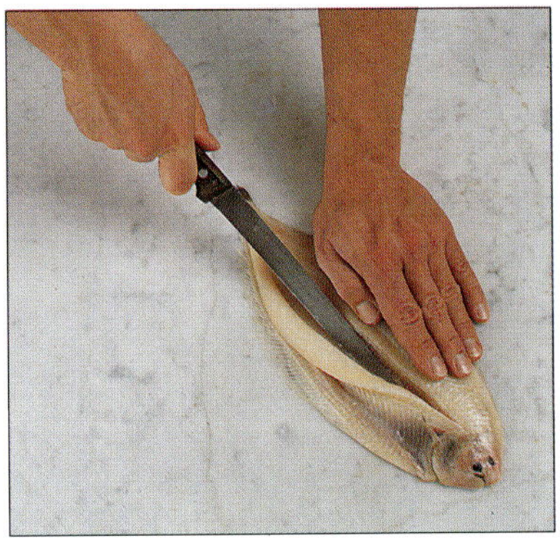

1 Cut along the backbone of the skinned fish as above, and free the flesh from the bones – but keep the outside edges of the fillets attached.

2 Fold the fish in half, open fillet side up, until the backbone snaps. Ease bones away from bottom fillets along the length of the fish with a filleting knife. Snip through the backbone at the head and tail with scissors, and remove.

3 Holding the piping bag in your left hand, fold back a cuff, and then fill the bag with *mousseline* filling.

4 Unfold the cuff and force the filling down in the bag with your right hand.

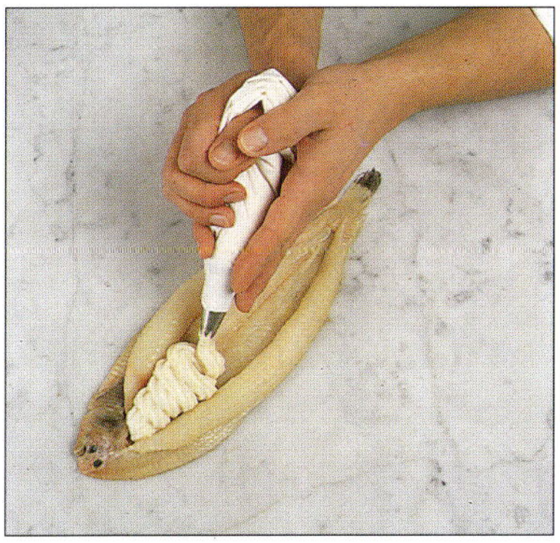

5 Pipe the *mousseline* carefully into the opening in the fish, and continue as directed in the recipe.

Poaching a Fish

Poaching is particularly good for large fish such as salmon, as pictured here. Properly poached, a salmon will not fall apart, so it can be cooked the day before and served cold. Either follow the instructions here or those in the recipe for Saumon à la Riga *(see page 90).*

1 If your fish is large, truss the head so that it holds its shape, and the mouth stays shut. Criss-cross a length of string over the head, under the chin and behind the gills. Put the fish on the perforated rack in the fish kettle.

2 Either prepare enough *court-bouillon* for the size of your fish (see page 32), or put 2-3 sliced carrots, a couple of roughly chopped leeks, a leafy stick of celery cut into chunks, a little salt, 6 black peppercorns, a bayleaf and a pinch of thyme into a large pan. Cover with about 2.75-4.5 litres (5-8 pt) water and bring rapidly to the boil. Simmer for 30 minutes, cool a little, then strain through a chinois sieve over the fish.

3 In a pestle and mortar, work together a handful of black peppercorns, and a teaspoon each of fennel, coriander and caraway seeds and sea salt. Fill the kettle with white wine and/or water, according to the recipe, so that the fish is completely covered with liquid. Add the spice mixture from the mortar.

4 Add ½ sliced lemon, 2-3 bayleaves, some parsley sprigs and 2-3 large dill sprigs.

(continued)

Poaching (continued)

5 Put the kettle on the cooker and bring gently to the boil.

6 As soon as it boils, remove the kettle from the heat and cover with a clean tea-towel.

7 Secure the tea-towel with the lid. If you want to serve the fish cold, leave off the heat in a cool place for 12-15 hours. The fish will poach in the stock. Lift the rack with the fish on it from the kettle and let it drain for an hour. The fish is then ready to be prepared for serving.

8 If you want to serve the fish hot, as soon as you have put the lid on the kettle (see above), return it to the heat, and simmer for a further 5-6 minutes. Be very careful to ensure that no part of the cloth hangs near the heat source. Remove the kettle from the heat and leave the fish to 'cook' for a further 20 minutes. Remove the rack and let the fish drain for a couple of minutes. The fish is then ready to serve.

Boning a Chicken

1 Place the chicken, breast up, on a chopping board, and insert a large knife inside the chicken. Cut through, downwards, on one side of the backbone.

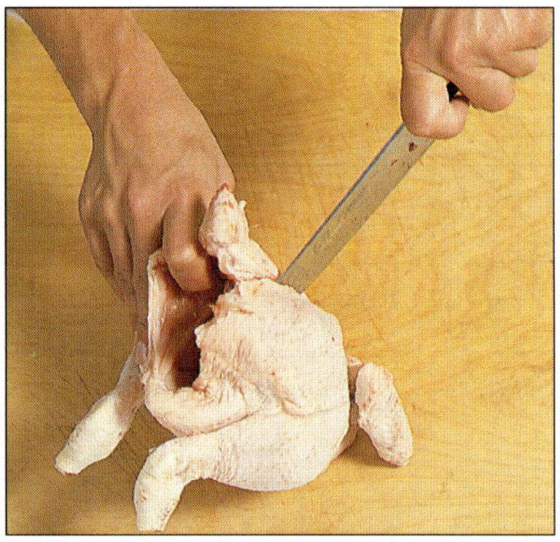

2 Turn the chicken over, and finish cutting along the backbone to open up the bird.

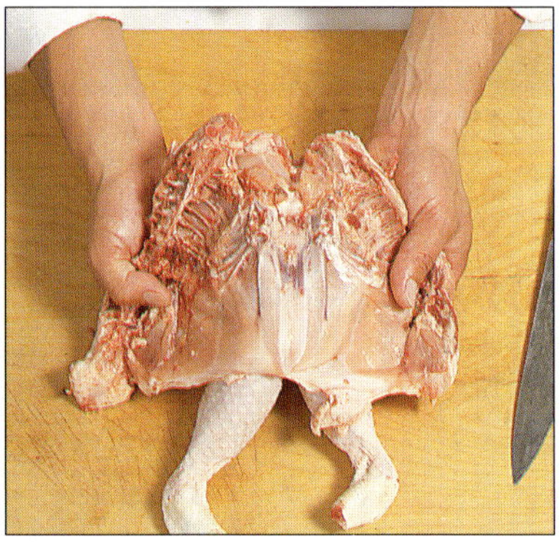

3 Spread the bird open so that the breastbones are exposed and point upwards.

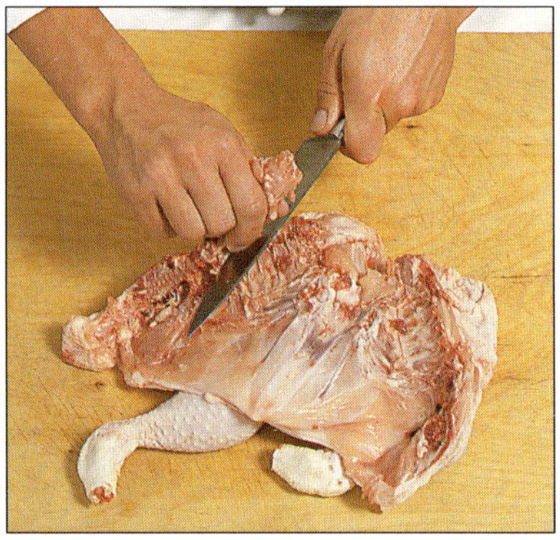

4 Cut out the backbone, including the parson's nose.

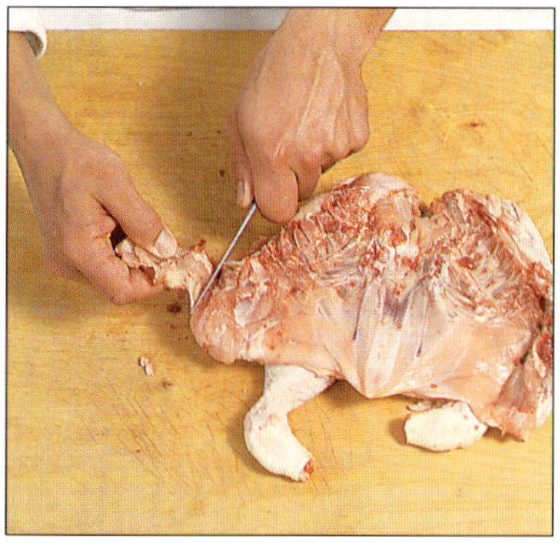

5 Cut through the thighbone joint and remove the bone attached to the thighs.

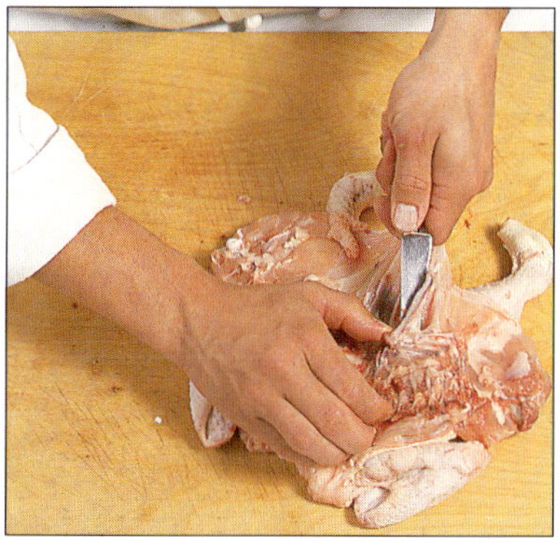

6 Insert a small knife under the rib cage and remove all the bones on both sides.

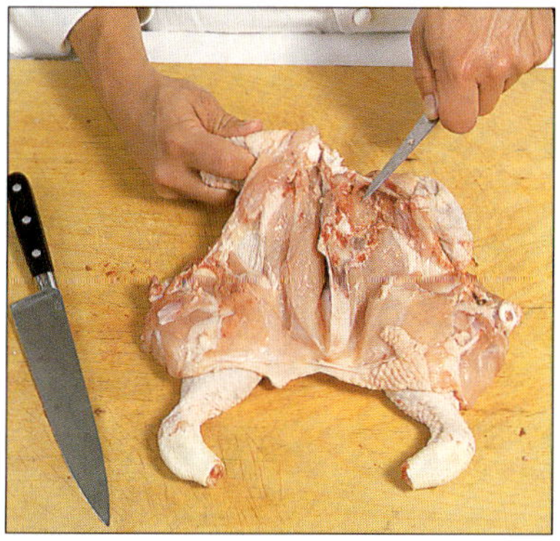

7 Ease the joints of the collarbone and remove the wishbone carefully so as not to damage the flesh.

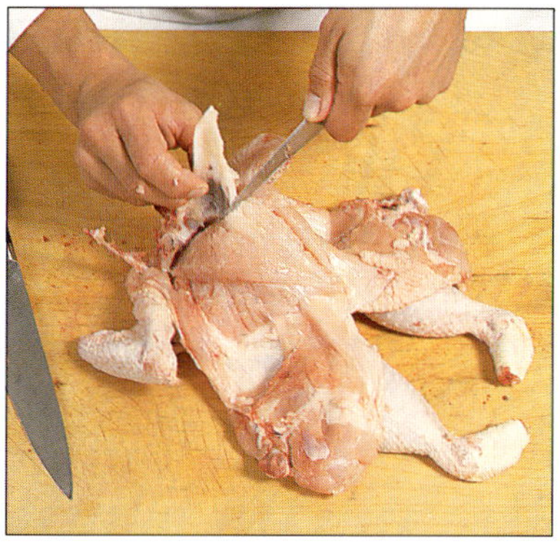

8 Ease the flesh from the breastbone on both sides and gently pull away the breastbone.

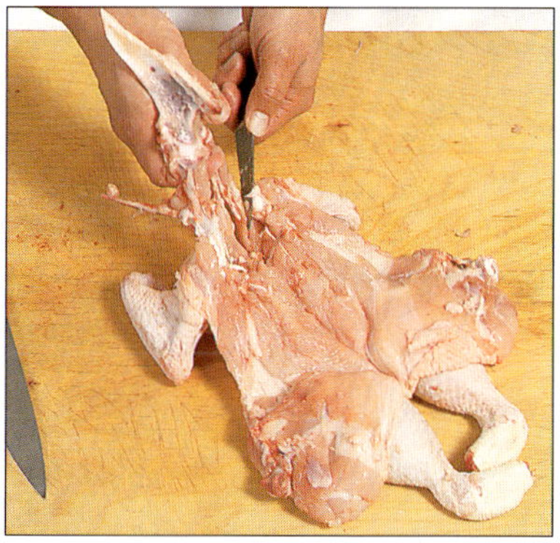

9 Completely free the breastbone and collarbone. Search all over with your fingers for any remaining bones (apart from thighs and drumsticks), and remove.

10 Turn the chicken over, pierce a hole through the skin near the thigh and tuck the drumstick through the hole. The chicken is now ready for marinating (see *Poulet Grille au Citron Vert*, page 134) or for stuffing.

11 For stuffing, have the chicken, breast side towards you, and insert two fingers between the skin and flesh to ease a space for stuffing. (Be careful not to break the skin in between the two breasts.) Separate the skin and flesh of the thighs and drumsticks and stuff these in the same way (see *Poulet Farci Fendu au Four*, page 131).

Deglazing

To deglaze is to add a liquid (wine, alcohol or stock) to a hot pan after meat or fish has been sealed in it. The liquid dissolves the juices and encrustations attached to the bottom of the pan and transfers the flavour to the liquid.

Jointing a Chicken

Jointing a chicken is simple once you know how, and it is a very useful technique to learn. You no longer need to rely on the butcher – and it is cheaper to buy whole chickens than portions.

1 Place the whole chicken on a chopping board, with its legs nearest you, and grasp the left leg in your left hand. With a sharp knife cut through the skin, and on towards the joint.

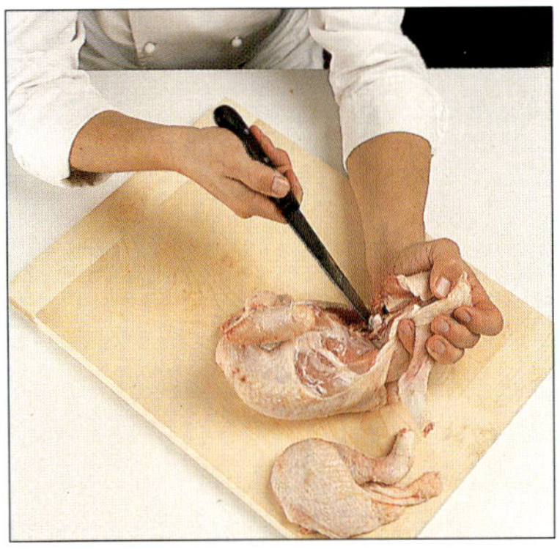

2 Cut the white tendons between thigh and body, twist the joint, and then pull the leg free. Turn the bird over and repeat on the other side.

3 To remove the breasts, carefully cut down each side of the breastbone using a sharp knife. Cut along the breastbone towards the wishbone and right down to the wing joint. Cut down through this to free both breast and wing. Repeat on the other side of the bird.

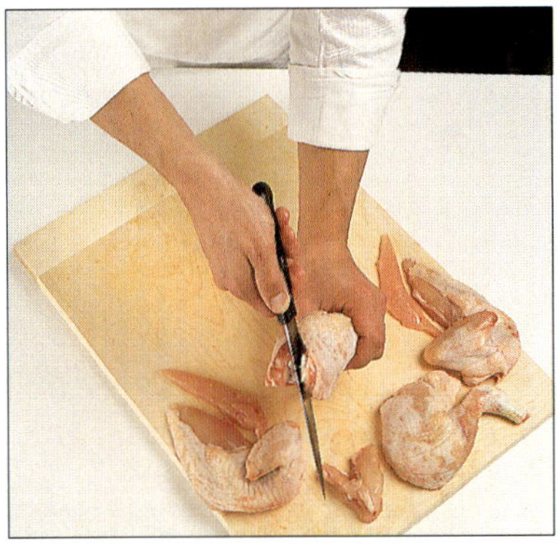

4 Cut the wingbone and the wing tips from the carcass and use for stock. Remove the fillets from the breasts and cut the breasts in half. Divide the legs into thighs and drumsticks by bending each leg back until the skin is taut, then cutting right down the middle.

Boning a Turkey Thigh

This is vital for a recipe such as Gigot de Dinde Farcie *(see page 142).*

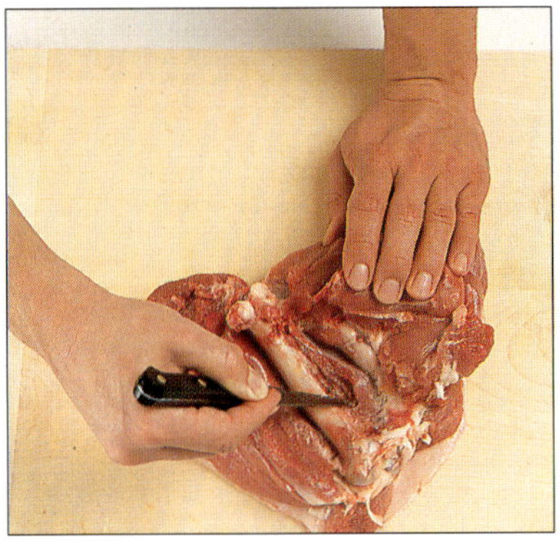

1 Lay the turkey thigh on a board and cut through the skin and flesh lengthwise to expose the bone. Cut in along the bone to release the flesh. Remove the bone, and any sinews or tendons.

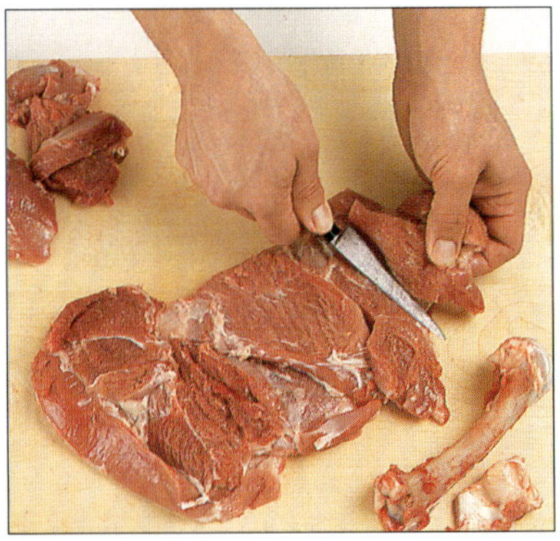

2 Trim any ragged pieces from the meat so that the bulk of the meat is as flat as possible. Use the trimmings in the stuffing.

Jointing and Boning a Rabbit

The most important thing to remember when jointing a rabbit is not to cut through *the bones if at all possible. The bones splinter very easily and are extremely sharp.*

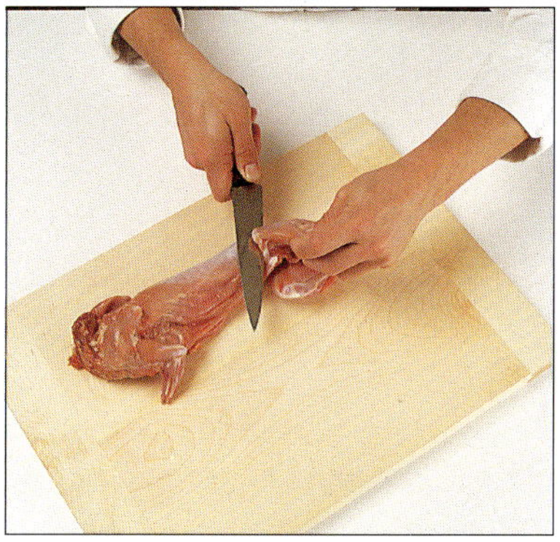

1 Lay the rabbit on a board and work the blade of a sharp knife around each of the four leg joints. Separate each leg from the body.

2 Cut the rabbit in two where the saddle meets the ribs. (Reserve the rib cage for stock.)

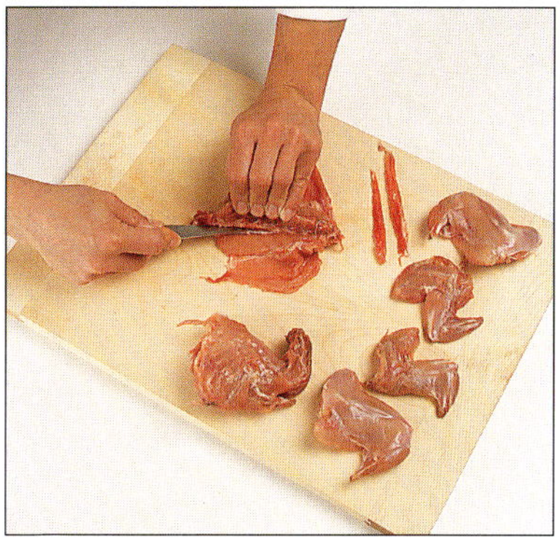

3 Cut away the two small fillets from the saddle. Then, bone the saddle by easing the flesh away from the saddle bone. Use a sharp knife, but be careful not to cut through the flesh.

4 Bone the four legs as described for boning a turkey thigh (see above). Keep the bones for stock.

Sweating

This is a method of cooking used mainly for vegetables, which are cooked in their own moisture without browning, and with hardly any fat.

Start by heating up the cooking vessel slowly over a low heat. Add a very little fat (usually 1 teaspoon), and then the prepared vegetables. Toss well and cover immediately to keep in the moisture. If more than one vegetable is to be sweated, add one at a time, starting with those with the highest water content (onions, for example). It is essential to cover the pan as it is the steam created inside which cooks the vegetable. Toss once in a while, keeping the cover on, and always keep on a very low heat. The sweating is finished when all ingredients are soft and not browned.

Braising/ Wet Roasting

This method combines the moisture-retaining qualities of braising with the browning quality of roasting, and is more usually used for meat. First, season with a little salt and pepper and then seal the meat very quickly in a well preheated skillet in a little oil. This retains the moisture, and colours the outside. Then put the meat aside, wipe the skillet and place it back over the heat. Sweat a *mirepoix* in the skillet, then deglaze with stock and/or white wine. Place the meat back on to the *mirepoix* and put, uncovered, into the oven. During cooking, the fat, if any, will run down into the juices; these are ultimately freed of fat and reduced before serving.

Washing Herbs and Leaves

All herbs and leaves should be washed this way before use. Place in a bowl of cold water and leave to soak for 5 minutes. This should be enough time for the grit and dirt to soak off and settle on the bottom of the bowl. Pick leaves or sprigs up delicately so as not to disturb the grit. Repeat once or twice with clean water.

Bouquet Garni

A fresh bouquet garni *is used in a great number of recipes and, although pre-packed versions are now available, the flavour is nothing like as good.*

Take a leek – using the green only or the white too if you like – and cut in half lengthways. Remove a few centre leaves from each side to make a groove, then fill one groove with about 10 black or white peppercorns, cracked. Top with some parsley sprigs, a thyme sprig and a bayleaf, and cover with the other half leek. Tie together with string.

Chiffonade

Chiffonade *is a word describing leaves cut into fine strips or ribbons. It is especially used with spinach (as here), lettuce and sorrel.*

1 To cut spinach into *chiffonade*, wash it well first (see above), then drain. Remove the stalks. Lay several leaves at a time on a board, and roll them up into a cigar shape.

2 Holding the shape firmly with one hand, chop crosswise into strips with a sharp knife.

Chopping an Onion

It may be something you do every day – but this is the correct *way of doing it!*

1 First peel the onion *without* trimming the root and shoot ends. Cut in half through the root then place one half, cut side down, on a board. Slice from the root end to the stem with a sharp knife, but take care not to cut *through* the root.

2 Keeping the onion in the same position, cut in towards the root horizontally, that is, with the knife parallel to the board, still not cutting through the root.

3 Cut down through the onion to form cubes. The size of the cubes will depend on the width between cuts.

Peeling Tomatoes

Remove the stalk and cut round the growth end – the '*mouche*' – with a small sharp-pointed knife. Remove. Cut a criss-cross on the other end of the tomato and plunge into a saucepan of boiling water. Leave for 10-30 seconds (the time depends on the size and ripeness of the tomatoes), then remove immediately with a slotted spoon to a bowl full of extremely cold water. The difference in temperature will help remove the skin and preserve the firmness of the tomato.

Skinning Peppers

Preheat the grill and cut off the stem end of the peppers. Remove the pith and seeds, then grill the peppers until their skins brown and burst here and there. Wrap them in a wet tea-towel or place in a plastic bag – where they will 'steam' slightly – and leave to cool. When almost cold, the skins will peel off very easily and the peppers will be nearly cooked.

Crushing Garlic

This is the best way to extract all the flavour from garlic.

Peel a clove easily by crushing it first with the palm of your hand on the counter. Remove the middle green part (which is difficult to digest) and place the white flesh inside a garlic crusher. Press over a plate, distribute the remains inside the pierced part of the crusher and squeeze again. Remove the shreds from the crusher and add to the dish.

Duxelle of Mushrooms

Heat a skillet and sweat a chopped shallot in 1 teaspoon grapeseed oil for 1 minute. Add a crushed garlic clove and sweat for a further minute. Add the finely chopped mushrooms (the quantity is specified in individual recipes) and season with a little salt and pepper and 1 teaspoon lemon juice. Put over a high heat, tossing well, and when the juices of the mushrooms start to run, reduce the heat to medium. Leave to reduce until nearly dry, then add 1 dessertspoon tomato concentrate. Stir well over the heat for 1 minute and then reserve on a plate.

Cutting Vegetables

Vegetables for any dish should always be cut into even-sized pieces so that they cook evenly. Vegetables cut in the ways described here also make attractive garnishes for sauces and soups. Always wash the vegetables well before use, and reserve any trimmings for stocks, sauces, mirepoix, *etc.*

JULIENNE

Julienne *vegetables are mostly used for garnishing meat or fish dishes. Many vegetables and some meats can be cut into* julienne *(matchsticks).*

First wash and trim the vegetable, then square off and cut lengthwise into thin 3 mm (⅛ in) slices (discard the rounded outside slices). Slice lengthwise into tiny matchsticks and cut in half if necessary. The vegetable *julienne* here are (clockwise) carrot, courgette, leek, turnip and asparagus.

BRUNOISE

Brunoise *vegetables make attractive garnishes for soups, particularly if made with different coloured vegetables.*

Cut the vegetables into *julienne* as described above, and then chop the matchsticks into very fine dice. The vegetable *brunoise* here are (clockwise) carrot, asparagus, turnip, courgette and leek.

PAYSANNE

Paysanne *vegetables can also be used to garnish soups.*

Trim and cut the vegetables into 3 mm (1/8 in) slices, as described for *julienne* (above). Then cut into small squares. The vegetable *paysanne* here are (clockwise) carrot, courgette, leek, turnip and asparagus.

MIREPOIX

A mirepoix *is a mixture of vegetables – onion, carrot and celery – which is used in many meat and fish dishes to enhance the flavour, and as a bed upon which to braise meat or fish.*

Mirepoix can be roughly (*paysanne*) or finely (*brunoise*), chopped – depending on the recipe – and the proportions are usually 1 part onion to 1 part carrot and 1 part celery. The individual recipes specify the quantities of each vegetable to be used.

Lichettes de Légumes

VEGETABLE TONGUES

Simply peel or prepare the vegetables, then drag them across the back of a sharp cheese slicer or vegetable mandolin. The vegetable *lichettes* here are (clockwise) courgette, carrot and turnip.

Turned Vegetables

These are vegetable chunks 'carved' into barrel shapes, which make attractive garnishes.

Cut larger prepared and peeled vegetables (like potatoes, turnips and carrots) into fairly even-sized pieces, and then carve with a sharp knife to a rounded barrel or oval shape. Cut large courgettes into quarters lengthwise, then carve.

Use any trimmings for stock, or for a vegetable purée or soup.

Onion Leaves

These are easy to prepare and make a delicious and unusual casing for vegetable or meat fillings (see Oignons Farcis, *pages 60 and 62).*

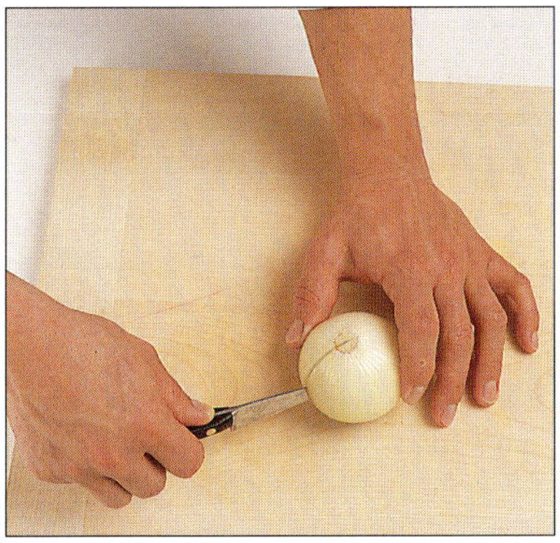

1 Peel and make a single cut into a whole onion from the shoot to the root, cutting right into the core of the onion.

2 Place the onion in boiling water and simmer for 10 minutes, then refresh in cold water. Cut off the root end with a sharp knife and discard, then separate the onion into leaves.

3 Chop the heart of the onion to use in the filling, then put some filling into each onion leaf. Curl the leaves around the filling to enclose it.

Garnishes

CROÛTONS

To serve four, stack two or three slices of 1-2 cm (½-¾ in) thick bread and trim off the crusts. Cut at 1-2 cm (½-¾ in) intervals horizontally and vertically into cubes. Toast the cubes under the grill, turning them every so often so that all faces are browned. These *croûtons* are very much healthier than those fried in fat!

GLACÉ MINT LEAVES

These are ideal as a garnish for a fruit dessert or sorbet. Dip the leaves in a little beaten egg white and dip again in a bowl containing either granulated, caster or icing sugar. Leave in a cool dry place to set, or place in the freezer for 3 minutes.

CAPER FLOWERS

To make a caper flower garnish, simply peel back the leaves of the caper very carefully. These flowers are an attractive garnish for many fish dishes.

ONION FLOWERS

Small onions and spring onions can both be cut to blossom forth into flower shapes.

Take a small peeled onion and stand it on its root. Make a series of narrow vertical cuts into the onion towards the root, but do not cut through the root. Turn the onion 90°, and make another series of cuts at right angles to the first ones. Again, be careful not to cut through the root. Place in iced water for about 1 hour to open out.

For spring onions, remove the root and trim off most of the green. Either cut the bulb alone as for the onion above, or cut the bulb and green stalk, leaving the middle section uncut. Leave in iced water as above.

TOMATO ROSES

Take a firm tomato and a small, sharp knife. Starting from the end opposite the stalk, and working round the tomato, cut through the skin carefully to make a continuous strip of skin about 1 cm (½ in) wide. Start from the end first cut and curl the skin (flesh inwards) into a rosebud, and finally into an open rose.

Quenelles

Most soft foods – vegetable purées (as here), ice-cream, sorbet or meringue – can be shaped into ovals with the aid of 2 dessertspoons.

1 Take some of the mixture on to a spoon. Place the second spoon over the mixture in the first and slide it between the mixture and the bowl of the first spoon. Scoop the mixture towards you to transfer it to the second spoon. Keep this action going until the mixture is well shaped.

2 Transfer to the plate by inserting one spoon underneath the mixture on the other spoon, and easing off gently.

Fruit Garnishes

ZESTING A CITRUS FRUIT

Either use a zester to remove very fine strips, or use a potato peeler to remove larger *julienne* strips.

SCORING LEMONS (OR CUCUMBERS)

Use a citrus scorer or decorator, or a cannelle knife, and run it along the sides of an unpeeled lemon (or cucumber) at regular intervals. When the lemon (or cucumber) is sliced, the grooves have a decorative effect (see lemon below).

LEMON GARNISHES

A selection of various lemon garnishes (clockwise from top): a wedge of lemon, the peel slightly separated from the flesh top and bottom, slotted on to the side of an individual salad bowl; a half lemon which has been scored, with the scoring tied in a knot, inserted in the centre of the cut face; a lemon twist made from a slice of scored lemon, cut halfway through its diameter and twisted; a half lemon with a knot of rind – run a sharp knife narrowly around the whole diameter of the lemon half in a continuous piece, leaving 1 cm (½ in) attached, and tie in a knot; a lemon basket – cut a thin slice from the bottom for stability and mark a 1 cm (½ in) wide strip halfway up and over the top of the fruit for a handle. Cut into the fruit to slice through, keeping the handle whole, and remove the flesh and peel to reveal the handle.

Cutting a Pineapple

These are two attractive ways to prepare pineapple to serve decoratively on its own as a dessert or to use when preparing Ananas Princesse *(see page 180) and* Sorbet à l'Ananas *(see page 173).*

ANANAS PRINCESSE

Cut the leafy top off the pineapple and reserve. Cut a thin slice off the bottom for stability but do not expose the flesh. Run a long, sharp and thin-bladed knife between the flesh and shell all the way down from the top to within 2.5 cm (1 in) of the bottom of the pineapple. Cut all round the open top this way. Insert a small thin-bladed knife on one side of the bottom, about 2.5 cm (1 in) up, and slice across the pineapple. Turn the knife over, re-insert into the hole, and slice in the opposite direction. Try not to enlarge the hole in the shell too much. Repeat this operation on the other side of the pineapple – if you have cut in the right places, when you invert the pineapple, a cylinder of flesh will come out of the top! Remove the 'eyes' and slice the flesh then replace, in the correct order, inside the shell. Dust the leaf section with icing sugar and put it back on top. With this method, the fruit does not dry up between preparation and serving.

SORBET À L'ANANAS

Cut the pineapple into quarters, cutting through the leafy top as well. Run a small sharp knife in between the flesh and skin at a good distance from the skin to avoid the 'eyes'. Check you have avoided them, then cut the quarters into thick slices. For an attractive presentation, push the slices out alternately to right and left.

Segmenting Citrus Fruit

This technique is ideal for preparing fruit salads and desserts (see Gratin d'Oranges à la Maltaise, *page 167).*

1 Cut a slice off the top and bottom of the fruit to make it stable, then cut down the side of the fruit, to remove the peel and pith, following the curve of the fruit.

2 Holding the peeled fruit in your left hand over a bowl, slice down between the membrane and flesh on both sides of each segment. Let the freed segments and juice drop into the bowl, then squeeze in the juice from the remaining membrane.

Bain-marie

This is a double boiler consisting of a pan of water at the base with another pan on top. It is used to cook gently, reheat or even keep warm a sensitive sauce. Often a roasting tin filled with hot water, in which a bowl or pan of food is placed, will work as well.

Liquidizing

When liquidizing a soup, for instance, always put the solid ingredients into the machine first, using a slotted spoon, then pour in enough liquid just to cover them. Liquidize, and add the remaining liquid in a steady stream while the machine is running.

Correcting a Sauce

MAYONNAISE OR VINAIGRETTE: If either has curdled, place ½ dessertspoon Dijon mustard – as an alternative to an egg yolk – in another bowl. Slowly add the curdled mixture, whisking vigorously.

YOGHURT SAUCE: If this has curdled, liquidize in a food processor for 1 minute.

Folding

When two mixtures of different consistencies are to be folded together – for a soufflé, say – first mix 1 tablespoon of the softer mixture into the stiffer one to lighten and thin it. Then, put all the soft mixture on top of the stiffer one and cut, scoop and turn the mixture over, using a rubber spatula, while turning the bowl with your other hand. Never *over*fold.

Papillotes

A papillote *is a well-sealed envelope of greaseproof paper, usually used for meat or fish dishes. The advantage of cooking* papillotes *is that they concentrate the aromas and flavours, and the meat or fish cooks in its own juices. Fold a 40 cm (16 in) square of greaseproof paper in half and cut a half-heart shape from it and unfold.*

1 Open out the paper and place all the recipe ingredients on the half nearer to you, beside the fold. Spread a stiff flour and water paste in a 1 cm (½ in) border along the edge of one side of the heart.

2 Fold the half further from you over the filling. Starting from the broader end, fold over the pasted border twice to seal, making tucks around the curve.

3 Brush oil over the top of the *papillote* and place, oiled side up, in the oven.

Cutlet Frills

These are used to garnish the ends of cutlets or poultry bones.

1 Cut greaseproof or Bakewell paper into strips 25 cm (10 in) long and 12.5 cm (5 in) wide. Fold in half lengthways. Cut into the fold at 3 mm (⅛ in) intervals halfway through the width.

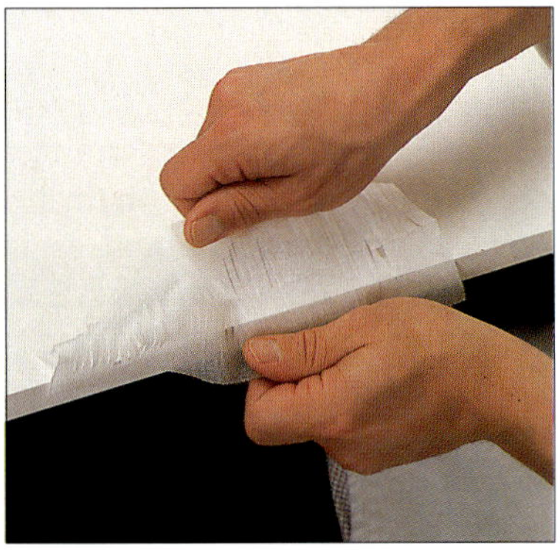

2 Unfold, and open out flat, pressing against a table or counter edge to erase the fold.

3 Re-fold inside-out, lining up the edges, then roll around your finger. Secure with flour and water paste or sticky tape.

Greaseproof Paper Circles

These are used for lining the bottoms of cake tins to ease turning out, and for lining the base of a tart or quiche so that the baking beans do not touch the dough.

1 First take a square of paper larger than the diameter of the chosen tin. Fold it in half diagonally, then in half again, and again. Continue folding over from the centre point of the square until you can no longer fold the paper.

2 Measure the radius of the tin against the paper – from the *centre* to the outside edge – and mark this across the folds. Tear or cut at the mark, then open the paper out to form a circle.

Napkin Gondola

This is the best way to present large, round fish like salmon, Saumon à la Riga *(see page 90) for example. You will need three large napkins.*

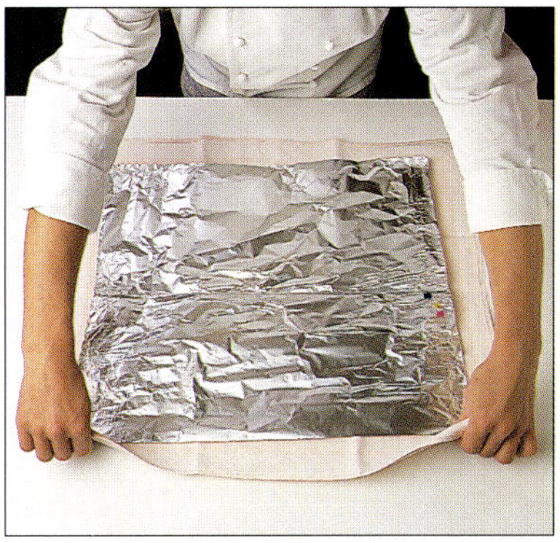

1 Lay a napkin flat on a surface and cover with a square of kitchen foil. Fold in half horizontally, fold away from you.

2 Fold one side into the centre of the fold, followed by the other side, to form a large triangle. Fold twice more in the same way on each side.

3 Bring the two sides together for the last fold.

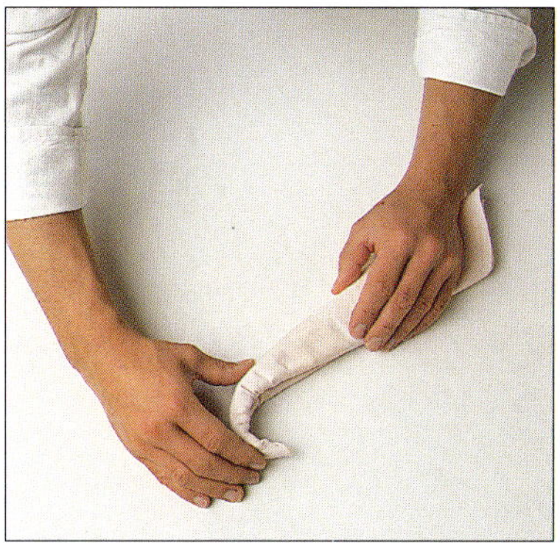

4 Hold the napkin with your left hand and shape the point to form the curved end of the gondola.

5 Repeat with a second napkin and lay them at opposite ends of a platter. Place a third napkin folded into quarters in the centre.

STOCKS, SAUCES AND DOUGHS

French cuisine is built upon several important bases: stocks, sauces and doughs. Usually these traditional building blocks have been very high in fat, but here we have shown you how to make delicious alternatives that are much lighter. In the sauces, we have replaced cream either partially or completely with Greek yoghurt, and the pastries use smaller quantities of butter, which can be further reduced by using semi-hard polyunsaturated sunflower oil. Our stocks not only use less fat than normal, but are also left in the fridge overnight, then skimmed of the fat that forms on the top.

Fonds de Volaille

CHICKEN STOCK

There is no good cuisine which does not rely on good stocks. This basic stock is used in most main course and starter recipes and is a vital ingredient to prepare regularly and freeze. Never skimp on the recipe as the result just will not be the same.

Whenever you have a chicken carcass, clean it well, remove and discard all the fat along with the parson's nose and either place the carcass in the freezer for later use, or prepare a stock immediately. Preparing healthy dishes such as Poulet Farci Fendu au Four *or* Poulet Sauté à l'Estragon *(see pages 131 and 135) should ensure you have a regular supply of carcasses.*

This stock freezes well. Place in ice-cube trays or ramekin dishes to freeze. Store in freezer bags ready to be used in small quantities when needed. Most stocks can be kept for up to 2 days in the fridge.

GLUTEN FREE
MAKES 900 ML (1½ PT)

1 chicken carcass plus neck, washed
2 chicken wing tips plus feet, washed
mirepoix *(1 carrot, 1 onion and 1 celery stick)*
1 litre (1¾ pt) cold water
salt
freshly ground black pepper
1 bouquet garni
1 bayleaf
1 thyme sprig

1 Drain all the chicken bones, then cut into small pieces and place in a saucepan.

2 Place the roughly chopped *mirepoix* vegetables in the saucepan with all the remaining ingredients.

3 Bring to the boil slowly, skimming off all the impurities as they rise to the surface.

4 Simmer partially covered over a low heat for 1 hour. Skim off the impurities as they rise to the surface (this is important for the clarity of the stock). Cover and leave to cool, then place in the fridge overnight.

5 The next day, remove the layer of fat set on the surface. Bring to the boil again and skim off the impurities. Simmer for 5 minutes, then strain.

Court-Bouillon

VEGETABLE STOCK WITH WINE

A court-bouillon *is a wine-flavoured vegetable stock, very useful for poaching or steaming fish. It is particularly valuable for vegetarians, as is the vegetable stock which follows, and should be used whenever a stock is called for in the various vegetarian recipes in the book. Don't use this* court-bouillon *as the basis for a sauce to be reduced, however, as the wine will make it too bitter.*

This stock can be frozen as Fonds de Volaille *on page 31.*

GLUTEN FREE
MAKES 900 ML (1½ PT)

mirepoix *(2 carrots, 2 onions and 2 celery sticks)*
250 ml (8 fl oz) white wine
750 ml (1¼ pt) cold water
salt
freshly ground black pepper
1 bouquet garni

1 Place the finely chopped *mirepoix* vegetables in a saucepan with the wine, water and remaining ingredients.

2 Bring to the boil slowly, skimming off all the impurities as they rise to the surface.

3 Simmer over a low heat for 20 minutes. Cover and leave to cool before straining.

Bouillon de Légumes

VEGETABLE STOCK

This stock, while as useful as the court-bouillon *for vegetables, is also delicious and beneficial when used as a soup. Drink it, minus the vegetables, or with them puréed into the liquid, to help a cold, an upset stomach, or general malaise.*

This stock can be frozen, as Fonds de Volaille *on page 31.*

GLUTEN FREE
MAKES 900 ML (1½ PT)

mirepoix *(4 carrots, 1 onion, 2 celery sticks)*
1 litre (1¾ pt) cold water
salt
finely ground black pepper
1 bouquet garni
1 small bunch fines herbes, *washed*

TO SERVE AS SOUP
50 g (2 oz) vermicelli or wild rice
100 ml (3½ fl oz) whipping cream and/or 50 g (2 oz) Greek yoghurt
fines herbes

1 Place the finely chopped *mirepoix* vegetables in a saucepan with the water, 2 pinches salt, a little pepper, the *bouquet garni*, and the bunch of *fines herbes*.

2 Bring to the boil slowly, skimming off all the impurities as they rise to the surface.

3 Simmer over a low heat for 20 minutes, then cover and leave to cool before using. If to be used as a stock, strain when cold.

TO SERVE To serve as a soup, strain the stock, bring to the boil and cook the vermicelli or wild rice in it. For a richer soup, liquidize the strained vegetables with the stock, and add the whipping cream and/or yoghurt. (The cream or yoghurt is optional, and could be replaced by milk.) Sprinkle with finely chopped *fines herbes* just before serving.

RIGHT *Fumet de Poisson*

Fumet de Poisson

FISH STOCK

There are several ways of making a traditional fumet *or fish stock. In one method, the vegetables and bones are sweated in butter, wine and water are then added and the mixture is simmered for 20 minutes. This gives a very good stock, but one which is often cloudy. The version which follows does not use any fat at all, therefore the vegetables are not sweated. The flavour is slightly different as a result, but the* fumet *is not as cloudy, and is always better when used for a sauce. The proportion of wine used could be increased – up to half water, half wine – which will give a more bitter stock (not particularly advisable if the stock has to be reduced for a sauce).*

This stock can be frozen, as Fonds de Volaille *on page 31.*

GLUTEN FREE
MAKES 900 ML (1½ PT)

1 kg (2¼ lb) fish bones (sole, plaice, turbot)
mirepoix *(1 carrot, 1 onion and 1 celery stick)*
1 bouquet garni
salt
freshly ground black pepper
250 ml (8 fl oz) white wine
750 ml (1¼ pt) cold water

1 Wash the fish bones well – if possible, leave them for 20 minutes in a bowl under cold running water. This is known as *dégorger*.

2 Place the finely chopped *mirepoix* vegetables in a saucepan with the bones, the *bouquet garni*, a pinch of salt and a little pepper. Add the white wine and water.

3 Bring to a bare simmer over a low heat (this can take up to 15 minutes), skimming off all the impurities as they rise to the surface. Simmer over this very low heat for 20 minutes, then remove the saucepan from the heat and leave to cool. Strain through muslin.

Sauce Diable

DEVILLED SAUCE

This sauce is an ideal accompaniment for braised vegetables, or for robust main course meats or fish. As it's quite spicy, don't use it with delicately flavoured dishes. (If serving with fish, replace the chicken stock used in the tomato sauce with half fish stock, half vegetable stock.)

Doubled in quantity and thinned down with stock, this sauce makes a delicious soup.

GLUTEN FREE
SERVES 4

1 recipe Sauce à la Tomate *(see page 36)*
1 hot chilli pepper, washed and seeded
4 sweet red peppers, washed and seeded
4 shallots, peeled and finely chopped
100 ml (3½ fl oz) white wine
50 ml (2 fl oz) cold water
1 dsp tarragon vinegar
salt
cayenne pepper
freshly ground black pepper

1 While preparing the tomato sauce, chop the chilli pepper and one of the red peppers, and add them to sweat with the other ingredients.

2 Place the shallots in a saucepan with the wine, water, vinegar, a pinch each of salt and cayenne, and some pepper. Bring to the boil over a low heat, and leave to reduce until only about 2 dessertspoons of liquid are left.

3 Meanwhile, seed the remaining sweet peppers and skin them as described on page 23.

4 Liquidize the flesh of two of the peppers. Chop the third one finely and reserve. Add the pepper purée to the reduced shallot mixture and cook slowly without burning for 10 minutes to thicken the purée. Add the chopped pepper.

5 Press the tomato sauce through a chinois sieve and pour into the pepper sauce. Bring to the boil and simmer for 5 minutes. Adjust the seasoning if necessary.

Sauce Calypso

CALYPSO SAUCE

A delicious sauce, this is reminiscent of the commercially famous 'Thousand Island' dressing, which is, in fact, a traditional Haute Cuisine sauce. Prepare it in this way and you will never want to buy a ready-made variety again! It can be used as a salad dressing, with poached eggs or with a 'prawn cocktail' for which the sauce was originally designed.

GLUTEN FREE
SERVES 4

25 ml (1 fl oz) tarragon vinegar
Tabasco sauce
Worcestershire sauce
1 dsp tomato ketchup
1 tsp tomato concentrate
salt
freshly ground black pepper
1 egg yolk
1 garlic clove, peeled and crushed
150 ml (5 fl oz) grapeseed oil
50 g (2 oz) Greek yoghurt
1 dsp cognac

1 Leave all the ingredients to reach room temperature before you begin.

2 In a bowl, mix together the vinegar, a dash each of Tabasco and Worcestershire sauce, the ketchup, tomato concentrate, a pinch of salt and some pepper. Add the egg yolk and garlic and whisk in well.

3 Pour the oil into the mixture very slowly, a few drops at a time to start with, whisking continuously. As the sauce starts to thicken, the oil can be poured in a little more quickly.

4 Add the yoghurt, a spoonful at a time, stirring in well, and flavour with the cognac. Correct the seasoning if necessary.

Sauce Vinaigrette

SALAD DRESSING

This is the basic salad dressing we always use. Prepared once a week, it keeps well in a large screw-topped jam-jar. All you need to do is shake the jar well before using, and place a small amount of the dressing in the bottom of the salad bowl. Layer the various ingredients for the salad on top. Toss just before serving.

GLUTEN FREE
MAKES 500 ML (18 FL OZ)

50 g (2 oz) Dijon mustard
½ tsp sea salt
freshly ground black pepper
100 ml (3½ fl oz) tarragon vinegar
4 shallots, peeled and finely chopped
2 garlic cloves, peeled and crushed
25 g (1 oz) fines herbes, *washed*
250 ml (8 fl oz) grapeseed oil
50 ml (2 fl oz) olive oil

1 Place the mustard, salt, a generous amount of pepper and vinegar in the jar. Close the jar and shake well for a minute to combine the ingredients well.

2 Add the shallots and garlic to the jar. Dry the herbs well, then chop them finely and add to the jar.

3 Pour in all the oil, close the jar again and shake well for 2 minutes. Leave to marinate for at least 20 minutes before using, and remember to shake again before pouring into the salad bowl.

4 Alternatively, this dressing can be made in a food processor. Process the shallots, garlic and herbs for 30 seconds, then add the vinegar, mustard and seasoning. Process again for 30 seconds. With the machine running, pour in the oil. Process for another minute and pour into the jar.

5 For daily use, just shake well before using.

LEFT *Sauce Vinaigrette*

Sauce à la Tomate

TOMATO SAUCE

This tomato sauce has not been much modified for Cuisine Santé as this is the way we have always made it. A traditional recipe would contain a lot more oil and use flour to thicken it, but here just the pulp of the tomatoes is used. If available, flavour with basil.

This tomato sauce can be used to accompany a gratin of vegetables, cooked meats or, more traditionally, home-made pasta – when grated Parmesan cheese is the best garnish. This sauce takes longer to make than a simple coulis, *so make a large amount at a time. It can be bottled, or frozen in ice-cube trays, ready for last-minute use.*

GLUTEN FREE
SERVES 4

1 tsp olive oil
mirepoix *(1 onion, 1 carrot and 1 celery stick)*
1 garlic clove, peeled and crushed
1 dsp tomato concentrate
100 ml (3½ fl oz) white wine
1 litre (1¾ pt) Fonds de Volaille *or* Bouillon de Légumes *(see pages 31 and 32)*
450 g (1 lb) tomatoes, washed and quartered
salt
freshly ground black pepper
1 bouquet garni
herbes de Provence

1 Heat the oil in a heavy saucepan and sweat the finely chopped *mirepoix* over a low heat, covered, tossing once in a while. It should not colour. Add the garlic and sweat for 1 minute. Add the tomato concentrate, stir well and sweat for a further minute. Add the white wine, stir, and leave to reduce until nearly dry.

2 Add the stock, tomatoes, 2 pinches of salt, some pepper and the *bouquet garni.* Stir well and bring to the boil over a medium heat, skimming off the impurities as they rise to the surface. Add a pinch of *herbes de Provence*, stir and cover. Simmer very gently for 20 minutes, then remove the lid and simmer for another 20 minutes; again skim off the impurities as they rise.

3 Leave the sauce to cool for an hour, then press through a chinois sieve. If too thin, reduce over a medium heat.

Sauce au Curry

CURRY SAUCE

This sauce goes wonderfully with steamed, poached or papillote-*cooked fish or poultry, or with a baked vegetable. A good stock (*fumet *or* court-bouillon *for fish, and* fonds de volaille *for poultry) is essential.*

GLUTEN FREE
SERVES 4

1 onion, peeled and finely sliced
100 ml (3½ fl oz) white wine
50 ml (2 fl oz) water
1 tsp butter
salt
freshly ground black pepper
1 tsp Madras curry powder
300 ml (10 fl oz) stock (as above, see pages 31-3)
½ tsp crème de riz *(rice flour)*

1 Place the onion slices in a saucepan with the wine, water, butter, a pinch of salt and a little pepper. Cover and place over a medium heat. Simmer for 5 minutes with the lid on, then remove the lid and cook until the liquid has almost completely evaporated (about 5 minutes).

2 Add two-thirds of the curry powder and sweat the mixture for 5 minutes over a low heat, tossing well so it does not stick or burn. Add the stock and bring to the boil, stirring well. Simmer for 10 minutes, uncovered, skimming off the impurities as they rise.

3 Liquidize in a food processor or push through a hand food mill, then return to the heat. Bring back to the boil, stirring occasionally.

4 Place the rice flour in a bowl and dilute with half the milk. Stir in a little of the hot sauce, then pour this mixture back into the sauce. Bring back to the boil, stirring, and leave to simmer for 2 minutes. Add the remaining milk and remove from the heat.

5 Mix the cream, yoghurt, and remaining curry powder together, then stir in a little sauce. Pour it back into the sauce, mixing well.

6 Adjust the seasoning if necessary with a little salt and pepper, and serve immediately.

100ml (3½fl oz) milk
50ml (2fl oz) whipping cream
25g (1oz) Greek yoghurt

Marinade Café de Paris

MEAT MARINADE

This marinade can be used for many different meat recipes, especially white meats like veal, chicken, turkey or pork.

Fermentation develops the unique flavour of the marinade, which is why it should be left overnight at room temperature. Although the ingredients' list is long, the quantity is enough for only a few slices of meat – four veal escalopes, for instance (see Escalopes de Veau Woronoff, *page 123). For more, multiply the ingredients in proportion.*

GLUTEN FREE

1 Place all the ingredients except the oil in a china bowl, and mix well together with a wooden spoon for 3 minutes. Cover with a piece of cling film and leave overnight to marinate at room temperature.

2 The next day, mix with the oil and liquidize in a food processor. Use to marinate meat or as a basis for a sauce.

1tsp each of tomato ketchup, Dijon mustard, chopped capers, parsley, chives, tarragon, Madeira, Worcestershire sauce and lemon juice
1 pinch each of marjoram, dill, paprika, curry powder and cayenne pepper
1 thyme sprig
1 garlic clove, peeled and crushed
1 shallot, peeled and chopped
1 anchovy fillet, chopped
salt
freshly ground black pepper
grated zest of ½ orange
4dsp grapeseed oil

Marinade Café de Paris

Coulis de Tomates

TOMATO COULIS

Traditionally, the vegetables for this sauce are fried in a lot of olive oil. Here we sweat the vegetables instead, making the sauce much lighter and easier to digest.

Because it is so 'santé', *we use it often in meat, fish and vegetable dishes. It's also good on top of a poached egg.*

GLUTEN FREE
SERVES 4

3 tsp olive oil
1 garlic clove, peeled and crushed
450g (1lb) tomatoes, washed and quartered
herbes de Provence
salt
freshly ground black pepper

1 Heat a heavy saucepan, add 1 teaspoon of the olive oil and add the garlic. Sweat for 1 minute, then add the tomatoes, a pinch each of salt and *herbes de Provence* and a little pepper. Sweat for 3 minutes, tossing over a low heat.

2 Cover and simmer for a further 10-15 minutes or until soft enough to purée.

3 Push through a sieve and reduce if too liquid.

Sauce Verte

GREEN SAUCE

The traditional recipe uses a rich mayonnaise, but we have cut down on the number of egg yolks used and increased the amount of herbs, adding raw spinach and sorrel which add to the fibre, vitamin and iron content of the sauce. We also replace some of the oil with Greek yoghurt, which gives a creamy taste but is less rich.

This sauce is especially good served with steamed or poached fish, but it can also be a base for salad dressing, a dip for vegetables, or a spread for canapés or sandwiches.

GLUTEN FREE
SERVES 4

25 ml (1 fl oz) tarragon vinegar
salt
freshly ground black pepper
1 egg yolk
150 ml (5 fl oz) grapeseed oil
1 shallot, peeled and very finely chopped
1 garlic clove, peeled and crushed
50g (2 oz) fines herbes, *washed*
25g (1 oz) spinach, washed and tough stems removed
2 sorrel leaves, washed and tough stems removed
50g (2 oz) Greek yoghurt

1 Leave all the ingredients to reach room temperature before you begin.

2 Mix the vinegar, a pinch of salt and some pepper in a bowl. Add the egg yolk, and whisk in well. Pour the oil into the bowl very slowly, whisking constantly, a few drops at a time at first, then in a thin stream as the sauce thickens.

3 Add the shallot and garlic to the sauce. Drain and dry the herbs, spinach and sorrel, then chop them very finely. Add to the sauce, mix in well, and correct the seasoning if necessary.

4 Add the yoghurt, a spoonful at a time, and mix in gently.

5 Leave at room temperature for at least 10 minutes before using to allow the herbs to flavour the sauce well.

Sauce Tartare

TARTARE SAUCE

This sauce normally uses two or three egg yolks; here only one is used. The oil is pure and high in polyunsaturated fats, but don't over-indulge in the sauce, it still contains a lot of oil! Do not add more salt than stated as the pickles, tarragon vinegar and parsley provide a good substitute for it.

It is the pickles which give Sauce Tartare *the unique taste which goes so well with grilled fish or meat, but the sauce can also be used as a spread for canapés or sandwiches.*

GLUTEN FREE
SERVES 4

25 ml (1 fl oz) tarragon vinegar
salt
freshly ground black pepper
1 egg yolk
150 ml (5 fl oz) grapeseed oil
1 shallot, peeled and very finely chopped
1 garlic clove, peeled and crushed
1 dsp capers
4 cocktail gherkins
15 g (½ oz) parsley, washed

1 Leave all the ingredients at room temperature for at least 30 minutes before you begin.

2 Mix the vinegar, a pinch of salt and some pepper in a bowl. Add the egg yolk, and whisk well. Pour the oil into the bowl very slowly, whisking constantly, a few drops at a time at first, then in a thin stream as the sauce starts to thicken.

3 Add the shallot and garlic to the sauce. Drain and dry the capers, gherkins and parsley well. Chop them very finely, and stir into the sauce. Correct the seasoning if necessary.

4 Leave at room temperature to marinate for at least 20 minutes before using.

Sauce Moutarde / Sauce Cumberland

MUSTARD (CUMBERLAND) SAUCE

The original recipe for mustard sauce, which had a mayonnaise base and mustard added at the end, contained two or three egg yolks. We have eliminated the yolks completely, and used the mustard alone to emulsify the oil.

A spoonful of redcurrant jelly can be added to the mustard (a recipe given by a British general to a chef during the Napoleonic Wars), and it becomes a Cumberland Sauce, the Cuisine Santé way, of course!

Both sauces are good served with cold meats and fish, and can be used as salad dressings too, but neither keeps at all well.

GLUTEN FREE
SERVES 4

2 dsp Dijon mustard
salt
freshly ground black pepper
1 dsp redcurrant jelly (for Cumberland Sauce only)
100 ml (3½ fl oz) grapeseed oil

1 Place the mustard, a pinch of salt and a little pepper in a bowl and mix. Add the redcurrant jelly (for the Cumberland Sauce only) and mix well.

2 Pour in the oil very slowly, drop by drop at first, then in a thin stream as the sauce thickens. Whisk well at the same time.

3 Adjust the seasoning, if necessary, and serve immediately.

Sauce Colombo

COLOMBO SAUCE

This sauce is adapted from a very famous dish from the French Caribbean islands of Guadeloupe and Martinique which settlers from Sri Lanka brought with them to the islands in the last century.

The flavour is quite strong and spicy, so the sauce is best served with a piece of grilled or poached meat (chicken, pork, or lamb), a baked vegetable, or a poached egg on a bed of wild rice (see Oeufs Pochés Colombo, *page 55).*

GLUTEN FREE
SERVES 4

2 pinches sea salt
10 coriander seeds
½ tsp mustard seeds
5 each of black peppercorns, white peppercorns and caraway seeds
½ tsp Madras curry powder
1 pinch each of turmeric, ground ginger and saffron
½ hot red chilli pepper, seeded and chopped
2 garlic cloves, peeled and crushed
1 onion, peeled and very finely chopped
2 dsp olive oil
50 g (2 oz) aubergine
juice of 1 lime
300 ml (10 fl oz) Fonds de Volaille *or* Bouillon de Légumes, *as appropriate (see pages 31 and 32)*
1 dsp creamed coconut

1 To prepare the Colombo paste, place the salt, coriander and mustard seeds, black and white peppercorns, caraway seeds, curry powder, turmeric, ginger and saffron into a mortar. Work well together with the pestle. Add the chilli pepper and garlic to the mortar, and work again until a paste.

2 Sweat the onion in 1 teaspoon of the olive oil.

3 Peel the piece of aubergine, cut the flesh into cubes and sprinkle with half the lime juice. Add to the onion and sweat, covered, until soft.

4 Add two-thirds of the Colombo paste to the saucepan, mix well, and sweat for 3 minutes without colouring. Add the stock, a little at a time to start with, to dissolve the paste well. Bring slowly to the boil, skimming off the impurities as they rise to the surface.

5 Simmer for 30 minutes, then reduce to a purée in a liquidizer, food processor or hand food mill. Return to the heat, bring back to the boil, stirring, and simmer for another 5 minutes.

6 Add the coconut to the reserved third of the paste in the mortar. Stir in the remaining lime juice and olive oil, then add a little of the sauce, and pour this mixture back into the sauce. Remove from the heat, and stir well to mix the flavours. Pour the sauce over the meat or fish and leave to marinate for 5 minutes before serving.

RIGHT *Sauce aux Fines Herbes*

Sauce Beurre Blanc

BUTTER SAUCE

This 'white butter' sauce is traditionally 95 per cent butter, with double cream added. Here the butter is reduced by half, and single cream is used instead of double. To finish, Greek yoghurt is used and the sauce is seasoned with only a drop of lemon juice and a little salt and pepper.

This sauce can be used to accompany poached eggs or fish, grilled, braised or poached meat, or even a gratin of vegetables.

GLUTEN FREE
SERVES 4

4 shallots, peeled and finely chopped
25 ml (1 fl oz) water
50 ml (2 fl oz) dry white wine
1 dsp tarragon vinegar
50 ml (2 fl oz) single cream
100 g (4 oz) butter, diced, at room temperature
100 g (4 oz) Greek yoghurt
1/2 tsp lemon juice
salt
freshly ground black pepper

1 Place the shallots in a saucepan with the water, wine and vinegar. Reduce over a low heat until only 2 dessertspoons of liquid are left (about 6 minutes).

2 Add the cream, and reduce again until nearly evaporated.

3 Reduce the heat as much as possible, and add the butter, a few dice at a time, shaking the pan at the same time. The butter should melt and emulsify but it must not boil.

4 Off the heat, add the yoghurt, a spoonful at a time. Adjust the seasoning with a drop of lemon juice and some salt and pepper. Do not heat again.

Sauce aux Fines Herbes

HERB SAUCE

This is a very simple sauce, which can be used in various ways: to dress a salad (about 3 dessertspoons would be enough for an average salad for four); to accompany a hot or cold vegetable dish, or poached, steamed or grilled fish or poultry; as a spread for canapés and sandwiches; or as a dip for vegetables.

The fines herbes *give a delightful flavour (and are full of goodness), but any one of these herbs, or others such as dill, thyme or savory, could also be used instead and give their name to the sauce. If fresh herbs are not available, use dried herbs reconstituted in cold water for a few minutes beforehand.*

GLUTEN FREE
SERVES 4

150 g (5 oz) Greek yoghurt
25 ml (1 fl oz) tarragon vinegar
salt
freshly ground black pepper
1 dsp olive oil
25 g (1 oz) fines herbes, *washed*

1 Beat the yoghurt for a minute to make it completely smooth.

2 Place the vinegar with a pinch of salt and some pepper in a bowl. Mix well, so that the salt and pepper dissolve. Add the oil, whisking well.

3 Add the yoghurt, a spoonful at a time, whisking constantly.

4 Dry the herbs well, and chop them very finely. Add to the sauce, and leave to marinate at room temperature for at least 20 minutes before serving.

Pâte Feuilletée

PUFF PASTRY

In the traditional puff pastry recipe, equal amounts of butter and flour are used; here we use one-third less butter. You could substitute hard vegetable fat for the butter, with good results, but do not expect a buttery taste!

SERVES 4

200 g (8 oz) plain flour
100 g (4 fl oz) ice cold water
½ tsp salt
130 g (5½ oz) unsalted butter

1 Sieve the flour into a bowl, and make a well in the centre. Place the water, salt and 25 g (1 oz) of the butter in the well and work into a dough. Wrap in cling film or foil and rest in the fridge for at least 20 minutes.

2 Roll the dough in a star shape and place the remaining butter in a lump in the middle of the star. Wrap the dough over the butter and, using the rolling pin, spread the butter out over the dough, flattening the dough into a rectangle 15 cm (6 in) × 30 cm (12 in). Fold in three, then turn the dough so that the opening is to one side. Roll the dough again to the same size. Fold in three again and rest in the fridge for at least 20 minutes. The dough now has two 'turns'.

3 Place the dough with the opening on the same side again, and repeat the rolling and turning so that the dough has four turns. At this stage the dough can be kept in the fridge for two or three days or put in the freezer for six to eight months.

4 When you are ready to use the dough, repeat the rolling and turning so that the dough has had six turns all together. Roll down to the thickness required.

Pâte à Choux

CHOUX PASTRY

This pastry uses butter, of course, but when you consider that each recipe – whether for a gougère, swans or for profiteroles – will serve from four to six people, it's not too sinful!

PREHEAT OVEN TO 400°F/200°C/GAS 6
MAKES 50 PROFITEROLES, 1 GOUGÈRE OR 4 SWANS

2 eggs
water (see method)
25 g (1 oz) butter
salt
75 g (3 oz) plain flour, sifted on to a piece of paper

1 Weigh the whole eggs in their shells. Measure out an equivalent weight of water.

2 Place the water, butter and a pinch of salt in a medium pan and heat gently until the butter is melted. Bring to the boil, remove from the heat and add the flour all at once. Stir well to form a dough. Dry this dough over a low heat, beating well, for 1 minute.

3 Off the heat, add the eggs, one at a time, beating well between each addition. Make sure that the dough has absorbed one egg before adding the other.

4 Spoon or pipe the dough on to greased baking trays as required (see pages 78 and 174).

5 Bake in the preheated oven for the recommended time.

TO MAKE PROFITEROLES

1 Put the pastry in a piping bag and, using a straight 1 cm (½ in) nozzle, pipe small amounts (about 2 cm/1 in in diameter) on to a baking tray.

2 Brush with a little egg wash.

3 Bake for 15 minutes, then open the oven door a little, and bake for 5 more minutes.

Pâte à Pissaladière

YEAST DOUGH

For this recipe, the butter has been replaced with olive oil, the egg yolks have been reduced by half, and we use 50 per cent wholemeal flour, which still allows the gluten of the strong flour to rise and make the dough lighter.

The recipe makes enough pastry for two quiche tins, but if you want to make only one pissaladière, *use the leftover dough to make rolls to serve with your next meal.*

FILLS 2 × 25 CM (10 IN) QUICHE TINS

150 g (5 oz) strong white flour
150 g (5 oz) wholemeal flour
150 ml (5 fl oz) lukewarm water
25 g (1 oz) fresh yeast
1 egg yolk
1 dsp olive oil
¼ tsp salt
freshly ground black pepper

1 Sieve the white and wholemeal flours together into a bowl. Sprinkle in the bran left in the sieve. Make a well in the centre of the flour.

2 Gently dissolve the yeast in the lukewarm water. Place the egg yolk, olive oil, salt and pepper into the well and add the dissolved yeast. Mix together with a little of the flour to form a wettish paste. Stir in the rest of the flour and work the dough very well until it becomes elastic – this helps it to rise.

3 Place the dough in a bowl, cover with plastic – a plastic food bag cut at the base and on one side – and leave in a warm room to prove. If you are in a hurry, warm up the oven to the lowest temperature and turn it off. Bring a saucepan of water to the boil and place it in the oven with the dough above it. The damp atmosphere will help it rise, but make sure that the oven door is not opened too frequently. Bring the water back to the boil once or twice during the proving time. The dough should double in size in about 15-20 minutes.

4 A second proving is necessary and it is best to do this after shaping the dough. If you want to make rolls, for instance, the shaping should be done now. (Bake for 15 minutes.) For the *pissaladière*, press half of the dough into a quiche tin or on to a baking tray with your hands. Cover with the plastic and leave to prove in the same manner as above.

5 Arrange the topping on the dough (see page 76) and bake as soon as possible or the dough will deflate.

Pâte Brisée

SHORT PASTRY

The butter content of this pastry has been reduced by 25 per cent from a more traditional recipe, which makes the dough less flaky, but it is a good compromise. In a lot of the recipes, using pâte brisée *throughout the book, the amount of flour is mentioned. In order to calculate the amount of fat, divide the quantity of flour by half and then subtract a quarter of it. A whole egg is used in all recipes, and the more (or less) flour, the more (or less) water.*

FILLS A 25 CM (10 IN) QUICHE TIN

200 g (8 oz) wholemeal flour
½ tsp salt
1 egg
3 dsp water
75 g (3 oz) butter or hard polyunsaturated fat, softened and cubed

1 Push the flour into a circle on the work surface, make a well in the centre, and place all the remaining ingredients in the well. Mix the ingredients in the well roughly together, taking in a little flour at a time, until crumbly. Use a plastic scraper or your hand. Bring all the ingredients together and with the palm of your hand push the dough down on to the work surface to blend it all evenly. (Do not *over*work or it will become tough.)

2 Knead lightly, roll lightly into a ball, and wrap (in cling film or foil if the pastry is being prepared a long time in advance; with greaseproof paper if using within the hour). Always rest the dough for at least 20 minutes in the fridge before rolling.

3 If the pastry has been prepared a long time in advance, remember to take it out of the fridge at least 20 minutes before use.

4 This pastry freezes very well. Defrost it overnight in the fridge or for 1 hour at room temperature.

TO MAKE A *TIMBALE*

This is a marvellous way to present a casserole of meat or fish. Once the pastry would have been thrown away, but now it can be enjoyed as part of the meal.

Preheat the oven to 350°F/180°C/Gas 4.

1 Roll out the pastry and use some to line a straight-edged *génoise* tin about 18 cm (7 in) in diameter. Prepare a lid separately, slightly larger in diameter. Make an egg wash by mixing an egg yolk with a little water (for a glossy egg wash) and brush over the lid; decorate it with the remaining dough cut into leaves, etc. Egg wash again.

2 Line the pastry-lined tin with paper and baking beans, and bake for 10-15 minutes until well cooked, then remove the paper and beans and brush well with egg wash. Take the pastry out of the tin and egg wash the outside. Place on a baking tray and cook for a further 2 minutes. Repeat this egg washing and baking twice more.

3 Bake the lid on a baking tray for 10-15 minutes and egg wash similarly.

Pâte à Nouilles

PASTA DOUGH

This is the original Italian pasta dough, except that here healthier wholemeal flour is used. For a lighter texture, plain white flour could be substituted for some of the wholemeal flour.

The proportions of the recipe can be increased easily – 1 egg to each 100g (4oz) flour, 1 pinch salt and 1dsp olive oil. Do prepare a good amount at a time and freeze the remainder in small quantities to be used on separate occasions.

The dough can also be attractively coloured using spinach, beetroot, or saffron. If you intend to do this, it is best to use a plain white flour, and the amount of flour should be increased by about 50g (2oz) to make up for the extra moisture of the colouring or flavouring.

SERVES 4

200g (7oz) 75% wholemeal flour
2 eggs
2 pinches salt
2dsp olive oil

TO COOK
1dsp olive oil

1 Put the flour in a large bowl, make a well in the middle, and place the remaining ingredients in this (including the colouring or flavouring).

2 Work the wet ingredients well together first (especially the colouring or flavouring) and gradually take in a little flour at a time. Carry on, gradually combining the rest of the flour, until the dough forms a ball. Work the dough well for 3 minutes, then cover with cling film or foil and rest in the fridge for at least 30 minutes.

3 Roll the dough into strips 10cm (4in) wide, 60cm (24in) long and 4mm (1/16in) thick, either by hand or in a pasta machine. Leave to dry naturally for 20 minutes (a broom handle placed between two tables or two chairs is ideal to hang the strips over). If using any of the colours, be prepared to use a lot more flour for dusting than normal, as there will be a lot more moisture.

4 To cook the pasta, bring a large saucepan of salted water to the boil, then add 1 dessertspoon olive oil.

5 Cut the pasta into the shape required (noodles, spaghetti, etc.) and plunge into the rapidly boiling water. Stir well, bring back to the boil and time 3 minutes. Taste the pasta to see if it is done to your liking (*al dente* is the best texture). Stop the cooking by removing from the heat and adding a large glass of ice-cold water to the pan. Do not rinse, and leave the pasta in the water until ready to serve.

TO SERVE Drain the pasta through a sieve, *do not rinse*, and transfer to a heated dish. Serve immediately.

SOUPS AND STARTERS

Soups and starters are very important: they are supposed to titillate the appetite, without being too filling, and they should look good enough to arouse delighted expectations for what is to come. They should be delicate, light and sophisticated, and our Cuisine Santé starters and soups are meant to be a combination of all these factors. In addition, they are *santé* because of the reduction of fat and the preponderance of vegetables.

A number of the starters, especially the *tourtes* and quiches, can also be served with a salad as a main course. The soup recipes are basic formulas with which you can experiment: use your imagination and create your own variations.

Crème Capucine

MUSHROOM CREAM SOUP

This is a delicious soup which can be prepared ahead of time, and reheated. The mushrooms contain protein, and their fibre content aids digestion.

GLUTEN FREE (EXCEPT FOR THE CROÛTONS!)
SERVES 6

375g (13oz) button mushrooms
juice of ½ lemon
1tsp grapeseed oil
1 onion, peeled and thinly sliced
1 white of leek, thinly sliced
1 garlic clove, peeled and crushed
40g (1½oz) crème de riz *(rice flour)*
1.5 litres (2½pt) Fonds de Volaille *(see page 31)*
100ml (3½floz) whipping cream
50g (2oz) Greek yoghurt
salt
freshly ground black pepper

GARNISH
grilled wholemeal bread croûtons (optional)
25g (1oz) parsley, finely chopped

1 Wash the mushrooms, then chop and sprinkle with the lemon juice.

2 Heat the oil in a large saucepan, and sweat the onion and leek until soft, covered, about 10 minutes. Add the garlic and sweat a minute longer, then add the mushrooms. Turn the heat up high to sauté them, tossing them often. Continue cooking the mushrooms until only 2 tablespoons of liquid remain in the pan.

3 Add the rice flour and mix well, not letting it stick to the bottom of the pan. Add the stock, mix well to dissolve the flour, and bring to the boil, skimming off all the impurities that rise to the surface. Cover with a lid and simmer for 20 minutes.

4 Strain the soup and liquidize the solids, gradually adding in some of the liquid. Pass the soup through a chinois sieve, then add the cream and bring to the boil again. Simmer for 5 minutes.

5 Thin the yoghurt with a little of the soup and stir the mixture back into the soup. Season to taste with salt and pepper.

TO SERVE Serve the croûtons (if using) separately. Add the parsley to the soup just before serving.

Consommé à l'Estragon

TARRAGON CONSOMMÉ

A consommé is usually made with meat that contains quite a lot of fat. Here we remove all the fat and use very lean meat, which still gives a certain richness and strong flavour. The tarragon lends its own distinctive flavour, and is extremely good for the digestion; it also stimulates the appetite and permits the use of less salt.

You could use the leftover cooked beef and vegetables as the base of a stuffing for vegetables.

SERVES 6

mirepoix *(1 carrot, 1 onion and 1 celery stick)*
100g (4oz) fillet of beef, minced
100g (4oz) lean rump steak, minced
2 tomatoes, washed and quartered
1 green of leek, washed and thinly sliced
1 carrot, washed and finely chopped
2 garlic cloves, peeled and crushed
4 black peppercorns, crushed
2 egg whites
50g (2oz) ice cubes
1.5 litres (2½pt) Fonds de Volaille *(see page 31)*
40g (1½oz) fresh tarragon
100ml (3½fl oz) Madeira or port

TO SERVE
50g (2oz) carrots, cut into julienne
50g (2oz) turnips, cut into julienne

1 Place the finely chopped *mirepoix* in a large bowl with all the remaining ingredients except the chicken stock, half the tarragon leaves and all the stems and the Madeira or port. Mix the ingredients well by hand until the ice cubes have melted.

2 Bring the chicken stock to the boil.

3 Add the boiling stock to the contents of the bowl, stir well, then transfer the mixture into the stock pan and return to the heat. Keep stirring slowly so it does not stick to the bottom of the pan. As soon as it boils, turn the heat down and let it simmer, untouched and uncovered, for 30 minutes.

4 Pour carefully into a clean pan through a chinois sieve lined with muslin, and let it drip. Do not hurry the process by pressing, or the consommé will become cloudy.

5 Reheat, adding the Madeira or port. Steam the vegetable *julienne* for 3 minutes. Skim the surface of impurities as they rise to the top, then add the remaining tarragon leaves and the vegetable *julienne* and bring just to the boil. Turn off the heat and leave to infuse for 5 minutes.

TO SERVE Serve from a heated soup tureen into heated soup bowls or consommé cups.

RIGHT *Consommé à l'Éstragon*

Potage Crécy

CARROT SOUP

This soup traditionally contains far fewer carrots, with more cream and egg yolks. At home, my mother adapted this soup to a much healthier version which virtually reached the consistency of a purée when we were too ill for solid food. The addition of yoghurt gives it a certain tartness, similar to the flavour of crème fraîche, *but without the richness. Carrots are high in Vitamin A, good for the skin, liver and digestion.*

GLUTEN FREE
SERVES 4

1 dsp safflower or grapeseed oil
1 onion, peeled and thinly sliced
1 leek, cleaned and thinly sliced
450 g (1 lb) carrots, washed and roughly sliced
salt
freshly ground black pepper
1 litre (1¾ pt) Fonds de Volaille *or* Bouillon de Légumes *(see pages 31 and 32)*
50 g (2 oz) Greek yoghurt
1 dsp milk

GARNISH
a small bunch of fresh chives

1 Heat the oil and sweat the onion and leek for 5 minutes in a covered saucepan. Add the carrots, salt and pepper and sweat for a further 5 minutes, covered.

2 Meanwhile, heat up the stock, then add it to the sweated vegetables. Simmer slowly for 1 hour.

3 Strain and purée the vegetables in a liquidizer, gradually adding the liquid. Adjust the seasoning if necessary.

4 Mix the yoghurt and milk to a thinnish batter, and pour half into the soup. Heat through briefly but do not allow to boil.

TO SERVE Pour the soup into a warmed tureen or into individual bowls, and snip the chives finely with scissors over the top. Pour the rest of the thinned yoghurt over the soup in a spiral pattern starting from the centre. Draw the blade of a knife over the surface of the soup, from rim to centre alternately, to feather the yoghurt.

Potage Orge Perlé Brunoise

BARLEY SOUP

Instead of using refined 'pearl' barley, we use the 'whole' or 'pot' version available in health-food shops, complete with its bran.

SERVES 6

100 g (4 oz) each of onion, leek, celery and carrot brunoise
1 tsp grapeseed oil
50 g (2 oz) whole barley
1.5 litres (2½ pt) Fonds de Volaille *(see page 31)*
salt
freshly ground black pepper

TO SERVE
50 ml (2 fl oz) single cream
50 g (2 oz) Greek yoghurt

1 Heat the oil in a pan, and sweat the onion *brunoise*, covered, for 5 minutes. Add the leek, carrot and celery and sweat for a further 15 minutes, covered.

2 Add the barley and sweat for 5 minutes.

3 Add the stock, a pinch of salt and a little pepper. Bring to the boil and simmer for 30 minutes, skimming off all the impurities that rise to the surface.

TO SERVE To serve hot, mix the cream and yoghurt together in a bowl and stir in a little of the soup. Pour this mixture back into the soup, off the heat. Adjust the seasoning and serve immediately.

To serve cold, thin with a little more stock and chill in the fridge.

LEFT *Potage Crècy*

Potage Minestrone

MINESTRONE SOUP

This soup is actually more like a complete meal than a starter! Serve it on a cold winter evening with large chunks of crusty garlic bread. You could follow it with a plate of cold meats – perhaps Parma or honey-roast ham, or cold poached chicken (use the poaching stock for the soup) with a Cumberland Sauce (see page 39).

The finishing sauce, pistou *– also known as* pesto *– can be used in many other dishes, and it carries the unmistakable signature of the south of France. Try it on pasta, salads and ratatouille.*

GLUTEN FREE
SERVES 6

50g (2oz) haricot beans
1 onion, peeled and sliced
1 bouquet garni
freshly ground black pepper
1dsp grapeseed oil
100g (4oz) each of onion, leek, carrot and potato paysanne
50g (2oz) each of cabbage and celery paysanne
50g (2oz) tomato concentrate
1.5 litres (2½pt) Fonds de Volaille *(see page 31)*
25g (1oz) spaghetti
salt

PISTOU
2 garlic cloves, peeled
2dsp parsley, finely chopped
2dsp basil, finely chopped
4dsp olive oil

1 Soak the beans overnight in cold water. Drain, and place them in a saucepan with fresh water to cover, the onion, *bouquet garni* and pepper. Cover and leave to simmer over a low heat for 2 hours until tender.

2 Heat the grapeseed oil in a large pan, and sweat all the *paysanne* vegetables except the potatoes, covered, for 15-20 minutes.

3 Add the tomato concentrate, mix in and sweat for 1 minute. Add the stock and bring to the boil. Simmer very gently for 30 minutes, skimming off the impurities as they rise to the surface.

4 Break the spaghetti into little pieces by wrapping in a tea-towel, holding each end, and running the tea towel down the edge of a table very quickly. Add the potatoes, beans and short pieces of spaghetti to the soup and simmer for another 10 minutes.

5 Meanwhile, make the *pistou*. Work together the garlic and herbs using a pestle and mortar or small food processor. (Chop the herbs at the last moment to keep all their flavour.) Add the oil, a little at a time, whisking to emulsify the sauce.

6 Adjust the seasoning of the soup, and add the *pistou* slowly. Do not boil or the *pistou* will separate.

RIGHT *Potage Minestrone*

Gaspacho Andalous

COLD VEGETABLE SOUP

This cold soup, Spanish in origin, has been 'revamped' by us. It is already awash with vitamins and fibre, but we have cut down on the time it takes to make: a traditional gaspacho could take up to 3 hours to prepare; done our way, it only takes 10 minutes!

SERVES 4-6

450g (1lb) ripe tomatoes
1 small cucumber, washed
1 green pepper, washed
1 red pepper, washed
1 onion, peeled
1 litre (1¾pt) pure tomato juice
salt
freshly ground black pepper
2 pinches cayenne pepper
25g (1oz) fines herbes, *washed*
1 dsp tarragon, washed
2 garlic cloves, peeled
25ml (1floz) olive oil
2 dsp tarragon vinegar

GARNISH
grilled wholemeal bread croûtons

1 Trim all the vegetables as necessary and cut into small pieces. Reserve 4 dessertspoons of each for garnishing (rinse the chopped onion in cold water before use). Place the remainder in a food processor or liquidizer and reduce to a purée.

2 Add the tomato juice slowly, plus 2 pinches of salt, some pepper, the cayenne, half the *fines herbes*, and the tarragon. Place in the fridge or freezer to chill well.

3 When ready to serve, using a pestle and mortar, work the garlic, a pinch of salt, a little pepper and the remaining herbs together to a thick paste. Add the olive oil slowly.

4 Blend the chilled gaspacho again in the food processor, adding the garlic paste and the vinegar, a little at a time, alternately.

TO SERVE Correct the seasoning if necessary, and serve in a large bowl. Serve immediately – this soup quickly loses its goodness and flavour. Arrange the croûtons, along with the reserved chopped vegetables, in bowls from which the guests can help themselves.

Oeufs Pochés Colombo

POACHED EGGS WITH COLOMBO SAUCE

This poached egg recipe uses a Sauce Colombo *which contains no cream or butter, just a blend of spices, onion, garlic and a little olive oil. Served with a salad, this will make an ideal light meal.*

SERVES 4

4 eggs, poached (see page 15)
150g (5 oz) wild rice

TO SERVE
1 recipe Sauce Colombo *(see page 40)*
4 parsley sprigs or small bunch chives

1 Prepare the poached eggs and keep in a bowl of cold water.

2 Cook the rice.

TO SERVE Trim off the excess egg white and discard. Place the eggs in a bowl of hot water for 3 minutes to reheat, then strain off the water and pour the sauce over them. Leave for 2 minutes. Spoon the rice on to a large serving dish or individual plates and make a nest for each egg. Lift the eggs from the sauce with a slotted spoon, and drain for a moment. Place on the rice, and pour a little sauce over the top of each and around the bed of rice. Garnish with parsley or chives and serve immediately. Pour the remaining sauce into a gravy boat.

If you want a smoother sauce, strain it, and push through a chinois sieve.

Oeufs en Cocotte à l'Aveyronaise

BAKED EGGS WITH BLUE CHEESE

This recipe evolved when everyone at home was fighting over the last piece of Roquefort cheese. An oeuf en cocotte *is traditionally an egg covered with double cream and baked. Here it is a much lighter preparation, and needs care as there is virtually no means of checking its consistency as it cooks. Do not hesitate to use leftover vegetables in the base if you have any. This dish can be served cold.*

GLUTEN FREE
SERVES 4
PREHEAT THE OVEN TO 350°F/180°C/GAS 4

1 tsp soft butter
100g (4 oz) Roquefort (or other blue cheese)
100g (4 oz) Ricotta (or other low-fat soft cheese)
5 eggs
100g (4 oz) Greek yoghurt
salt
freshly ground black pepper
paprika

1 Use the butter to grease four ramekin dishes, then put them in the fridge to set.

2 Mix the cheeses together roughly and push through a sieve into a bowl.

3 Break one of the eggs into a cup, beat lightly, and add to the cheese mixture a little at a time, along with the yoghurt and seasoning.

4 Spoon a little of the cheese mixture into the greased ramekins, break an egg into each, and cover carefully with the rest of the mixture.

5 Bake in a bain-marie lined with a sheet of greaseproof or Bakewell paper and half-filled with hot water until set – approximately 10-15 minutes.

TO SERVE Serve immediately in the ramekins on a small plate lined with a doily. Eat with a spoon.

LEFT *Gaspacho Andalous*

Rouleau aux Épinards

SPINACH ROLL

Once you have mastered the recipe for home-made pasta, use your imagination and you will be able to serve it in many different shapes and flavours. Rolling the dough is a little difficult (like strudel pastry), but be patient!

In this recipe we combine meat and vegetables (use the leftovers of a previous meal). Alternatively, you could increase the amount of spinach used by about 175g (6oz) and omit the meat completely. A fish kettle is ideal for cooking this, as it can take the length of the rouleau.

SERVES 6

Pâte à Nouilles *made with 250g (9oz) flour (see page 45)*
1 onion, peeled and finely chopped
1 shallot, peeled and finely chopped
1 dsp grapeseed oil
2 garlic cloves, peeled and crushed
1 kg (2¼ lb) spinach or Swiss chard (or a mixture), cut into chiffonade
150g (5oz) cooked meat (turkey, chicken, pork or lamb), minced
salt
freshly ground black pepper
1 egg
100g (4oz) low-fat curd cheese
grated nutmeg
egg wash

TO SERVE
Coulis de Tomates *(see page 38)*
parsley, chervil or watercress sprigs
tomato rose (see page 26)

1 Rest the pasta dough in the fridge for 20 minutes.

2 Sweat the onion and shallot in the oil for a few minutes in a pan, then add the garlic. Sweat for a further minute, then remove with a slotted spoon and keep to one side.

3 In the same saucepan sauté the spinach *chiffonade* very quickly. Add the onion, shallot and garlic mixture. Increase the heat and add the meat, and sauté for 1 minute. Keep on one side to cool, season and mix well.

4 Beat the egg in a bowl, add the vegetable and meat mixture, cheese and nutmeg, and mix thoroughly.

5 Roll the pasta dough very thinly into a rectangle roughly the size of a tea-towel. Finish the rolling *on* a clean tea-towel.

6 Brush the egg wash all over the dough and spread the filling evenly over it. Roll up the dough, with the help of the tea-towel, starting on the long side. (If a larger slice is wanted and/or your cooking pan is not long enough, start rolling from the narrow end.) Rinse and wring out the tea-towel, then wrap it around the roll. Tie the ends with string. It will keep like this overnight if you wish.

7 To cook, bring a saucepan or fish kettle of water to the boil. Add some salt and then put the roll in. Leave to simmer for 30 minutes. When done, add a little cold water to the pan to stop the cooking.

TO SERVE Heat the tomato *coulis.*

Remove the roll from the water only when you are ready to serve or it will dry up. Remove the tea-towel. Cut the roll into slices 1cm (½in) thick and arrange on individual plates on top of the tomato *coulis*. If you wish to serve on a platter, hand round the sauce separately. Garnish with parsley, chervil or watercress sprigs and a tomato rose.

RIGHT *Rouleau aux Épinards*

Gâteau d'Herbage à l'Ancienne

VEGETABLE GÂTEAU

This delicious starter or light evening supper, which we usually serve with a Coulis de Tomates, *can be prepared ahead of time and reheated. It can also be prepared in small ramekin dishes and presented on individual plates.*

GLUTEN FREE
SERVES 6
PREHEAT THE OVEN TO 350°F/180°C/GAS 4

salt
1 Savoy cabbage, separated into leaves
3 tsp grapeseed oil
1 onion, peeled and chopped
150 g (5 oz) leek, cleaned and chopped
100 g (4 oz) sorrel, cut into chiffonade
250 g (9 oz) spinach, cut into chiffonade
freshly ground black pepper
50 g (2 oz) fines herbes, *finely chopped*
grated nutmeg
2 eggs, separated
1 egg white
200 ml (7 fl oz) milk
100 ml (3½ fl oz) whipping cream

TO SERVE
1 recipe Coulis de Tomates *(see page 38)*
parsley sprigs

1 Bring a large saucepan of water with ½ teaspoon salt added to the boil. Blanch the cabbage leaves for 1 minute (time from when the water comes back to the boil). Cool them in a bowl of iced water, drain, and lay flat on a tea-towel. Cut out the main stalks.

2 Heat 1 teaspoon of the oil in a large saucepan and sweat the onion and leek, covered. Add the sorrel *chiffonade* and sauté briskly for 1 minute, stirring constantly. Place on a plate to cool.

3 In the same saucepan heat another teaspoon of the oil and sauté the spinach, seasoned with salt and pepper, over a high heat. Cook till soft, about 3 minutes, and stir continuously so that it does not stick. Place on the plate with the other vegetables and mix well.

4 Grease a 1 litre (1¾ pt) savarin mould with the remaining oil, and line it with the cabbage leaves, leaving an overhang of leaves all around to cover the top of the stuffing. Chop the remaining cabbage into *chiffonade* and add to the stuffing vegetables with the herbs. Season well with salt, pepper and nutmeg.

5 In a bowl, whisk together the eggs, the egg white, milk and cream. Add the vegetables and mix well (this should be done at the last minute or too much water will be drawn from the vegetables).

6 Spoon the mixture into the lined mould, fold the overhanging leaves over, and cover with a piece of Bakewell paper. Bake in a bain-marie in the preheated oven for 50 minutes.

TO SERVE Meanwhile, heat the tomato *coulis*.

Leave the mould to cool for 5 minutes out of the oven. Remove the paper covering and any dry leaves. Turn out on to a round serving dish, and clean up any custard which may have seeped through the leaf wrapping. Pour the *coulis* into the middle, and garnish the ring with parsley sprigs.

LEFT *Gâteau d'Herbage à l'Ancienne*

Oignons Farcis 1

STUFFED ONIONS 1

GLUTEN FREE
SERVES 6
PREHEAT THE OVEN TO 350°F/180°C/GAS 4

3 large onions, peeled
salt
300g (11oz) low-fat curd cheese
4dsp fines herbes, *finely chopped*
50g (2oz) Greek yoghurt
1 egg
freshly ground black pepper
½tsp grapeseed oil
50ml (2floz) whipping cream
50ml (2floz) Fonds de Volaille *(see page 31)*

TO SERVE
100g (4oz) carrot, cut into julienne
100g (4oz) broccoli florets
parsley or watercress sprigs (optional)
chives

These stuffed onions are delicious as well as healthy and economical. The herbs add to the vitamin and mineral content, and give a wonderful freshness; they also reduce the need for salt. Do be sure not to over-blanch the onions – if you do, they will be more difficult to stuff.

1 Bring a saucepan of water with ½ teaspoon salt added to the boil. Cut the onions as described on page 25, and blanch them for 10 minutes.

2 Sieve the cheese into a bowl, and mix in the herbs, yoghurt, egg and some pepper.

3 Refresh the onions under the cold tap and carefully separate the leaves. Chop the hearts, which cannot be stuffed, and add to the cheese stuffing. Stuff each leaf with 1 dessertspoon stuffing, then roll and place in a gratin dish, lightly greased with the oil, keeping the open part down so that the stuffing does not escape during cooking.

4 Mix the cream and chicken stock together and pour over the onions. Cover the dish with foil and bake in the preheated oven for 40 minutes, basting every 10 minutes. Uncover and bake for a further 10 minutes without basting.

TO SERVE Meanwhile, steam the vegetables until they are *al dente* – no longer than 3 minutes.

You can serve the onions in several ways. To serve from the gratin dish, clean the edges of the dish and place it on a platter lined with a napkin or doily. Arrange a garnish of steamed vegetables and a few parsley heads over the top of the onions. You could also remove the onions from the gratin dish and arrange around the edge of a hot serving platter with the garnish in the middle, or arrange the onions and the garnish alternately, with sprigs of parsley or watercress in the middle. Or, you could prepare large individual plates with the onions arranged in the shape of a flower, each onion leaf being a petal. Arrange the strips of carrots, twisted with chives, to make the stem, with the broccoli as the centre of the flower!

RIGHT *Oignons Farcis 1*

Oignons Farcis 2

STUFFED ONIONS 2

This second version of stuffed onions uses meat. It too is delicious, and is very economical as it uses leftovers. Try it with fish as well! If you are on a gluten-free diet, the breadcrumbs can be omitted.

SERVES 4
PREHEAT THE OVEN TO 350°F/180°C/GAS 4

4 small onions, peeled
salt
1 small dessert apple
1½ tsp grapeseed oil
150 g (5 oz) cooked lean meat
25 g (1 oz) dry wholemeal breadcrumbs
25 g (1 oz) Emmenthal cheese, grated
2 fresh sage leaves, finely chopped, or ½ tsp dried sage
freshly ground black pepper
100 ml (3½ fl oz) Fonds de Volaille *(see page 31) or 50 ml (2 fl oz)* Fonds de Volaille *and 50 ml (2 fl oz) whipping cream*

1 Prepare the onions as described in the previous recipe, blanching them and separating the leaves.

2 Chop the onion hearts finely. Mince the meat.

3 Peel and core the apple, and cut into very small cubes.

4 Heat 1 teaspoon of the oil in a skillet and sauté the onion heart briskly. Add the meat, breadcrumbs, apple cubes, cheese and the sage. Season well with salt and pepper and remove to a large plate to cool down.

5 Stuff the onion leaves with the meat stuffing as described in the previous recipe and arrange in the gratin dish, greased with the remaining oil.

6 Pour the chicken stock over the onions, cover the dish with foil and bake in the preheated oven for 40 minutes, basting every 10 minutes.

TO SERVE Serve in one of the ways outlined in the previous recipe.

Oeufs Pochés à la Chantilly

CHANTILLY POACHED EGGS

The 'Chantilly' garnish is traditionally a purée of peas and a Sauce Beurre Blanc *which contains 95 per cent butter and double cream. We have kept the peas but replaced half the butter of the sauce with Greek yoghurt and the double cream with single. The peas contribute vitamin C and fibre if the purée contains the skins (although the texture is more refined if they are sieved out).*

SERVES 4
PREHEAT THE OVEN TO 350°F/180°C/GAS 4

Pâte Brisée *made with 150g (5oz) flour (see page 44)*
4 eggs, poached (see page 15)
1 onion, peeled and finely chopped
1tsp grapeseed oil
½ round lettuce, cut into chiffonade
salt
freshly ground black pepper
150g (5oz) frozen petits pois
50ml (2fl oz) Fonds de Volaille *or* Court-Bouillon *(see pages 31 and 32)*
1dsp fines herbes, *finely chopped*
50ml (2fl oz) milk

TO SERVE
1 recipe Sauce Beurre Blanc *(see page 41)*
parsley sprigs or chervil leaves

1 Rest the pastry for 10 minutes in the fridge, then roll out and use to line four tartlet tins 7.5cm (3in) in diameter. Bake blind in the preheated oven until golden brown, about 5 minutes, then remove the baking beans, and bake for another 10 minutes. Keep warm.

2 Reserve the poached eggs in a bowl of cold water.

3 Sweat the onion in the oil in a saucepan, covered, for 5 minutes. Add the lettuce *chiffonade* to the onion along with a pinch of salt and a little pepper. Sweat for 5 minutes until tender. Add the frozen peas and toss with the other ingredients for 1 minute. Add the stock, herbs, and another small pinch of salt. Cover the top of the vegetables with a circle of paper, and the pan with a lid. Leave over a low heat for 7 minutes. Check to see if the peas are tender enough to be puréed: if not, let them cook for 1-2 minutes longer.

4 Reserve a few whole peas for garnish and purée the remainder of the mixture in a food processor or run through a hand food mill. Bring the milk to the boil and add to the purée. Its consistency should be that of a very thick soup.

TO SERVE Trim the excess white from the eggs when they are cold, and reheat by placing them in a bowl of hot water for 3 minutes.

If serving immediately, place a napkin or doily on a serving plate. Divide the pea purée between the tartlets, place a drained egg on top, and spoon a little of the *Sauce Beurre Blanc* over the egg. Garnish with a pea and/or parsley sprig or chervil leaf. Place on the serving plate, and serve the remaining sauce in a gravy boat.

If serving on individual plates, pour a little sauce over the base of the plate and place the filled tartlet on the sauce. Garnish the plate with a few peas, and the egg with a parsley or chervil leaf. Serve the remaining sauce separately.

LEFT *Oeufs Pochés à la Chantilly*

Terrine de Lapin

RABBIT TERRINE

This terrine was originally wrapped in pork fat and streaky bacon, and also contained pork fat. For the filling we use low-fat pork tenderloin, and the dish is lined with spinach leaves which are non-fatty, protect the meat from drying out, and make the dish look good!

For the best results, prepare over 3 days as advised in the recipe: on the first day, prepare the forcemeat and stock; on the second, cook the terrine; and do not serve it before the third day.

GLUTEN FREE
SERVES 6-8

1 × 1 kg (2¼ lb) rabbit (with liver)
250 g (9 oz) lean veal
150 g (5 oz) lean pork tenderloin
salt
freshly ground black pepper
25 ml (1 fl oz) cognac
herbes de Provence
2 tsp grapeseed oil
2 shallots, peeled and chopped
2 garlic cloves, peeled and crushed
100 g (4 oz) livers (the rabbit's, plus some chicken livers to make up the weight)
50 g (2 oz) shelled hazelnuts, roasted
25 g (1 oz) shelled pistachio nuts, blanched and skinned
2 dsp fines herbes, *finely chopped*
mirepoix *(1 onion, 1 carrot and 1 celery stick)*
100 ml (3½ fl oz) white wine
1 dsp tomato concentrate
600 ml (a good pt) Fonds de Volaille *(see page 31)*
1 bouquet garni
1 egg
450 g (1 lb) spinach, washed and stalks removed, or lettuce leaves (if spinach is not available)

GARNISH
lettuce leaves
gherkins
tomato roses (see page 26)
spring onion flowers (see page 25)

TWO DAYS BEFORE SERVING

1 Joint the rabbit as described on page 21, leaving the saddle whole. Remove the meat from the hind and forequarters and the belly, and reserve the bones and sinews. Cut the meat into cubes and mince with the veal and pork.

2 Remove the meat from the saddle in two long fillets (see page 21). Cut off the remaining meat attached to the saddle, mince it, and mix with the rest of the minced meat.

3 Place the fillets on a plate and sprinkle with salt, pepper, 1 teaspoon of the cognac, and a pinch of *herbes de Provence*.

4 Heat half the oil in a skillet and sweat the shallot and garlic until soft, covered, about 5 minutes. Add the rabbit and chicken livers and sauté briskly over a high heat for 2 minutes. Add half the remaining cognac and set alight. Leave on a plate to cool, and mince when cold.

5 Roughly chop half of the hazelnuts and pistachios and mix into the forcemeat with some salt and pepper, half the fresh herbs, the remaining cognac (except for 1 teaspoon), and the minced livers. Chill in the fridge overnight.

6 Heat the remaining oil in a saucepan and sauté the rabbit bones with the roughly chopped *mirepoix*. Deglaze with the wine and then reduce for 2 minutes. Add the tomato concentrate and mix well over the heat for another 2 minutes, then deglaze again with the stock. Add the *bouquet garni* and leave to simmer for 1½ hours, skimming off the impurities as they rise to the surface. Strain and reduce by simmering until 100 ml (3½ fl oz) is left. Leave to cool, and then place in the fridge to chill overnight.

THE DAY BEFORE SERVING

Preheat the oven to 325°F/160°C/Gas 3.

1 Mix together the forcemeat, reduced stock and beaten egg, and season with pepper, a little salt, and the remaining fresh herbs.

2 Blanch the spinach leaves in salted boiling water for about 1 minute and refresh under the cold tap. Line a 20 × 10 cm (8 × 4 in) terrine with the leaves, leaving enough overhang to cover well the top of the forcemeat. Chop up the remaining spinach and add it to the forcemeat. Place half of the forcemeat into the base of the terrine, and arrange the two rabbit fillets in the middle, with the remaining whole nuts on either side. Pile high with the remaining forcemeat and leaves of spinach.

Terrine de Lapin

3 Cover the terrine with a lid or foil, and place in a bain-marie lined with a sheet of greaseproof or Bakewell paper and a little hot water. Bake in the preheated oven for 1 hour. Turn the oven off and let the oven cool with the terrine inside. Remove the lid, put weights on top of the meat, and leave in the fridge for at least 12 hours.

TO SERVE Dip the base of the terrine dish into hot water in a bain-marie, and turn out on to a platter lined with lettuce leaves. Cut the first three slices and leave the remainder intact. Garnish with gherkins, tomato roses, and spring onion flowers.

For individual servings, place a slice on a lettuce leaf, and garnish in the same way.

Pâté Chaud Paysan

PÂTÉ BAKED IN PASTRY

This is an ideal dish for making use of leftover raw meat. Assorted pieces of meat, stored in the freezer, can be transformed into this pâté en croûte. *Although the pâté is wrapped in a rich puff pastry, the amount consumed by each guest is minimal. It can be served hot or cold.*

SERVES 8 AS A STARTER, 6 AS A MAIN COURSE

- Pâte Feuilletée *made with 350g (12oz) flour (see page 42)*
- mirepoix *(1 onion, 1 carrot, and 1 celery stick)*
- *500ml (18floz) red wine (Côtes du Rhône type)*
- *1 thyme sprig*
- *1 bayleaf*
- *2 parsley sprigs*
- *1dsp olive oil*
- *5 each of black and white peppercorns and coriander seeds, crushed*
- *1 clove*
- *200g (7oz) each lean beef, veal and pork, cut into strips*
- *100g (4oz) lean beef, cubed*
- *150g (5oz) lean pork, cubed*
- *1tsp grapeseed oil*
- *1 onion, peeled and finely chopped*
- *2 shallots, peeled and finely chopped*
- *2 garlic cloves, peeled and crushed*
- *200g (7oz) chicken or duck livers, well trimmed*
- *2dsp cognac*
- *1 egg*
- *25g (1oz)* fines herbes, *finely chopped*
- *salt*
- *cayenne pepper*
- *freshly ground black pepper*
- *1tsp butter*
- *egg wash*
- *1 egg yolk*

TO SERVE

- *1 recipe* Sauce Diable *(see page 34)*
- *1 recipe* Salade de Champignons de Sabine *(see page 160)*

TWO DAYS BEFORE SERVING

1 Prepare the puff pastry up to the four-turn stage (see page 42), then leave to rest, well wrapped, in the fridge.

2 Place the finely chopped *mirepoix* in a roasting tin with the wine, thyme, bayleaf, parsley sprigs, olive oil, crushed spices and the clove. Mix all these ingredients well together by hand so that the flavours blend. Place the meat strips and cubes in this marinade and mix well. Place a piece of Bakewell paper directly on top of the meat and cover the tin with foil.

3 Leave to marinate at room temperature for 2 hours, then toss again and place in the fridge overnight.

THE DAY BEFORE SERVING

1 Heat a skillet, then heat the grapeseed oil. Sweat the onion and shallot over a low heat until soft, about 5 minutes. Add the garlic and sweat for 1 minute. Remove any green bits, nerves and fat from the livers, then add the livers to the pan. Turn the heat up and sauté, tossing well, before adding the cognac. Set it alight, then leave to cool.

2 Give the pastry two more turns and return it to the fridge to rest.

3 Drain the meat and discard the marinade. Dry the meat well on paper towels, leave the strips to one side, then mince the cubes. Place in a bowl with the egg, herbs, 2 pinches each of salt and cayenne, and some pepper, and work well together by hand.

4 Mince the cooled livers, add to the minced meat, and mix well together by hand.

5 Butter a baking tray lightly and sprinkle with a few drops of water. Cut the pastry in two, one part slightly bigger than the other, and roll out both pieces into rectangles, the larger roughly 25 × 35cm (10 × 14in), the smaller 15 × 25cm (6 × 10in). Lay the larger piece on the baking tray.

6 Brush with egg wash all over, and then spread a third of the mince over the rectangle on the baking tray, leaving wide borders. Arrange half the meat strips all over it lengthwise, then cover with another third of the mince. Arrange the remaining strips over it, and cover finally with the remaining mince. Fold the borders of the dough up over the meat, and brush with egg wash. Lay the smaller rectangle on top of this, pressing well to stick the layers together. Brush with egg wash all over thickly, and let it set for 5 minutes. Add the egg yolk to the remaining egg wash (with a little water if it is too thick) and brush again. Leave to set, then cover loosely with foil.

7 Place in the fridge overnight to marinate, along with the remaining egg wash (covered as well).

THE DAY OF SERVING

Preheat the oven to 450°F/230°C/Gas 8.

1 Mix the egg wash with a fork and brush over the pastry. Lay any leftover dough in a lattice on top of the pastry.

2 Place the baking tray in the preheated oven, and turn it down immediately to 350°F/180°C/Gas 4. Bake for 1 hour. If the pastry starts to brown too much, cover it with a piece of foil.

TO SERVE Meanwhile, keep the *Sauce Diable* warm.

Leave the pâté in the turned-off oven for 15 minutes, then transfer to a warm serving dish. Cut into portions with a sharp knife. Serve the sauce separately in a gravy boat. Serve with *Salade de Champignons*.

Pâté Chaud Paysan with *Salade de Champignons de Sabine*

Tourte aux Épinards

SPINACH PIE

The spinach, which is the base of this tourte, *should be washed three times in different water; it can be very gritty, and it also will have traces of nitrates if not organically grown. Spinach is a healthy vegetable, with a high content of iron, phosphorus, copper, cobalt and vitamins A, B and C. This* tourte *can be served hot or cold.*

SERVES 6 AS A STARTER,
4 AS A MAIN COURSE
PREHEAT THE OVEN TO 350°F/
180°C/GAS 4

Pâte Brisée *made with 250g (9oz) flour (see page 44)*
egg wash
300g (11oz) Ricotta (or other low-fat soft cheese)
2 eggs
saffron
25g (1oz) fines herbes, *finely chopped*
1 thyme sprig
salt
freshly ground black pepper
grated nutmeg
450g (1lb) spinach, cut into chiffonade
4dsp skimmed milk (optional)

TO SERVE
1 recipe Coulis de Tomates *(see page 38) or salad leaves*
parsley sprigs

1 Rest the pastry in the fridge for 20 minutes. Roll out the pastry and line a 20cm (8in) loose-bottomed *tourte* tin (a pie tin will do), leaving a lip all around the edge. Roll out the remaining pastry to make a lid. Brush both parts with egg wash, but do not assemble yet.

2 Heat the oil in a large saucepan. Add the spinach *chiffonade* and toss over a high heat for two minutes. Place on a large serving dish, and spread out so that it cools quickly.

3 Push the cheese through a sieve into a bowl. Mix in the eggs, one by one, and a pinch of saffron. Add the herbs, the leaves from the sprig of thyme, a pinch of salt, some pepper and some nutmeg.

4 Mix in the spinach *chiffonade*. Pour the batter into the pastry case and place the pastry lid on top. Press both pieces of pastry together well, using the egg wash to help them stick. Cut off the excess pastry with a knife, and crimp all round the edges with your fingers. Brush with egg wash again, and decorate the top with any leftover pastry. Make a small hole in the centre of the lid, and keep it open with a chimney made of foil (rolled around the handle of a wooden spoon).

5 Bake in the preheated oven for 40 minutes. After 30 minutes, take out of the oven, remove the sides of the tin and brush the sides of the pastry with egg wash. Return to the oven to finish cooking. Repeat the operation twice to obtain a good golden brown colour.

TO SERVE Turn the *tourte* out on to a cooling rack, and leave in the turned-off oven to cool for 10 minutes or for 5 minutes at room temperature. Serve with tomato *coulis*. Alternatively, leave to cool completely, and serve with salad leaves. Garnish the top with parsley.

RIGHT *Tourte aux Épinards*

Peperonata

PROVENÇAL PEPPER SALAD

This very traditional Provençal dish is usually cooked in olive oil, which we have replaced with wine and water or chicken stock. If you have already had your quota of eggs for the week, you can omit the ones in this recipe. The dish is full of vitamins, and low in calories; if you left the pepper skins on, the fibre content would be increased, but they would be more difficult to digest.

This dish can also be served as a side salad, either tepid or cold, but leave to marinate for at least a few hours to enhance the flavours.

GLUTEN FREE
SERVES 4

2 green peppers and 2 red peppers, skinned (see page 23)
2 dsp olive oil
2 onions, peeled and thickly sliced
4 garlic cloves, peeled and crushed
50 ml (2 fl oz) white wine
50 ml (2 fl oz) water or Fonds de Volaille *(see page 31)*
herbes de Provence
salt
freshly ground black pepper
4 eggs
2 dsp tarragon vinegar
5 fresh basil leaves, chopped, or 1 tsp dried basil

1 After skinning the peppers, cut the flesh into strips.

2 Heat half the olive oil in a large pan, and sweat the onion, covered, for 5 minutes. Add the garlic, and sweat for 2 minutes.

3 Sweat the strips of pepper with the onion and garlic for 5 minutes. Add the white wine, water or stock, a pinch of *herbes de Provence*, salt and pepper and simmer, covered, for 5 minutes.

4 Take the lid off the pan, and continue simmering until the liquid has reduced by half. Leave to cool.

5 Boil the eggs in boiling water for 5 minutes, then refresh under cold water to stop the cooking. (If you are preparing well in advance, cut the cooking time for the eggs by 1 minute and do not refresh them.)

6 Add the vinegar to the peppers and adjust the seasoning if necessary. Place in a serving bowl, and mix in the basil.

TO SERVE Shell the eggs, quarter them, and place on top of the *Peperonata*. Serve lukewarm or cold – both are delicious.

Paupiettes de Choux

CABBAGE ROLLS

These paupiettes *are one of our own creations rather than a modification of an existing recipe, and are therefore already healthy! Serve cold as a starter, on cocktail sticks as* amuses-gueules, *or hot in the winter months as a garnish for meat... there are endless possibilities.*

GLUTEN FREE
SERVES 4

1 Savoy cabbage, small
1 round lettuce
1 leek, washed
2 spring onions, washed
100g (4oz) brown rice
salt
2 parsley sprigs
1 thyme sprig
1tsp grapeseed oil
75g (3oz) sorrel, cut into chiffonade
1 tomato, skinned, seeded and finely chopped
25g (1oz) Emmenthal cheese, grated
freshly ground black pepper
50g (2oz) Greek yoghurt
50ml (2floz) Sauce Moutarde *(optional, see page 39)*

TO SERVE
1 recipe Coulis de Tomates *(optional, see page 38)*
lemon twists (see page 26)

1 Remove some of the leaves from the cabbage, for garnishing. Cut the cabbage into quarters through the heart, and reserve the heart pieces. Divide the lettuce into leaves, reserve the heart, and chop the rest into *chiffonade*. Wash all the vegetables very carefully. Chop the white of the leek and the spring onion bulbs finely. Chop the lettuce and cabbage hearts.

2 Cook the rice in plenty of salted boiling water with the green of the leek and spring onions, the parsley sprigs and thyme.

3 Cook the cabbage leaves and quarters in a steamer above salted boiling water for 10 minutes with the lid on, and for a further 15 minutes without the lid.

4 Heat the oil in a frying pan and sweat, one after the other, the spring onion, leek, lettuce and cabbage hearts, and the *chiffonade* of lettuce and sorrel. Keep them well covered, and allow 2 minutes between each addition. Add the tomato and sweat for 1 more minute. Add the cheese, the rice, a pinch of salt and some pepper. Mix well and put on a plate to cool. When it is cold, add the yoghurt and adjust the seasoning if necessary. If you want to serve the *paupiettes* cold, add the mustard sauce to the filling and leave to marinate for at least one hour.

5 Divide the cabbage quarters into leaves and lay on a board covered with paper towels to absorb the excess moisture. Divide the stuffing between the leaves, fold in the sides, and roll.

TO SERVE If serving hot, preheat the oven to 350°F/180°C/Gas 4. Lay the *paupiettes*, opening side down, in a greased 25cm (10in) gratin dish. Cover with foil and place in the oven for 5 minutes to reheat. Serve with a warm tomato *coulis* if you like.

When serving cold, arrange on a serving dish lined with the cabbage leaves, and garnish with lemon twists.

RIGHT *Paupiettes de Choux*

Feuilletés aux Champignons

MUSHROOMS IN PASTRY

SERVES 4
PREHEAT THE OVEN TO THE MAXIMUM SETTING, NORMALLY 475°F/240°C/GAS 9

Pâte Feuilletée *made with 300g (11oz) flour (see page 42)*
egg wash

FILLING
25g (1oz) butter
450g (1lb) button mushrooms, thinly sliced
1tsp lemon juice
salt
freshly ground black pepper
75ml (3floz) white wine
100ml (4floz) whipping cream

GARNISH
2dsp chopped parsley

These puff pastry feuilletés *are always a huge success. They are simple to make, economical, and taste delicious. You can, if you prefer, prepare one large* feuilleté, *in which case the cooking time should be increased by 5-10 minutes.*

1 Prepare the *feuilletés* as shown on page 14.

2 Bake in the preheated oven for 5 minutes, then turn the temperature down to 350°F/180°C/Gas 4, and bake until the pastry is golden brown, approximately 15-20 minutes. The centre part of the pastry cases will rise. When cooked remove the upper layers with a sharp knife, and use these top parts as lids. Dry out the bases a little more in the oven.

3 For the filling, melt the butter and sauté the mushrooms over a high heat, adding the lemon juice, salt, pepper and white wine. Cover with a lid as soon as the juices of the mushrooms start to run, turn the heat down to medium and leave them, covered, for 5 minutes. Remove the lid and add the cream. Leave to reduce slowly, for about 10-15 minutes. There must still be a little sauce, or the filling will be too dry.

TO SERVE When the mushrooms are cooked, mix in half the parsley. Spoon the mushrooms into each *feuilleté*, and sprinkle with parsley.

If you have prepared one large *feuilleté*, bring it to the table, slice off the ends with a serrated knife, and cut into four portions.

Feuilletés aux Champignons

Pudding de Courgettes Soufflé

SOUFFLÉD COURGETTES

This delicious starter is halfway between a soufflé and a courgette terrine 'au gratin'. *Prepared individually in ramekin dishes and served with a tomato* coulis, *it looks very pretty.*

The basic soufflé can be prepared up to a day in advance and reheated in a very hot oven for a few minutes before serving.

If you replace the wholemeal flour with potato flour, the recipe is gluten free.

SERVES 4

PREHEAT THE OVEN TO 350°F/180°C/GAS 4

300g (11oz) courgettes, washed, topped and tailed
salt
1tsp butter
1dsp olive oil
2 garlic cloves, peeled and crushed
150ml (5floz) milk
freshly ground black pepper
cayenne pepper
grated nutmeg
25g (1oz) Emmenthal or Gruyère cheese, grated
1 heaped dsp wholemeal flour
1 egg, separated
1dsp fines herbes, *finely chopped*
3 egg whites

TO SERVE
25g (1oz) Parmesan cheese, grated
1 recipe Coulis de Tomates *(see page 38)*

1 Grate the courgettes finely (by hand or in the food processor). Layer in a bowl with a teaspoon of salt sprinkled between the layers. Leave for 20 minutes. Butter four ramekin dishes lightly and refrigerate to set.

2 Rinse the courgettes under cold running water to rid them of the salt. Take small amounts at a time in your hand and squeeze well to eliminate as much water as possible. Heat a skillet, add the oil, and sauté the courgettes very quickly for 2 minutes to evaporate the remaining moisture. Add the garlic and sweat for 1 minute more. Reserve on a plate to cool.

3 Mix the milk, a pinch of salt, a little pepper, a pinch of both cayenne and nutmeg in a pan and bring to the boil. Mix the Emmenthal with the flour in a bowl. Pour a third of the boiling milk into the bowl, mixing well, then return this mixture to the milk in the pan. Bring back to the boil, whisking vigorously, and take off the heat. Add the egg yolk and mix well, then add the courgettes and herbs and mix again. Reserve, covered, in a warm place.

4 Whisk the 4 egg whites until they form soft peaks (almost runny). Mix 1 tablespoon into the courgette batter, then gently fold in the remainder.

5 Dust the buttered ramekins with extra plain white flour, and tap upside-down on the work surface to eliminate the excess. Fill them three-quarters full with the courgette batter. Line a roasting tin with a sheet of paper (greaseproof or Bakewell) and place the dishes on it. Pour enough boiling water into this bain-marie to come halfway up the dishes.

6 Bake in the preheated oven for 15 minutes. Take out and leave to cool for 5 minutes. The soufflés will fall. Turn each ramekin out on to a serving plate. If you are serving more than 1 hour later, leave in the ramekins until ready to reheat.

TO SERVE Preheat the oven to 450°F/230°C/Gas 8.

Pour some tomato *coulis* over the soufflés and sprinkle evenly with the Parmesan. Bake in the hot oven for 5 minutes and serve immediately.

Soufflé au Fromage

CHEESE SOUFFLÉ

This version of a classic cheese soufflé excludes the butter normally used for the roux. *The cheese itself contains enough fat.*

This mixture fills a 2 litre (3½pt) soufflé dish, so measure your dish and adjust the quantities accordingly.

SERVES 6

PREHEAT THE OVEN TO 350°F/ 180°C/GAS 4

400ml (14floz) milk
salt
freshly ground black pepper
grated nutmeg
60g (scant 2½oz) plain flour (plus extra, to dust)
75g (3oz) Gruyère cheese, grated
5 eggs, separated
2 egg whites
1dsp fines herbes, *finely chopped*
15g (½oz) butter

1 Bring the milk, salt, pepper and nutmeg to the boil in a saucepan.

2 Butter the soufflé dish, and dust it lightly with a little flour.

3 In a bowl, mix together the flour and cheese. Pour the boiling milk over this mixture, whisking hard and continuously. Add the egg yolks, one by one.

4 Whisk all the egg whites until they form very soft peaks, and fold gently into the cheese batter. Add the herbs.

5 Pour into the soufflé dish, and bake in the preheated oven for 20-30 minutes.

TO SERVE As with all soufflés, make sure your guests are seated at the table waiting for it (not the other way around!). Place the soufflé dish on a plate lined with a folded napkin or a doily and serve *immediately*!

Soufflé au Saumon Fumé

SMOKED SALMON SOUFFLÉ

This soufflé uses no butter, and with a minor change of method, works very well. In fact, the soufflé becomes so much lighter that one wonders why butter was used in the first place!

SERVES 6

PREHEAT THE OVEN TO 350°F/ 180°C/GAS 4

1tsp grapeseed oil
1 medium onion, peeled and finely chopped
300ml (10floz) skimmed milk
salt
freshly ground black pepper
75g (3oz) smoked salmon
3 capers, drained and finely chopped
40g (1½oz) flour
4 eggs, separated
1 egg white

1 Heat the oil in a skillet, and sweat the onion over a low heat, covered, until tender, about 10-15 minutes. Leave to cool briefly.

2 Bring the milk, salt and pepper to the boil in a saucepan.

3 Process the smoked salmon in a food processor or hand food mill, then mix with the capers in a bowl. Place the flour in another bowl, and pour the boiling milk into it, whisking hard and continuously. Add the egg yolks one by one, then season with a pinch of salt and plenty of pepper. Add the salmon mixture, and mix well.

4 Whisk all the egg whites until they form very soft peaks, and fold gently into the mixture. Add the sweated onions.

5 Pour into a 1 litre (1¾pt) soufflé dish that has been oiled and lightly floured, and bake in the preheated oven for 30 minutes.

TO SERVE As with all other soufflés, serve *immediately*!

Quiche aux Oignons

ONION TART

This quiche originated in Alsace where it is called 'zewelwai'. *Fewer onions were used, and a larger quantity of eggs, cream, ham and butter. Onions cooked this way have an extraordinarily good flavour.*

SERVES 8 AS A STARTER, 6 AS A MAIN COURSE
PREHEAT THE OVEN TO 350°F/ 180°C/GAS 4

1 recipe Pâte Brisée *(see page 44)*
egg wash
700g (1½lb) onions, peeled and thickly sliced
50ml (2fl oz) water
50ml (2fl oz) white wine
1 thyme sprig
1 bayleaf
salt
freshly ground black pepper
25g (1oz) butter
1tsp grapeseed oil
100g (4oz) gammon ham or green bacon (fat and rind removed), diced
2 eggs
100ml (3½fl oz) whipping cream
100ml (3½fl oz) skimmed milk

GARNISH
parsley sprigs

1 Rest the pastry in the fridge for 20 minutes, then use to line a 25cm (10in) loose-bottomed quiche tin. Prick the base of the pastry with a fork, line with a circle of Bakewell or greaseproof paper, then cover with baking beans. Bake blind in the oven for 10 minutes. Remove the beans and foil, brush a little egg wash all over the pastry base, and bake again for 2 minutes. Repeat this twice more.

2 While the pastry is cooking prepare the filling. Put the onions in a saucepan with the water, white wine, thyme, bayleaf, salt, pepper and butter. Cover with a lid and simmer very gently for 10 minutes. Remove the lid and let the juices reduce completely. Be careful once the juices have evaporated. The onions need to colour a little, but stir regularly so they do not stick or burn.

3 While the onions are cooking, heat the oil in a skillet and sauté the ham until golden brown. Place on paper towels to drain off the fat. (If you want to allow yourself a little treat, omit the butter from the filling, and add this fat to the onions while they cook!)

4 When both the onions and pastry base are ready, mix the eggs, cream and milk together in a bowl. Off the heat, add to the onions, then add the ham. Remove the bayleaf and thyme, and mix very carefully but thoroughly before transferring to the pastry base. Spread evenly all over and bake for 20-30 minutes in the preheated oven until golden brown on top.

TO SERVE Transfer the tin on to a cooling rack, remove the base and sides, and leave to cool for 5-10 minutes before serving. Garnish with parsley sprigs.

Quiche aux Oignons

Pissaladière à la Niçoise

PROVENÇAL ONION TART

A pissaladière *is usually served as a snack in the markets of the south of France, and is the southern version of the onion quiches of Alsace. It can be served as a main course, with an accompanying salad.*

We use oregano in the filling which, like many herbs, is reputed to help digestion and many internal disorders.

SERVES 8

PREHEAT THE OVEN TO 450°F/ 230°C/GAS 8

1 recipe Pâte à Pissaladière *(see* *page 43)*
700g (1½lb) onions, peeled, halved and thickly sliced
salt
1 bayleaf
1 thyme sprig
1 dsp olive oil
1 garlic clove, peeled
12 black olives
100ml (3½fl oz) white wine
freshly ground black pepper
1 dsp dried oregano or 12 fresh leaves
10 anchovy fillets, drained

1 Leave the dough to prove in a warm place. Knock it back and use half of it to line a 25cm (10in) quiche tin. Leave in a warm place to prove again. (With the leftover dough, make a few rolls to serve with your next meal!)

2 Meanwhile, place the onion slices in a saucepan with a pinch of salt and all the remaining ingredients except the oregano and anchovies. Simmer over a low heat, covered, for 5 minutes, and then simmer uncovered until the liquid has evaporated. Continue cooking over the same low heat to brown slightly. Remove the garlic, bayleaf and thyme. Add half the oregano, and mix well.

3 When the dough has proved, cover the top with the onions and arrange the olives evenly around, with the anchovy fillets between them. Sprinkle the remaining oregano over the top.

4 Bake in the preheated oven for 30-40 minutes. Remove from the tin and cool for a few minutes before serving, or serve cold.

Tourte de Courgettes et d'Aubergines

COURGETTE AND AUBERGINE PIE

This is a delicious tourte *or pie which can be prepared ahead of time and reheated, and can also be served cold for a buffet or a picnic. It is a very good way to use up the livers which come with chickens, and are usually thrown away. We store them in a jam-jar in the freezer and when the jar is full, it is time to make this* tourte*!*

Do seal the vegetables well initially or their moisture will come out while the tourte *is cooking and will make the pastry soggy.*

SERVES 6 AS A STARTER, 4 AS A MAIN COURSE
PREHEAT THE OVEN TO 450°F/230°C/GAS 8

Pâte Feuilletée *made with 300g (11oz) flour (see page 42)*
750g (a good 1½lb) aubergines
150g (5oz) courgettes, washed topped and tailed
salt
olive oil
4 spring onions, thinly sliced
2 garlic cloves, peeled and crushed
100g (4oz) chicken livers
1 egg
freshly ground black pepper
40g (1½oz) fines herbes, *chopped*
egg wash

TO SERVE
1 recipe Sauce à la Tomate *(see page 36)*

1 Rest the puff pastry in the fridge for 20 minutes.

2 Slice the aubergine and courgettes, salt them well and leave them to drain for 15 minutes. Rinse them to remove the salt, and dry on paper towels. Heat 1 dessertspoon oil in a large frying pan and sauté the aubergine and courgette briefly over a high heat to seal the slices. Be careful not to put too much oil in the pan as both vegetables will absorb as much as you give them. Put aside to cool.

3 Sweat the onions and garlic in a little more olive oil in the same pan, and put aside to cool.

4 Remove any nerves and greenish parts from the livers. Chop them very finely, almost to a purée consistency. Place in a bowl, beat the egg into them and season well with salt, pepper and the herbs.

5 Roll out the puff pastry and cut a round shape for the top of the pie. Roll out the rest and use to line a 20cm (8in) loose-bottomed pie tin. Mix the vegetables with the liver and pour into the pastry base. Brush the edges of the pastry with egg wash and place the lid on top. Crimp the edges with your fingers to stick them together, and make a hole in the centre of the lid. Keep it open with a chimney of foil (rolled around a wooden-spoon handle). Brush the top with more egg wash and place in the fridge to rest for 10 minutes. Make a decoration on the lid with the back of a knife.

6 Place in the preheated oven, and turn it down immediately to 350°F/180°C/Gas 4. Bake for 40 minutes.

7 Remove the sides of the tin, brush the pastry sides with egg wash, and leave to brown for a further 5 minutes. Repeat once more.

TO SERVE Remove the base of the pie tin, and leave the *tourte* to cool for 5 minutes on a cooling rack, then serve warm with the tomato sauce.

LEFT *Pissaladière à la Niçoise*

Gougère

CHOUX PASTRY RING

SERVES 4
PREHEAT THE OVEN TO 400°F/200°C/GAS 6

100 g (4 oz) Emmenthal cheese
1 recipe Pâte à Choux *(see page 42)*
egg wash

TO SERVE
salad leaves
1 recipe Sauce Vinaigrette *(see page 35)*

ABOVE *Gougère*

A gougère, a choux pastry ring flavoured with cheese, is traditionally served during wine tastings in Burgundy – but even if you don't have such a pleasant task to perform, you can indulge in this light and tasty confection. If you serve it with a salad as the main part of a meal with a fruit dessert afterwards, it makes a delicious and satisfying lunch or dinner.

1 Cut the cheese in half. Cut one piece into very small cubes (they need to go through the nozzle of the piping bag), and the other into thin slices with a cheese slicer. Add the cubes to the choux dough and place in a piping bag fitted with a 6 mm (¼ in) plain nozzle.

2 Pipe four small rings of 7.5 cm (2 in) in diameter, or one larger one 40 cm (10 in) in diameter, on a greased baking tray. Brush with a little of the egg wash, and place the slices of cheese on top.

3 Bake in the preheated oven for approximately 10 minutes, and then for 5 minutes at 350°F/180°C/Gas 4 with the door ajar (prop it open with the handle of a wooden spoon). Increase these times by 5 minutes if you are making the larger ring.

TO SERVE Prepare a few salad leaves using different varieties – try lettuce, radicchio, chicory, watercress, etc. – ready to be dressed in the vinaigrette, and place in the middle of the rings. As soon as the *gougères* are ready, arrange the dressed salad leaves and serve immediately. The quantity of salad used depends on whether the *gougères* are to be served as a starter or a main course.

Terrine de Foies de Volaille

CHICKEN LIVER PÂTÉ

Don't be alarmed by the amount of butter and cream used here: it has already been reduced by half and it is shared by 10 people! The stock used should be of the highest quality and should be quite strong before being reduced. The terrine will be at its best 24 hours after cooking, as the flavours will have combined well by then.

This dish can also be used as a warm first course. Reheat slowly in a bain-marie, then slice and serve on a bed of Coulis de Tomates *(see page 38), with a few chopped skinned and seeded tomatoes, and chopped parsley.*

If you are on a gluten-free diet, omit the breadcrumbs, and add one more egg instead.

SERVES 10

PREHEAT THE OVEN TO 300°F/150°C/GAS 2

450 g (1 lb) chicken livers
1 litre (1¾ pt) Fonds de Volaille *(see page 31)*
90 g (3½ oz) dry wholemeal breadcrumbs
4 garlic cloves, peeled and crushed
100 g (4 oz) soft butter
3 eggs, beaten
100 ml (4 fl oz) whipping cream
25 ml (1 fl oz) cognac
salt
freshly ground black pepper
cayenne pepper
paprika

GARNISH
aspic
parsley sprigs
tomato rose (see page 26)

1 Wash and drain the livers and lay on a work surface to separate them. Remove the nerves, and any green parts or fat.

2 Reduce the stock by simmering to obtain 250 ml (8 fl oz), about 20 minutes, then add the breadcrumbs. Mix well to make a dough or *panade*. Cook over a low heat for 2-3 minutes, then add the garlic.

3 Using a food processor or a hand food mill, purée the livers. Add the *panade*, the butter (reserving about 1 teaspoon), the eggs, cream and cognac and season well to taste. Blend thoroughly and then push through a sieve (this will eliminate any nerves still left in the livers).

4 Grease a 11 × 25 cm (4 × 10 in) terrine dish with the remaining butter, and line the bottom with a strip of greaseproof paper (to ease turning out).

5 Pour the liver mixture into the dish, cover with foil and place in a bain-marie. Bake in the preheated oven for 30 minutes, until the pâté sets. Turn off the oven and leave the pâté to cool in the oven. Refrigerate for 24 hours before serving.

TO SERVE Turn out on to a serving dish garnished with chopped aspic and cut two or three slices. Do not slice ahead of time, however, since without colouring and preservative of any sort, oxydization will take place, changing the colour of the livers from pink to greenish. Garnish with some parsley sprigs and a tomato rose.

FISH AND SHELLFISH

Cuisine Santé uses a lot more fish than traditional cuisiné because it is lower in fat than meats, and what fat there is, is polyunsaturated. White fish (skate, rainbow trout, sole, haddock, monkfish, turbot and bass) contain less fat than oily ones (salmon and sea trout), and both types are high in protein, vitamins and minerals.

Shellfish, although unfortunately expensive, should be healthy, but they are only worth considering when at their freshest, and when they come from unpolluted waters. They spend their life filtering water for nutrients but, alas, in the process, they also retain the filth we put in that water.

Truites Farcies Grillées

STUFFED GRILLED TROUT

This trout dish has always been a success – ask the BBC team who came to Clapham House to film A Taste of Health! *The boning can take a long time, but once you have mastered the technique (see page 15) it will become easier and quicker. The combination of prunes and spinach – if unusual – is particularly delicious and nutritious.*

GLUTEN FREE
SERVES 4
PREHEAT THE GRILL TO ITS MAXIMUM

4 trout
salt
freshly ground black pepper
50g (2oz) flaked almonds
½tsp grapeseed oil
1 onion, peeled and chopped
450g (1lb) spinach, cut into chiffonade
50g (2oz) button mushrooms, sliced
50g (2oz) pitted prunes, chopped

SAUCE
150g (5oz) Greek yoghurt
2dsp olive oil
25g (1oz) chives, freshly snipped

TO SERVE
450g (1lb) new potatoes, scrubbed

1 For the stuffing, grill or roast the almonds until golden, then leave to cool.

2 Heat the oil in a large pan, and sweat the onion over a gentle heat for 1 minute, then add the spinach *chiffonade* and cook over a high heat for 2 minutes. Add the mushrooms and cook for a minute more. Leave to cool, and then add the almonds and prunes. Season well with salt and pepper.

3 Gut the trout and remove the backbones. Remove all the smaller bones with tweezers. Rinse well under cold running water, dry with paper towels, and season with salt and pepper.

4 Stuff the trout with the cooled spinach mixture, packing it in well, and then place the fish on lightly oiled foil on the grill rack.

5 Place under the preheated grill for 4 minutes each side, and leave for a further 4 minutes to rest before serving.

6 For the sauce, put the yoghurt into a bowl and whisk in the olive oil. Season well to taste, then add the chives. Pour into a gravy boat.

TO SERVE Meanwhile, steam the new potatoes.

Remove the top skin from each trout and arrange them on individual warmed serving plates with the potatoes.

Truites Bendor

TROUT BENDOR

These trout are traditionally accompanied by a very rich sauce made of double the amount of cream and egg yolks that we have used. The sauce is now much lighter although it retains the original aniseed flavour, using dill and Pernod. A little trick is to add a teaspoon of potato flour to the Greek yoghurt – this allows the sauce to reach boiling point without curdling.

To keep the fish in the best possible shape (whole), ask the fishmonger to gut them through the gills.

These trout can be served hot or cold – leave to cool in the stock – with the sauce.

GLUTEN FREE
SERVES 4
PREHEAT THE OVEN TO 350°F/180°C/GAS 4

4 × 150g (5oz) pink trout, gutted through the gills and cleaned
salt
freshly ground black pepper
5 tsp Pernod
5 small fresh dill sprigs
½ lemon, sliced and quartered
1 litre (1¾pt) Court-Bouillon *(see page 32)*
5 each of black peppercorns, dill, caraway and fennel seeds, crushed
2 parsley sprigs
1 small bayleaf
1 small thyme sprig
5 ice-cubes
100ml (4fl oz) milk
50ml (2fl oz) whipping cream
2 egg yolks
100g (4oz) Greek yoghurt
1 tsp potato flour

TO SERVE
450g (1lb) vegetables of your choice
fresh dill, finely chopped
25g (1oz) flaked almonds, toasted

1 Cut the tails of the fish into a 'V' shape for decorative purposes, then dry the insides using paper towels. Season the insides through the gills with salt and pepper, 1 teaspoon of the Pernod per fish, a dill sprig and the lemon slices.

2 Place the fish in an ovenproof dish and cover with the cool *court-bouillon*. Add a pinch of salt and the peppercorns and seeds to the *court-bouillon* along with the parsley sprigs, bayleaf and thyme. Cover with a lid or foil, and bake in the preheated oven for approximately 10 minutes, or until the flesh of the fish is firm and the eyes have become opaque.

3 When the fish is done, add the ice-cubes to the stock to stop the cooking.

4 For the sauce, combine the milk, cream and 100ml (3½fl oz) of the strained fish stock in a saucepan, and bring to the boil. Beat the egg yolks, yoghurt and potato flour together, then add a little of the boiling liquid. Pour it all back into the boiling liquid, and whisk over a very low heat (to get air into it). Let it come to the boil, but immediately remove from the heat, or the yolks will curdle. Add the remaining Pernod, a little at a time. Finely chop the remaining sprig of fresh dill and add it to the sauce. Correct the seasoning if necessary: the sauce should have a fresh taste of aniseed rather than tasting of too much salt and pepper.

TO SERVE Meanwhile, steam the vegetables, and sprinkle with the dill. The trout need to be skinned, but do this at the last moment as the skin preserves the moisture and tenderness of the flesh. Remove the brown fat attached to the flesh, being careful not to damage the flesh. Replace the trout in the stock when skinned.

While skinning the fish, reheat the stock in the preheated oven. Warm the fish through by placing in the stock for a minute only.

Arrange the trout on a warm serving dish, cover with some of the sauce and garnish with the flaked almonds. Surround with the steamed vegetables if there is room, or serve them in a separate warmed dish. Pour the remaining sauce into a gravy boat.

RIGHT *Truites Bendor*

Haddock Sauce aux Oeufs

HADDOCK WITH EGG SAUCE

In the classic recipe, the sauce is thickened with a roux *of butter and flour, but this is now removed and replaced with a small amount of Greek yoghurt plus, of course, the traditional hard-boiled egg. When served with basil – a 'natural tranquillizer' – the haddock becomes a lot more digestible.*

Start preparing the dish the day before you intend to serve it. Be sure to choose the best quality haddock with neither colouring nor preservatives; it should be pale yellowish in colour, not deep *yellow.*

GLUTEN FREE

SERVES 4

450g (1lb) smoked haddock fillet, cut into 4 pieces
1 litre (1¾pt) skimmed milk
1 litre (1¾pt) water
1 egg
freshly ground white pepper
parsley sprigs
1 thyme sprig
1 bayleaf
1 tsp crème de riz *(rice flour)*
50ml (2fl oz) whipping cream
50g (2oz) Greek yoghurt
salt
1 dsp parsley, finely chopped
2 dsp basil, finely chopped

TO SERVE

turned root vegetables and green vegetables as for Raie à l'Estragon *(see page 99)*
lemon slices

THE DAY BEFORE SERVING

1 Soak the haddock fillet in a mixture of half the milk and half the water overnight at room temperature.

2 Put the egg for the sauce into a saucepan of cold water and boil it for 5 minutes exactly. Leave it to cool, and keep in the fridge overnight.

THE DAY OF SERVING

1 Take the egg out of the fridge and bring it to room temperature.

2 Drain the fish on paper towels, and throw away the marinade. Place the fish in a saucepan and cover with the remaining milk and water. Season with white pepper and add the parsley sprigs, thyme and bayleaf. Bring slowly to the boil, cover, and cook for 1 minute, then remove from the heat and leave for a further 10 minutes to infuse and cook.

3 To make the sauce, pour the cooking liquid into another saucepan, leaving 100ml (3½fl oz) in the original pan to keep the fish moist. Keep the fish warm. Simmer to reduce this liquid by half, about 15-20 minutes. Mix a little of the liquid with the rice flour in a small cup. Pour this mixture back into the liquid and simmer for 1 minute. Add the cream and simmer for a minute longer. Remove the herbs.

4 Shell the hard-boiled egg and separate the yolk from the white. Cut the white into *julienne* strips, and push the yolk through a sieve into the sauce. Add the egg white *julienne*, the yoghurt, parsley and basil. Season to taste with salt and white pepper. If necessary, thin the sauce with the liquid remaining in the fish pan.

TO SERVE Meanwhile, steam the vegetables.

To serve traditionally, lay the fish on a warmed serving dish and spoon the sauce over it. Surround with the vegetables and lemon slices.

To serve individually, arrange a piece of fish in the centre of a plate, and pour over enough sauce to cover the plate. Garnish with the egg white *julienne*, and arrange the vegetables and lemon slices around the rim of the plate.

LEFT *Haddock Sauce aux Oeufs*

Sole Farcie Soufflée

SOUFFLÉD STUFFED SOLE

Traditionally, this Haute Cuisine dish has a very rich mousseline *of fish as a stuffing, mixed with egg white and a lot of double cream. Here we have replaced the double cream with a little whipping cream, some Greek yoghurt and a little more egg white.*

The addition of spices gives it a slightly Oriental taste, but in the summer, you can replace these with a handful of chopped fines herbes *for a lighter flavour.*

GLUTEN FREE
SERVES 4
PREHEAT THE OVEN TO 350°F/180°C/GAS 4

1 × 1kg (2¼lb) Dover sole
250ml (8fl oz) water
200ml (7fl oz) dry white wine
mirepoix *(1 onion, 1 carrot, 1 celery stick)*
1 bouquet garni
100g (4oz) salmon, hake or cod, boned and skinned
1 egg, separated, and 1 extra egg white
100ml (3½fl oz) whipping cream
100g (4oz) Greek yoghurt
1 pinch each of ground allspice and ground cloves
a little grated nutmeg
freshly ground black pepper
freshly ground coriander
ice-cubes
50g (2oz) pistachio nuts, shelled
2tsp grapeseed oil
1 shallot, peeled and finely chopped

TO SERVE
450g (1lb) broccoli florets
150g (5oz) each of carrot, turnip and swede, cut into julienne
fresh chives

1 Skin the sole on both sides, and bone as described on page 16. Reserve the bones.

2 Place the bones in a saucepan, and add the water, half the white wine, the roughly chopped *mirepoix* and the *bouquet garni*. Bring to a simmer over a low heat, skimming off the impurities as they rise to the surface. Simmer for 10 minutes and then remove from the heat.

3 Using a pestle and mortar, or a food processor, work the salmon (or other fish) with one of the egg whites. A little at a time, add half the cream and yoghurt, plus the spices – the allspice, cloves, nutmeg, pepper and coriander. To eliminate any bones, nerves or pieces of skin, push the mixture through a sieve into a bowl on top of another one containing ice-cubes. Place in the freezer for 15 minutes, beating well every 5 minutes.

4 Rub the pistachio nuts in a cloth to remove the salt. (Alternatively, blanch them for 2 minutes in boiling water, to eliminate the skins and obtain the typical green colour.) Chop them finely, keeping four whole. Add the chopped nuts to the mixture. Beat the remaining egg white until stiff and fold delicately into the mixture. Place inside a piping bag with a fluted nozzle and (following the instructions on pages 16-17) pipe the *mousseline* inside the fish. Garnish with the remaining whole pistachios.

5 Drain the fish stock through a chinois sieve lined with a rinsed muslin cloth or tea-towel.

6 Oil a gratin dish with half the grapeseed oil, and place the fish in it. Pour 50ml (2fl oz) of the remaining white wine and 100ml (4fl oz) of the fish stock over the fish, and cover with foil. Bake in the preheated oven for 10 minutes, then strain most of the juices into a bowl, leaving about 1 tablespoon to prevent the fish from drying up. Return the fish to the turned-off oven, close the door, and leave for another 10 minutes.

7 Meanwhile, heat the remaining oil in a skillet, and sweat the shallot slowly for about 5 minutes. Deglaze with the remaining wine, and leave to reduce almost completely. Add the remaining fish stock and leave to reduce by half. Add the remaining cream and reduce for 2 minutes more. This takes in total about 15-20 minutes.

TO SERVE Steam the vegetables together for 2 minutes with the lid on, and 3 minutes with the lid off (this will keep the broccoli bright green).

Take the sauce off the heat. Mix the remaining yoghurt with the egg yolk and add a tablespoon of the sauce. Combine well, then pour back into the sauce, a little at a time, mixing well. *Do not reheat*.

Carefully transfer the sole on to a heated serving dish. With a knife, scrape off the bones from around the edges of the sole and discard. Clean the dish well and pour half the sauce over the sole. Pour the remainder into a warm gravy boat. Garnish with some of the vegetables, tied into bundles with a blanched chive, and present the remainder in a warm vegetable dish. Serve immediately.

Sole Farcie Soufflée

Darnes de Saumon en Papillote

SALMON STEAKS EN PAPILLOTE

By cooking en papillote *(in paper parcels), these salmon steaks can be flavoured to taste, or with whatever is in season.*

Do experiment with other herbs, fruit or vegetables, as they will add individuality to your cuisine. Here, the combination of asparagus and dill gives a spring-like flavour to the salmon. Any other 'hard' vegetable used will need to be steam-blanched, like the asparagus used here, for a few minutes before wrapping in the parcel.

GLUTEN FREE

SERVES 4

PREHEAT THE OVEN TO 450°F/230°C/GAS 8

4 asparagus spears about 225g (8oz) total weight
4 dill sprigs
salt
freshly ground black pepper
1tsp Pernod, Ricard or Ouzo
4 × 200g (7oz) salmon steaks
25ml (1floz) dry white wine

TO SERVE
1kg (2¼lb) baby new potatoes, scrubbed
600g (a good 1¼lb) asparagus
1 recipe Sauce Beurre Blanc *(see page 41)*

1 Prepare the asparagus for both the *papillote* and garnish at the same time. Peel the hard stems of the asparagus with a potato peeler, starting from the base to about three-quarters of the way up. If you've bought young, thin asparagus, this will not be necessary. Working with the four large spears only, cut the tips off diagonally, about 3cm (1¼in) down from the tip, then cut the stems diagonally into 1cm (½in) slices. Bring a steamer to the boil and steam the asparagus tips and slices for 3 minutes.

2 Using a pestle and mortar, work together half the dill, a pinch of salt, some pepper and the spirit. Rub the paste all over the salmon steaks and leave to marinate for at least 10 minutes.

3 Meanwhile, prepare the paper parcels (see page 28). On to each sheet of paper lay a salmon steak, 1 asparagus tip, a quarter of the asparagus slices, a quarter of the wine and a little sprig of the remaining dill. Close the parcels well and reserve until you are ready to cook. They can be prepared up to 2 hours before serving and kept in the fridge, in which case no additional marinating time is necessary.

4 When ready to cook, bake the *papillotes* in the preheated oven for 10 minutes only.

TO SERVE Meanwhile, steam the vegetables for about 10 minutes. Put the potatoes in a warmed dish with the remaining chopped dill, cover well and leave to marinate for 5 minutes before serving. Present the asparagus in a serving dish lined with a napkin.

Bring the *papillotes* to the table unopened on a large serving dish (or on individual plates), and let your guests enjoy the wonderful smell as they open their parcels. Serve the *Sauce Beurre Blanc* separately.

To remove the centre bone of the steaks easily, push the tip of a sharp knife deeply into the centre bone, and ease it around the bone with a twisting motion to loosen it. Pull the bone out, and remove the side bones in between the fillets on either side of the main bone.

LEFT *Darnes de Saumon en Papillote*

Saumon à la Riga

POACHED SALMON WITH GREEN SAUCE

This is a very traditional buffet-type dish originated by Pellaprat (author of the famous 'bible' of French cuisine of the same name), but instead of using a very rich mayonnaise, we have used a delicious Sauce Verte.

It is best to prepare this dish over 2 days, which leaves enough time for it to marinate in its court-bouillon *overnight. Other round fish, such as a trout, a small bass, a small cod or a small hake could be prepared in the same way.*

You can baptize a brand-new plant spray-mister for this dish – the final aspic needs to be sprayed on!

GLUTEN FREE
SERVES 4

5 litres (8¾pt) Court-Bouillon *(see page 32)*
1 × 2kg (4½lb) wild salmon, with head, gutted
salt
5 each of white and black peppercorns, coriander, dill and caraway seeds, crushed
2 fennel seeds, crushed
1 large dill sprig
5 parsley sprigs
200ml (7fl oz) white wine
1 lemon, washed and sliced
1 recipe Sauce Verte *(see page 38)*
1 cucumber, washed
2 gelatine leaves

GARNISH
2 tomato roses (see page 26)
2 lemons, sliced and halved
lemon twists
1tsp cognac
lemon twists (see page 26)

THE DAY BEFORE SERVING

1 Leave the prepared *court-bouillon* to cool.

2 If not done by the fishmonger, gut the fish carefully yourself. Clean well under cold running water, and place in the fish kettle. (If the fish is too long, cut the head off and cook it separately in water with some lemon juice, and 'attach' it later.)

3 Strain the cold *court-bouillon* into the fish kettle through a sieve. Add 2 pinches salt and the spices and seeds to the *court-bouillon*, along with the fresh dill, parsley sprigs, white wine and lemon slices. Mix well.

4 Place the fish kettle over a medium heat and bring slowly to the boil. At the first bubble, turn the heat off (remove from the heat if using electricity), and place a folded and rinsed tea-towel between kettle and lid (see pages 17-18). Leave to cool down completely.

THE DAY OF SERVING

1 Store the prepared *Sauce Verte* in the fridge.

2 Slice the cucumber thinly by hand or, better, in a food processor (you'll get thinner slices!). Arrange the slices in layers on a plate with a pinch of salt between layers. Cover and leave for 20 minutes.

3 Lift the fish on the tray out of the kettle, and drain for a moment. Reserve 200ml (7fl oz) of the stock and filter through muslin or a damp tea-towel. Soak the gelatine leaves in cold water until soft, about 5 minutes, then place in a sieve to drain. Place a third of the reserved stock in a saucepan with the gelatine, and melt over a low heat (no more than a minute). Pour into a plant spray-mister.

4 Cut a piece of cardboard to the length and shape of the fish and wrap it in foil.

5 Very carefully peel off the entire skin of the fish as well as the brown fatty layer under it to expose the pink flesh. Detach the flesh from the top fillet carefully, one section at a time, and keep to one side, re-assembled to shape. Transfer the bottom part of the fish to the foil-covered board. Remove the bones carefully, and discard.

6 Spread a thick layer of the *Sauce Verte* over the fillet on the board, and lay the top fillets over this, reshaping the fish as accurately as possible. Fix the head back in place.

7 Rinse the cucumber well and dry on paper towels. Starting at the tail end, arrange overlapping slices over the surface of the fish, and cover half the head too.

8 Place the fish in the freezer for 10 minutes to cool quickly (or 20 minutes in the fridge), then spray the aspic evenly all over. Return the fish to the freezer for 5 minutes and repeat the operation several times to build up a good layer of aspic which will help the fish and cucumber retain their freshness. If the aspic starts to set and block the spray, leave the spray nozzle in the sink with hot, soapy water for 5 minutes and rinse well; place the bottom part in a bowl of hot water for 1 minute, or until the aspic becomes liquid again. Place the remaining aspic on a shallow plate and set in the fridge.

TO SERVE Prepare the serving dish. Using two napkins and some foil, prepare a gondola (see page 29). Lay a third napkin in between the two napkins.

Just before serving, place the fish on its board on the serving dish. Garnish with the tomato roses, half slices of lemon, and lemon twists. Turn the reserved aspic out on to a tea-towel, chop roughly, sprinkle with the cognac and use to garnish all round the fish.

Huîtres au Gratin

OYSTERS AU GRATIN

This is a delicious way to use oysters, but beware, for oysters, like other shellfish, are very high in cholesterol. With the addition of the egg yolk too, this dish is not particularly healthy, so the yolk should be optional (although it gives a richer taste and better colour). In their favour, though, oysters are low in carbohydrate and high in protein, iron, and calcium. Make sure they come from unpolluted waters and are very fresh.

GLUTEN FREE

SERVES 4

PREHEAT THE OVEN TO 350°F/180°C/GAS 4, AND PREHEAT THE GRILL TO ITS MAXIMUM

24 oysters, washed well
1 tsp grapeseed oil
1 shallot, peeled and finely chopped
50 g (2 oz) each of leek, carrot, swede and celeriac, cut into julienne
100 ml (3½ fl oz) Bouillon de Légumes *or* Fumet de Poisson *(see pages 32 and 33)*
½ tsp lemon juice
salt
freshly ground black pepper
1 egg yolk
25 g (1 oz) Greek yoghurt
2 dsp whipping cream

1 Put the oysters on a tray in the oven for 2 minutes until they open. Remove from the shell and pour the juices into a bowl. Clean the hollow half shells well and reserve.

2 Heat the oil in a skillet and sweat the shallot until soft, about 5 minutes. Add the vegetable *julienne* and the oyster juice, and leave to simmer very gently for 5 minutes, covered.

3 Add the stock and reduce by half, about 5-10 minutes. Add the lemon juice and season lightly with salt and pepper.

4 Whisk the egg yolk with the yoghurt and cream mixed together, then pour in the boiling stock reduction and stir well for 1 minute.

TO SERVE Arrange the half shells in a roasting tin or baking tray the size of the grill and place a little of the vegetable *julienne* in the shells. Top with the oysters, cover with more vegetable *julienne* and some sauce. Cook under the grill for 1½ minutes, then transfer to a serving dish lined with a doily or folded napkin. Serve immediately.

Roulade Bicolore

SOLE AND SALMON ROULADE

These attractive sole and smoked salmon rolls can be served hot as a main course as here, hot or cold as a starter, or cold as canapés. If serving as a cold starter, do not make the sauce from the court-bouillon, *but serve the slices of fish on top of the cold cucumber salad. To serve as a canapé, arrange a little cold cucumber salad on a toast round, cover with a slice of fish, and top with a caper flower (see page 25).*

GLUTEN FREE
SERVES 4 AS A MAIN COURSE, 6 AS A STARTER

1 × 700 g (1½ lb) Dover sole, skinned and filleted
1 cucumber, washed
salt
1 shallot, peeled and chopped
1 spring onion, chopped
2 fresh mint leaves, chopped, or ½ tsp dried mint
100 g (4 oz) Greek yoghurt
freshly ground black pepper
½ lemon
1 dsp olive oil
4 slices smoked salmon, about 150 g (5 oz) in weight
1 dsp fines herbes, *finely chopped*
550 ml (a scant pt) Court-Bouillon *(see page 32)*
1 thyme sprig
1 bayleaf
parsley sprigs
5 coriander seeds
50 ml (2 fl oz) whipping cream
1 egg yolk

TO SERVE
450 g (1 lb) broccoli florets
dill sprigs

1 With a sharp knife, slash the shiny side of the fish to prevent shrinkage.

2 Score the cucumber and cut it in half lengthwise. Remove the seeds. Slice thinly, sprinkle with some salt and leave in a glass or earthenware bowl for 15 minutes.

3 Drain and rinse the cucumber and pat dry. Put in the rinsed bowl with the shallot, spring onion, mint and half the yoghurt. Season with pepper, add the juice of the ½ lemon (cut off and reserve a slice before squeezing), and the olive oil, and marinate for 10 minutes.

4 Place a slice of smoked salmon on a work surface and place one fillet of sole, shiny side down, on top. Cut away the excess smoked salmon with a knife. Sprinkle lightly with herbs, salt and pepper. Roll up and secure with a skewer. Prepare three more rolls in the same way.

5 Place the rolls in a steamer filled with the *court-bouillon* and its additional flavouring ingredients – the thyme, bayleaf, parsley sprigs, coriander seeds and the reserved lemon slice. Steam for 5 minutes. Remove from the heat, but reserve in the closed steamer to keep warm.

6 Strain 100 ml (3½ fl oz) of the *court-bouillon* into a saucepan and bring it to the boil. Mix the remaining yoghurt, the cream and egg yolk in a bowl, then pour in a little of the hot *court-bouillon*. Pour this mixture back into the *court-bouillon*.

7 Add the fish rolls and the cucumber salad carefully to the sauce and heat for a few minutes. Do not boil. Remove from the heat and season if necessary.

TO SERVE Meanwhile, steam the broccoli for about 5 minutes.

To serve traditionally, place a little of the sauce on a heated serving dish, then slice the four rolls and arrange across the middle of the dish, surrounded by the broccoli florets. Serve the remaining sauce in a gravy boat.

To serve individually, slice each roll and arrange on the warm plate with some broccoli florets and cucumber slices, with the sauce around. Garnish with a dill sprig.

RIGHT *Roulade Bicolore*

Charlotte de Saumon Verdurette

SALMON TERRINE

This can be cooked in a charlotte mould or terrine or in four small ramekin dishes or terrines, then turned out and served with a prawn garnish and a chiffonade *of lettuce sautéd very quickly. The salmon used can be fresh or left over from a poached salmon served the day before, an extremely good way to use up leftovers. Any cooked fish can be substituted for the salmon.*

GLUTEN FREE
SERVES 4
PREHEAT THE OVEN TO 300°F/150°C/GAS 2

1 lettuce, washed
salt
butter
250g (9oz) frozen petits pois
3 eggs
2 egg whites
100ml (3½fl oz) whipping cream
40g (1½oz) parsley, finely chopped
25g (1oz) sorrel, cut into chiffonade
freshly ground black pepper
cayenne pepper
200g (7oz) fresh or cooked salmon

SAUCE
4 shallots, peeled and finely chopped
500ml (18fl oz) Court-Bouillon *(see page 32)*
50ml (2fl oz) whipping cream
100g (4oz) Greek yoghurt

TO SERVE
300g (11oz) carrots, scrubbed
chervil leaves

1 Blanch the whole lettuce in a saucepan of boiling salted water for 1 minute, then plunge immediately into a bowl of ice-cold water to cool. Lay flat on a tea-towel to drain.

2 Butter the mould or terrines, and line with the blanched lettuce leaves (remove the stalks if too thick), leaving an overhang.

3 Cook the peas in a pan of boiling salted water until tender. Purée them in a food processor or hand food mill, reserving a dessertspoon whole for garnish. Remove from the processor and mix in one of the eggs beaten with one of the egg whites, a third of the cream, and the parsley and sorrel. Season well with salt, pepper and a little cayenne.

4 Remove any fat, bones and skin from the salmon and flake the flesh. Purée in a food processor or hand food mill. Remove from the processor and mix in the remaining eggs, egg white and cream and adjust the seasoning.

5 Whichever type of dish you have chosen, first put in a layer of the salmon purée, then a layer of pea purée and finish with another layer of the salmon. Alternatively, pour them from separate jugs into the dish for a marbled effect. Fold over the tops of the lettuce leaves, butter some foil or waxed paper and place over the top. Place in a bain-marie and bake in the preheated oven – 10-15 minutes for the individual portions and 30-40 minutes for the large mould.

6 Meanwhile, prepare the sauce. Put the shallots and *court-bouillon* into a pan and reduce by half, about 10-15 minutes. Add the cream and reduce for a further 3 minutes. Leave to cool for 2 minutes and, just before serving, add the yoghurt. Reheat if necessary, but do not overheat or it will curdle.

TO SERVE Meanwhile, steam the carrots – either young, with a little bit of stem left on them, or older, turned, or cut into *julienne* – until tender. Reheat the reserved whole peas.

Turn the charlotte out on to a round serving dish, surround with a little sauce, and garnish the top with the hot carrots and peas, and a little chervil. Do the same with the ramekins on individual plates.

LEFT *Charlotte de Saumon Verdurette*

Turbotin au Champagne

TURBOT WITH CHAMPAGNE

Turbot is a delicious fish, unique in taste and texture, but it is expensive and not always available. Fillets of Dover sole could substitute. The stuffing is made of spinach and sorrel; if sorrel is not available, you can duplicate its acidity by adding a teaspoon of lemon juice to the cooked spinach. Don't use your most expensive champagne for this, but a decent cheap one (and serve your special bottle with *the meal). The original sauce was a* beurre monté *using cream and butter in vast amounts; here again we use low-fat Greek yoghurt, seasoned with a little cream and some chervil.*

GLUTEN FREE
SERVES 4
PREHEAT THE OVEN TO 350°F/180°C/GAS 4

1 × 1.5 kg (3¼ lb) turbotin *(small turbot), skinned and filleted (keep the head and bones)*
mirepoix *(1 onion, 1 carrot, and 1 celery stick)*
salt
1 bouquet garni
250 ml (8 fl oz) cold water
½ bottle champagne
2 tsp grapeseed oil
400 g (14 oz) spinach, cut into chiffonade
100 g (4 oz) sorrel, cut into chiffonade
grated nutmeg
1 dsp pine nuts, dry roasted for 5 minutes in the oven
freshly ground black pepper
100 ml (3½ fl oz) whipping cream
1 egg yolk
1 dsp chopped chervil, a few whole leaves reserved
50 g (2 oz) Greek yoghurt

GARNISH
6 baby carrots, scrubbed and trimmed, or turned
3 young turnips, washed, quartered and turned
12 new potatoes, washed (optional)
12 spring onions, the green cut 2.5 cm (1 in) above the bulb (optional)

RIGHT *Turbotin au Champagne*

1 To make the fish stock, place the rinsed bones and head in a saucepan with the roughly chopped *mirepoix*, a pinch of salt and the *bouquet garni*. Add the water and 250 ml (8 fl oz) of the champagne, and bring to the boil slowly, skimming off the impurities. Simmer gently, uncovered, for 20 minutes, then cover, cool and strain.

2 Put a skillet over a low heat to heat up, then turn the heat up high. Pour in half the oil and sauté the spinach and sorrel *chiffonade* briskly. Add a pinch of salt and some nutmeg. Toss well over a high heat to eliminate the water. Reserve on a plate to cool. When cold add the pine nuts.

3 Lay the fish fillets on a board, shiny side up. Slash the skin diagonally along the length with a sharp knife. Season with a pinch of salt and some pepper. Arrange a quarter of the spinach/sorrel *chiffonade* in the centre of each fillet, and fold the sides over the middle in thirds.

4 Use the remaining oil to grease a gratin dish and put in the fillets, open sides down. Pour in enough strained fish stock to cover the fish, then cover the dish with foil and bake in the preheated oven for 10 minutes. Transfer the cooking liquid to a saucepan, leaving a small amount in the dish to keep the fish moist. Leave the fish covered with the foil in the turned-off oven to keep warm.

5 Add all the remaining champagne, except for 1 dessertspoon, to the cooking liquid and reduce by half, skimming off the impurities as they rise. Add the cream, and reduce again until it coats the back of a spoon lightly (this can take up to 15 minutes). Take the sauce off the heat and add the remaining champagne. Mix the egg yolk, chervil and yoghurt together in a bowl, stir in a small amount of the sauce, then pour back into the sauce. Do not reheat.

TO SERVE Meanwhile, steam the vegetables and keep warm.

To serve traditionally, arrange the fillets in the middle of a warm serving dish, and spoon a little sauce over each, pouring the remainder into a warm gravy boat. Surround with the vegetables, and garnish each fillet with a chervil leaf.

To serve individually, place a fillet to the front of a heated plate, and pour the sauce over it, to cover the base of the plate. Arrange the vegetables at the back of the plate like a crown, alternating the colours. Place a chervil leaf on top of the fillet.

Salade de Lotte aux Poivrons Rouges

MONKFISH WITH RED PEPPERS

GLUTEN FREE
SERVES 4

450g (1lb) monkfish fillet
550ml (a scant pt) Court-Bouillon *(see page 32)*
4 garlic cloves, peeled and crushed
salt
freshly ground black pepper
½ tsp lemon juice
75ml (3fl oz) olive oil
2 red peppers, washed, seeded and diced

GARNISH
lettuce leaves
parsley, finely chopped

This delightful recipe is full of colour and flavour and can be served in a variety of ways: as a warm starter, as a salad, or as part of a buffet. It is also delicious served as a canapé, stuffed inside a hollowed cucumber. It can also be presented in a feuilleté *(see page 14).*

1 Cut the monkfish fillet into slices and steam for 2 minutes over the *court-bouillon* containing 2 garlic cloves.

2 Place the remaining garlic into a bowl, add a pinch of salt, some pepper and the lemon juice. Mix well and beat in the olive oil.

3 Place the monkfish into the dressing to cool.

4 Add the peppers to the monkfish. Stir well, cover, and leave to marinate at room temperature for a few hours.

TO SERVE Serve on its own, cold, placed inside a bowl lined with lettuce leaves and sprinkled with parsley.

To serve as a warm starter or *salade tiède* (warm salad), reheat very gently in a pan. Arrange the slices of monkfish in a ring surrounded by the peppers on individual plates. Pour over some of the dressing through a chinois sieve.

To serve as a canapé, process the salad with 1 dessertspoon olive oil in a blender. Peel a cucumber, cut in half widthways and hollow out the seeds. Stuff the middle of the cucumber with the fish mixture. Slice and serve.

Raie à l'Estragon

SKATE WITH TARRAGON

This fish is traditionally served in France 'au beurre noir', *with a butter sauce browned to such an extreme that the butter becomes nearly black. This gives the dish a very high cholesterol content, so here the butter is replaced by a warm vinaigrette flavoured with tarragon, which helps in the digestion of this delicious but rich fish.*

GLUTEN FREE
SERVES 4

1kg (2½lb) small skate wings (4 wings)
1 onion, peeled and thinly sliced
1 clove
1 thyme sprig
1 bayleaf
parsley sprigs
½ lemon, sliced
1.5 litres (2½pt) cool Court-Bouillon *(see page 32)*
freshly ground black pepper

VINAIGRETTE
freshly ground black pepper
salt
2 dsp tarragon vinegar
2 dsp fresh tarragon, finely chopped
1 dsp parsley, finely chopped
4 dsp grapeseed oil

TO SERVE
450 g (1 lb) root vegetables (carrots, turnips, swedes, celeriac)
450 g (1 lb) green vegetables (broccoli, spinach, dwarf beans) or 225 g (8 oz) mangetout
8 caper flowers (see page 25)

1 Place the skate wings, dark side up, in a large square tin – a roasting tin is ideal – and add the onion, clove, thyme, bayleaf, parsley sprigs and lemon. Cover with the cool *court-bouillon*. If the fish is not completely covered, top up with some water. Add some pepper and bring slowly to the boil on top of the stove, skimming off the impurities as they rise to the surface.

2 Let it start simmering, then remove from the heat, place a damp cloth over the pan and cover with a lid or foil. Leave for 10-15 minutes.

3 To prepare the vinaigrette, put a little ground black pepper and a pinch of salt into a saucepan, add the vinegar and mix. Add the tarragon and parsley, and mix well. (If the herbs are dried, use half the amount, add a dessertspoon of water to them, leave to stand for 5 minutes, then drain.) Whisk the oil in gently, then place over a low heat to warm through. *Do not* boil.

4 Remove the fish from the *court-bouillon* and skin. If you have enough patience, remove the bones too, but work swiftly as the fish will cool rapidly. If it does become too cool, place it in a dish with a little *court-bouillon* and reheat in a low oven.

TO SERVE While the fish is cooking, turn the root vegetables, then steam until done. Steam the chosen green vegetables as well.

To serve traditionally, lay the fish on a warmed serving dish and spoon the sauce over. Garnish with the caper flowers. Arrange the vegetables around the fish and serve immediately.

To serve individually, bone each wing, and lay flat on a warmed plate. Pour a little sauce over, and garnish with the vegetables and caper flowers. Serve the remaining sauce separately.

LEFT *Raie à l'Estragon*

Gigot de Lotte Clouté

MONKFISH IN RED WINE

This delicious dish is very 'nouvelle' in the sense that a few years ago, no-one would have served fish in a red wine sweet and sour sauce. This is one of the dishes taught to me by Jean Bardet in Châteauroux. He serves it with a braised white cabbage, which makes an original garnish and complements the flavour of the fish and its sauce. If you prefer a more conventional dish, serve it with the vegetables suggested here.

SERVES 4
PREHEAT THE OVEN TO 350°F/180°C/GAS 4

2 large carrots, scrubbed
100 g (4 oz) dwarf beans
1 small white cabbage (optional)
salt
freshly ground black pepper
4 tsp grapeseed oil
mirepoix *(1 onion, carrot trimmings and 1 celery stalk)*
1 garlic clove, peeled and crushed
400 ml (14 fl oz) red wine (such as Beaujolais)
100 ml (3½ fl oz) Bouillon de Légumes *(see page 32)*
450 g (1 lb) monkfish fillet
1 shallot, peeled and chopped
1 dsp honey
1 dsp raspberry vinegar
1 tsp potato flour

TO SERVE (OPTIONAL)
2 medium turnips, peeled
2 medium carrots, scrubbed
250 g (8 oz) mangetout

1 Cut the carrots into *julienne* strips the same size as the beans, keeping the trimmings for the *mirepoix*. Steam the carrots and beans for 3 minutes.

2 If used, cut the cabbage into quarters through the stem and blanch for 5 minutes in boiling salted water.

3 Heat half the grapeseed oil in a saucepan, and sweat the finely chopped *mirepoix* for 5 minutes. Add the garlic and sweat for 1 minute, then deglaze with 100 ml (3½ fl oz) of the red wine and the stock (or water). Place the cabbage in the pan, season with salt and pepper, and braise in the preheated oven for 40 minutes.

4 Remove the skin from the monkfish and cut the flesh into chunks the same length as the beans. Reserve the trimmings for the sauce.

5 Using a larding needle, thread the carrots and beans through the fish. Lightly salt and pepper the fish, place on a skillet and sprinkle with half the remaining oil. Bake in the oven for 5-7 minutes. Remove, wrap in foil, and return to the turned-off oven.

6 Heat the remaining oil in the skillet, and sweat the shallot for 5 minutes. Add the monkfish trimmings and sauté. Deglaze with 50 ml (2 fl oz) of the red wine, and reduce until a dessertspoon is left.

7 Add the honey and simmer for 1 minute, then deglaze with the vinegar. Mix the potato flour with the remaining wine and transfer into the sauce. Simmer for 2 minutes.

TO SERVE Cut the monkfish chunks into thick slices. Arrange the cabbage on a heated serving plate and put the monkfish slices on the top. Spoon a little of the sauce over the fish and serve the remainder in a gravy boat.

Alternatively, cut the carrots and turnips into *lichettes*, and steam with the mangetout for 3 minutes. Place the fish on a plate, and surround with the sauce and the vegetables.

RIGHT *Gigot de Lotte Clouté*

Bar Farci en Chemise

BASS WRAPPED IN LETTUCE LEAVES

This bass is delicious hot or cold, and it's nutritionally rich. To serve hot, follow all the instructions below. To serve cold, omit all the steps for the sauce. Allow the fish to cool in its cooking juices in the foil, and serve with a Sauce Verte *(see page 38).*

If you are on a gluten-free diet, omit the breadcrumbs and sauté the stuffing for 5 minutes longer.

SERVES 6

1 × 900 g (2 lb) sea bass (hake or pike)
salt
freshly ground black pepper
100 ml (3½ fl oz) dry vermouth (Noilly Prat)
2 large heads lettuce, washed
3 tsp grapeseed oil
250 g (9 oz) spinach, cut into chiffonade
50 g (2 oz) sorrel, cut into chiffonade
25 g (1 oz) fines herbes, *finely chopped*
25 g (1 oz) breadcumbs
100 g (4 oz) Greek yoghurt
100 ml (3½ fl oz) white wine
100 ml (3½ fl oz) whipping cream
1 tsp potato flour

TO SERVE
parsley sprigs
2 lemons
150 g (5 oz) each of carrot and potato, cut into julienne

1 Scale the fish with the back of a knife inside a bin liner, working from tail to head. Remove the guts and gills and clean very well. Remove the bones as described on page 15.

2 Rinse the fish well under cold, running water, pat dry with paper towels and season inside with a pinch of salt, a little pepper and 1 teaspoon of the vermouth.

3 Blanch the whole lettuces for 30 seconds in boiling salted water, then refresh in a bowl of ice-cold water. Arrange the largest leaves on a board. Chop the hearts roughly and reserve.

4 Heat 1 teaspoon of the oil in a large pan and sauté the spinach quickly over a high heat. Add the chopped lettuce hearts, toss well over the heat for a minute, then add the sorrel and sauté for a further minute. Add the herbs and breadcrumbs and mix well. Season with a pinch of salt and a little pepper, and leave on a plate to cool. When cold add half the yoghurt.

5 Stuff the fish with the cold stuffing, then wrap it in the lettuce leaves leaving the head and tail uncovered.

6 Place the fish on a large piece of oiled foil on a baking tray. Fold the foil over so that it creates an open *papillote*, a package with an opening at the top. Pour in half the white wine and half the remaining vermouth. Dribble a little oil on to the head and tail so they do not dry out during cooking. Close the package a little more to leave just a small opening in the foil at the top, and place the baking tray in the preheated oven. Bake for 15 minutes, then turn the oven off. Remove the fish, and pour the cooking juices into a saucepan. Close the foil tightly and leave the fish in the still warm oven for 15 more minutes.

7 Simmer the cooking juices to reduce by half, then add the remaining wine and vermouth, and the cream. Reduce for 5 minutes. Mix the potato flour with the remaining yoghurt, stir a little of the sauce into it, and transfer it all back into the sauce. Allow to come just to the boil, correct the seasoning, and remove from the heat.

TO SERVE Replace the eyes of the fish with parsley sprigs.

Score one of the lemons and then cut into slices. Cut both ends off the other lemon and cut across in half. Carve out a length of the peel around the wider top, and twist it into a knot (see page 26).

Lay the fish on a serving dish, and arrange the lemon slices all around, with the halves at either side of the dish. Pour a little sauce over the fish and serve the remainder in a gravy boat. Garnish the dish with the vegetable *julienne*, steamed until just tender.

Filets de Sole Pochés au Vin Blanc

POACHED SOLE WITH WHITE WINE SAUCE

These delicious sole fillets are poached in fish stock and white wine in the oven. Instead of the original sauce, a velouté *made with butter and flour and a lot of double cream, here we use a reduced stock with a small amount of whipping cream and Greek yoghurt. The rosemary gives an unusual flavour to the sauce.*

GLUTEN FREE
SERVES 4
PREHEAT THE OVEN TO 350°F/180°C/GAS 4

2 × 450g (1lb) Dover sole
mirepoix *(1 onion, 1 carrot, 1 celery stick)*
1 bouquet garni
150ml (5fl oz) dry white wine
1 litre (1¾pt) cold water
1 tsp grapeseed oil
4 shallots, peeled and finely chopped
salt
freshly ground black pepper
75ml (3fl oz) whipping cream

TO SERVE
1 recipe Peperonata, *without eggs (see page 69)*
4 large potatoes, quartered and turned
50g (2oz) Greek yoghurt

1 Skin both sides of the sole and fillet them as described on page 16, reserving the bones.

2 Wash the bones well under cold, running water and place in a saucepan with the roughly chopped *mirepoix*, the *bouquet garni*, 100ml (4fl oz) of the white wine and the water. Bring slowly to the boil over a low heat, skimming off the impurities as they rise to the surface. Simmer for 15 minutes, then leave to cool, covered.

3 Heat the oil in a skillet over a low heat, then sweat the shallots, covered, for 2 minutes. Reserve on a plate to cool.

4 Place the fillets shiny side up on the work surface, and slash them across with a sharp knife at 5cm (2in) intervals. Season with a pinch of salt and a little pepper, and scatter the shallots over them evenly. Roll the fillets up along three-quarters of their length.

5 Place the fillets in a gratin dish, with the 'tongues' flat at the bottom of the dish. Cover with the stock and the remaining wine, then with a piece of foil, and place in the preheated oven. Poach for 10 minutes.

6 Transfer the juices to a saucepan to reduce, leaving a little in the fish dish. Put the fish back in the oven, cover well, turn the oven off, and leave the door ajar.

7 Reduce the stock until only 200ml (7fl oz) is left, about 15 minutes. Add the cream, and reduce for 5 minutes longer over a low heat.

TO SERVE Steam the potatoes for 10 minutes.

When ready to serve, reheat the sauce if necessary, and take it off the heat. Stir the yoghurt well, pour 1 tablespoon of the sauce into it and mix well. Pour back into the sauce, stirring well with a spoon. Do not boil again.

To serve traditionally, arrange the fillets on a warmed serving dish, 'tongues' either up or down (both look attractive), and cover with a little sauce. Pour the remainder into a warmed gravy boat. Arrange a cross of a slice each of green pepper and red pepper over each fillet, then place the remaining peppers all around the dish with the steamed potatoes over the top.

To serve individually, arrange two fillets with 'tongues' turned towards the outside of the plate, and cover both fillets and plate with the sauce. Arrange the peppers in crosses all around the plate, twirling a slice of red pepper into a spiral for the top of each fillet. Arrange the potatoes to north, south, east and west of the plate. Serve immediately.

MEAT, POULTRY AND GAME

Meat, especially red meat, contains a lot of saturated fat and a fair amount of cholesterol. In meat's favour, however, it contains good amounts of protein, vitamins and essential amino acids. Meat is not excluded from Cuisine Santé, but we would advise cutting down on red meat in favour of chicken, turkey and rabbit. Use the leanest cuts of all meats, and wherever possible both remove any visible fat before cooking, and discard cooking and rendered fats before preparing the sauce and serving the dish.

Côtes de Porc à l'Auvergnate

PORK CHOPS WITH SAGE

These pork chops are flavoured with their classic herb accompaniment, sage. Sage, the 'saviour', complements the pork, giving it goodness and flavour. It also helps digestion of both the pork and the cabbage.

GLUTEN FREE
SERVES 4
PREHEAT THE OVEN TO 400°F/200°C/GAS 6

4 pork loin chops
salt
freshly ground black pepper
1 tsp grapeseed oil
1 onion, peeled and finely chopped
1 shallot, peeled and finely chopped
2 garlic cloves, peeled and crushed
150 ml (5 fl oz) dry white wine
85 ml (3 fl oz) whipping cream
100 ml (3½ fl oz) Fonds de Volaille *(see page 31)*
8 fresh sage leaves, chopped, or 2 tsp dried sage
1 Savoy cabbage
25 g (1 oz) Emmenthal cheese

1 Season the chops on both sides, and heat the oil in a skillet. Seal the chops on both sides very quickly (about 2 minutes each side). Put on a plate to cool. When cool, remove the bones and all the fat.

2 Put the onion and shallot into the same pan and sweat for 5 minutes. Add the garlic and sweat for another minute. Deglaze with the wine and simmer for 1 minute before adding the cream, the stock and sage. Simmer this sauce for another minute.

3 Bring a steamer containing salted water to the boil. Trim off any damaged outer cabbage leaves, and quarter the head, cutting through the root to obtain sections which will hold together. Steam each quarter for 5 minutes, then plunge into a bowl of ice-cold water (to fix the colour). Drain thoroughly, and then remove the cores carefully.

4 Oil a gratin dish lightly and pour in half the sauce. Arrange the four pork chops on top. Place a cabbage quarter on top of each chop, and grate the cheese over all. Bake in the preheated oven for 25 minutes, basting with the sauce every 5 minutes after 10 minutes.

5 Drain the sauce, onion and shallots from the gratin dish into a saucepan, and add the remaining sauce. Simmer for 5 minutes, then liquidize. Keep the chops warm in the turned-off oven.

TO SERVE Arrange the chops, each with their cabbage topping, on a warmed serving dish or individual plates. Serve the sauce in a warmed gravy boat, and the carrots in a warmed vegetable dish. Garnish the dish with the sage leaves.

TO SERVE
1 recipe Carottes Vichy *(see page 160)*
4 fresh sage leaves, blanched

Médaillons de Porc à l'Aigre Doux

PORK MEDALLIONS WITH GINGER

These little pieces of pork fillet are sautéd very quickly to retain all their juices, and later coated with a sweet and sour sauce. We use a little honey, instead of sugar, to sweeten the sauce and instead of a traditional demi-glace *sauce thickened with flour, we use a simple reduction. The whole dish is a perfect adaptation of a traditional dish to a Nouvelle Cuisine look and a Cuisine Santé taste!*

If you omit the tartlets, the dish is gluten free.

SERVES 4
PREHEAT THE OVEN TO 375°F/190°C/GAS 6

Pâte Brisée *made with 150g (5oz) flour (see page 44)*
1 pork tenderloin, about 450g (1lb) in weight
salt
freshly ground black pepper
2tsp grapeseed oil
mirepoix *(1 onion, 1 carrot and 1 celery stick)*
1dsp tomato concentrate
100ml (3½fl oz) white wine
500ml (18fl oz) Fonds de Volaille *(see page 31)*
1 thyme sprig
1 bayleaf
2 parsley sprigs
25g (1oz) fresh root ginger, peeled and cut into tiny julienne
1 lime, peeled and cut into tiny julienne
100ml (3½fl oz) water
25g (1oz) golden granulated sugar
1 large Conference pear, peeled
1 large Cox's apple, peeled
150ml (5fl oz) red wine
ground cinnamon
1 clove
1dsp muscovado sugar
1dsp honey
25ml (1fl oz) vinegar

TO SERVE
8 pieces each of turned carrots and courgettes

RIGHT *Médaillons de Porc à l'Aigre-Doux*

1 Rest the pastry for 20 minutes in the fridge. Use it to line four small tartlet tins. Line with paper and baking beans and bake blind in the oven until golden brown, about 12 minutes.

2 Trim the fat and sinew from the tenderloin, and cut the meat into 2.5cm (1in) slices. Flatten the slices by beating. Salt and pepper lightly and set aside.

3 Heat half the oil in a skillet and sauté the meat trimmings until well browned. Add the roughly chopped *mirepoix* and sweat until soft. Add the tomato concentrate and sweat for 1 minute. Add the white wine and allow to reduce, about 5 minutes. Add the chicken stock, herbs, and a little salt and pepper, and simmer for a minimum of 30 minutes. Skim off the impurities as they rise to the surface. Strain through a chinois sieve and replace in the cleaned pan to reduce further until the sauce coats the back of a spoon lightly.

4 Put the ginger and lime *julienne* into a saucepan with the water and granulated sugar. Simmer gently for 5 minutes, then reserve on one side.

5 Using a melon baller, carve into the pear and the apple. Place the balls in a saucepan with the red wine, a pinch of cinnamon, the clove and the muscovado sugar. Bring slowly to a simmer and poach until the fruit is tender. Remove the fruit balls and leave the juice to reduce slowly so it forms a shiny glaze (for the fruit later).

6 In another saucepan, heat the honey and let it brown slightly (it will be ready when it exudes a marvellous smell of honey). Add half the vinegar, reduce for 1 minute, then add the sauce, ginger and lime *julienne* with their juices. Leave to simmer very gently for 3-5 minutes.

7 Heat a heavy skillet, and rub the remaining oil, and some salt and pepper, on to the pieces of pork. Sauté for 1 minute on each side, then reserve in a warm place. Deglaze the skillet with the remaining vinegar and the sauce. Adjust the seasoning, remove from the heat, and place the meat in the sauce to marinate.

TO SERVE Meanwhile, steam the carrots and courgettes, and arrange them on a heated serving plate or individual plates. Arrange the slices of pork on top, and garnish with the warm tartlets filled with the fruit balls reheated in their juices, and coated with the juice. Pour the sauce over the meat and to coat the plate, and serve the remainder in a gravy boat. Garnish with strips of lime and ginger.

Rôti de Porc aux Pommes

STEAM-ROAST LOIN OF PORK WITH APPLES

To prepare the pork, the meat is first steamed, then roasted. The steaming dissolves the fat, which runs into the steaming water, and the roasting completes the cooking and gives an attractive colour. This method of cooking may seem a little strange, but the result is tender and very delicious.

The addition of the prunes brings a little sweetness to the flavour of the pork, and the fruit helps to dissolve the fat, helping digestion.

GLUTEN FREE
SERVES 4

½ tsp lapsang souchong tea leaves
1 Indian tea bag
½ litre (1 pt) boiling water
100 g (4 oz) dried prunes, washed
1 kg (2¼ lb) loin of pork (4 chops), boned
salt
freshly ground black pepper
2 dessert apples (Cox's are good), washed
½ lemon
1 dsp redcurrant or apple jelly
mirepoix *(1 onion, 1 carrot and 1 celery stick)*
200 ml (7 fl oz) white wine
300 ml (10 fl oz) Fonds de Volaille *(see page 31)*
1 dsp grapeseed oil
tarragon wine vinegar

TO SERVE
200 g (7 oz) each of carrots, celeriac, turnips and parsnips, cut into julienne
400 g (14 oz) broccoli
1 cauliflower, cut into florets
parsley sprigs

THE DAY BEFORE SERVING

1 Prepare a pot of tea with the tea leaves, tea bag, and boiling water, let it infuse, then strain. Soak the prunes in the tea overnight in the fridge. The next day, remove the prune stones and chop the flesh roughly. Retain the tea.

THE DAY OF SERVING

1 Ask the butcher to bone the meat, or prepare it yourself, removing the skin, fat and each bone, one after the other.

2 Push a needle through the centre of the loin to make a hole, then enlarge this with a finger. Insert half of the prunes, pushing them well in. Salt and pepper the meat and tie it up with string into a roll. Rub with the remaining prunes (keep 1 dessertspoon for the sauce later). Leave to marinate for at least 2 hours at room temperature (or overnight in the fridge).

3 Preheat the oven to 450°F/230°C/Gas 8.
Weigh the roast and allow 15 minutes' roasting time per 450 g (1 lb), plus 10 minutes resting with the oven turned off (this does not include the steaming).

4 Bring some water and 100 ml (3½ fl oz) of the prune tea to the boil in the base of a steamer. Put the meat in the top, cover and leave over the heat for 2 minutes. Then, without uncovering, take off the heat, and leave for 10 minutes. Turn the meat over, replace the lid, and put back over the heat for 2 minutes. Remove from the heat, still covered, and leave for another 10 minutes. This slow steaming method will let the fat run out without toughening the meat.

5 Prick the apples all over with the tip of a knife to prevent the skin from bursting, then cut in half across their 'equators'. Remove the core carefully, leaving a base, and sprinkle each half with a few drops of lemon juice. Spoon the redcurrant or apple jelly into the core holes of each half.

6 Put the pork into a roasting tin and place in the preheated oven. Turn it around every 5 minutes to give an even colour. After 10 minutes, turn the oven down to 350°F/180°C/Gas 4 and add the *mirepoix*, the apples and half the wine. Cook for the remaining time, then rest the meat and apples on a plate.

7 Add the stock to the wine and *mirepoix*, and push through a chinois sieve into a fat-separator. Discard the *mirepoix* left in the sieve. Transfer the sauce to a saucepan and simmer to reduce by half, about 10 minutes.

8 Heat the oil in a small skillet and slowly sweat the remaining prunes to 'caramelize' them, about 5 minutes. Deglaze the pan with a dash of vinegar and the remaining wine. Reduce for 2 minutes, then add the reduced stock. Liquidize, then simmer for 5 minutes, removing the impurities as they rise to the surface, until the sauce coats the back of a spoon. Correct the seasoning if necessary, then, just before serving, add 25 ml (1 fl oz) of the reserved prune tea.

TO SERVE Meanwhile, prepare the vegetables. Steam the *julienne* of root vegetables, the broccoli and cauliflower florets for about 5 minutes.

Remove the strings from the roast and carve it. If carving in the kitchen arrange the meat slices and the vegetables on a warmed platter and garnish with the apples and a few parsley sprigs. (Pour the carving juices on the root vegetables to season them.)

If the meat is to be carved at the table, arrange the vegetables in warmed serving bowls. Serve the apples on a separate plate with some parsley sprigs in the middle. Pour a little sauce over the *julienne* and serve the remainder in a gravy boat.

Rôti de Porc aux Pommes

Carré de Porc Glacé

GLAZED RACK OF PORK

This is a slightly different way to serve pork loin, on the bone in a rack, and here again sage helps to make the meat more digestible. The sweet-sour sauce is made from an apple or redcurrant jelly, but do buy the diabetic one which contains much less sugar, and make sure it contains no artificial flavouring or preservatives. The best kind, of course, is the one you made yourself in the summer.

GLUTEN FREE
SERVES 4
PREHEAT THE OVEN TO 450°F/230°C/GAS 8

1 rack of pork with 4 chops
salt
freshly ground black pepper
1 dsp grapeseed oil
mirepoix *(1 onion, 1 carrot and 1 celery stick)*
200 ml (7 fl oz) dry white wine
100 g (4 oz) redcurrant or apple jelly
25 ml (1 fl oz) cognac
300 ml (10 fl oz) Fonds de Volaille *(see page 31)*

TO SERVE
2 apples
1 orange
8 pieces each of the following turned vegetables: carrots, turnips, celeriac and swede
4 cutlet frills (see page 28)

1 Remove the rind from the pork rack and chine the bones (your butcher can do this for you when you buy the meat) so that the joint carves more easily. Remove as much fat as possible, and weigh the meat. Calculate the cooking time, allowing 40 minutes per 450 g (1 lb). Season the meat with salt and pepper.

2 Heat the oil in a roasting tin in the preheated oven. Add the rack, skin side down, then turn over after 5 minutes. After 10 minutes, pour the fat out of the tin, and add the *mirepoix* and half the white wine. Turn the oven down to 350°F/180°C/Gas 4.

3 Put the redcurrant or apple jelly into a saucepan with most of the cognac (reserving 2 teaspoons for later) and heat gently. Brush this glaze over the top of the meat, and return to the oven. Repeat this operation at least three times to obtain a good glaze. Reserve 1 dessertspoon of jelly for later. Make sure, too, that the *mirepoix* does not burn; add some water as soon as the moisture evaporates.

4 Cut the apples in half through their 'equators'. Remove the cores carefully so that the apple halves are not 'holed' at the top or bottom, and prick the skin all over with a sharp knife to prevent the apple exploding while cooking. Put a teaspoon of jelly inside each hole, and place the apple halves in the roasting tin with the meat until tender, about 10 minutes. Peel the orange (see page 27), and slice across into 4 slices. Dribble the remaining cognac over and set aside, covered.

5 When the meat is cooked, put it on a plate and rest in the turned-off oven for at least 10 minutes. Add the rest of the white wine to the *mirepoix* as well as half the remaining jelly, and leave to reduce for 3 minutes on top of the stove. Add 200 ml (7 fl oz) of the chicken stock and reduce for 3 minutes more. Pour through a chinois sieve into a fat-separator. Pour the fat-free sauce into a saucepan, add the remaining stock and another teaspoon of jelly, and reduce again for 3 minutes. Pour into a gravy boat.

TO SERVE Meanwhile, steam the vegetables for 5-10 minutes, depending on size.

Put the meat, garnished with cutlet frills, in the centre of a warmed serving dish. Place the slices of orange in the steamer for a minute to heat, and arrange around the meat. Place the baked apple halves on top of the orange slices, and arrange the carrots in between. Serve the rest of the vegetables separately.

If you can, bring the whole roast to the table to be carved; if, however, you find it easier, carve it in the kitchen.

LEFT *Carré de Porc Glacé*

Filets Mignons de Porc à la Normande

PORK FILLET WITH APPLE

GLUTEN FREE
SERVES 4
PREHEAT THE OVEN TO 450°F/230°C/GAS 8

750g (a good 1½lb) pork tenderloin
salt
freshly ground black pepper
grapeseed oil
200g (7oz) each of carrot, turnip, leek and celery, cut into julienne
1 cooking apple, chopped
1 shallot, peeled and chopped
25ml (1floz) Calvados
150ml (5floz) cider
500ml (18floz) Fonds de Volaille *(see page 31)*
100ml (3½floz) whipping cream

This recipe is a combination of the Cuisine Bourgeoise and Cuisine Nouvelle. In the Bourgeoise the meat would have been a chop or cutlet and the sauce thickened with a butter and flour roux *or* beurre manié; *in the Nouvelle the sauce would have been a reduction of cream. Our Cuisine Santé version does not use any flour and only a little cream – the trick is the apple purée added at the end!*

1 Season the pork with a little salt and pepper. Heat 1 teaspoon of the oil in an oven- and heatproof pan or heavy skillet and sauté the pork quickly on all sides to seal. Place in the preheated oven for 15 minutes, then turn the oven off. Transfer the pork to a plate and leave to rest in the oven.

2 Meanwhile, steam the vegetable *julienne* until *al dente*, about 3 minutes. Cook the apple to a purée with 2 dessertspoons water, then sieve and discard skin and cores.

3 Put the pork back on to the heat, but discard the fat and clean the pan with paper towels. Add 1 dessertspoon oil and gently sweat the shallot and the vegetable *julienne*, covered, for 5 minutes. Deglaze the pan with the Calvados and set it alight. Add the cider and reduce by half by boiling. Add the chicken stock and the cream and again reduce by half. Add any juices that have run out of the pork. Remove the vegetables from the sauce and reserve with the pork.

4 Add the apple purée, and simmer for another minute. Season well.

TO SERVE Slice the meat and arrange it on a bed of the vegetable *julienne*. Strain some of the sauce through a chinois sieve over the meat, and strain the rest into a gravy boat. Serve immediately.

Filets Mignons de Porc à la Normande

Gasconnade d'Agneau

LAMB WITH GARLIC

This recipe is definitely for garlic lovers. Garlic is one of the best vegetables to ward off all sorts of illnesses: it lowers cholesterol, and helps digestion. Do remember to remove the green germ inside each clove: it is this that is responsible for a garlicky breath and makes garlic difficult to digest.

You could ask your butcher to take out the aitch-bone when you buy the meat. This makes both the cooking and the carving easier.

GLUTEN FREE

SERVES 6

PREHEAT THE OVEN TO 450°F/230°C/GAS 8

1 × 2 kg (4½ lb) leg of lamb
225 g (8 oz) garlic cloves, peeled
2 anchovy fillets
salt
freshly ground black pepper
olive oil
150 ml (5 fl oz) white wine
mirepoix *(1 onion, 1 carrot and 1 celery stick)*
200 ml (7 fl oz) Fonds de Volaille *(see page 31)*

TO SERVE

300 g (11 oz) dwarf beans
300 g (11 oz) broccoli florets
450 g (1 lb) carrots, cut into julienne

1 Remove the excess fat from the leg and take out the aitch-bone at the thick fillet end. Weigh the meat, and calculate the cooking time, allowing 15 minutes per 450 g (1 lb) for pink lamb, and 20-25 minutes for well done. Allow 10 minutes resting time in the turned-off oven to make carving easier.

2 Using a pestle and mortar, work together 4 garlic cloves, the anchovies, some salt and pepper and 1 teaspoon of the olive oil. Make a few slits in the flesh of the leg with a knife, and push in some of the garlic purée. Rub the rest over the outside of the leg, and leave to marinate at room temperature for 20 minutes.

3 Meanwhile, blanch the remaining garlic cloves in a saucepan of boiling water for 2 minutes. Drain and reserve.

4 When the meat has marinated, seal it in 1 dessertspoon of olive oil in a roasting tin on top of the stove, browning it all over. Place the tin in the preheated oven. After 5 minutes turn the meat over, and add the *mirepoix*, 100 ml (3½ fl oz) of the wine and the blanched cloves of garlic.

5 Turn the oven down to 400°F/200°C/Gas 6, and cook for the calculated time. Add a little water during the cooking to keep the vegetables moist. This will also ensure that the fat runs from the meat.

6 When the meat is cooked, turn the oven off. Leave the meat in the oven, wrapped in foil, on another dish to rest for 10 minutes. Pick out and reserve the garlic for the sauce. Add the stock to the pan, and then push this through a chinois sieve into a fat-separator. Leave the fat to separate.

7 Liquidize the fat-free stock with the garlic, and pour into a saucepan. Add the remaining white wine, and simmer to reduce to obtain the right consistency (it should coat the back of a spoon). This will take about 5 minutes.

TO SERVE Meanwhile, steam the beans, broccoli and carrot *julienne* for 5-7 minutes, depending on size.

Carve the meat, putting the juices into the sauce, and present on a warmed serving dish or individual plates, surrounded by the vegetables. Serve the sauce separately in a warm gravy boat.

Filet d'Agneau en Papillote

LAMB FILLET EN PAPILLOTE

This dish combines the sweet flavours of lamb fillet, dried apricots and rosemary, and using a paper parcel helps to retain the full flavour and savour of all the ingredients. The papillote *can be prepared ahead of time and need only be put in the oven 10-15 minutes before serving. This lamb is best served pink.*

Ask your butcher to bone the best end of neck for you.

GLUTEN FREE
SERVES 4
PREHEAT THE OVEN TO 450°F/230°C/GAS 8

600g (a good 1¼lb) best end of neck of lamb, boned
2 rosemary sprigs, about 10cm (4in) long
salt
freshly ground black pepper
grapeseed oil
100g (4oz) dried apricots, washed
100ml (3½floz) dry white wine
1 white of leek, washed, halved lengthwise and sliced across thinly
1dsp flour mixed with 3dsp water

TO SERVE
Sauce à la Tomate *or* Coulis de Tomates *(see pages 36 and 38)*
300g (11oz) each of carrots, turnips and swedes, cut into julienne
450g (1lb) spinach, cut into chiffonade

1 Trim the lamb well. Using a pestle and mortar, crush together the leaves of one sprig of rosemary, 2 pinches of salt, some pepper and 1 dessertspoon oil. Rub into the fillet of lamb and leave to marinate for 20 minutes.

2 Place the dried apricots and wine in a saucepan, bring to the boil and simmer for 2 minutes. Remove from the heat and soak for 20 minutes. Drain the apricots (keep the marinade), and chop roughly.

3 Heat a skillet well, and sauté the lamb very quickly all over, without adding any oil. This should take no longer than 2 minutes. Place the lamb on a plate to cool.

4 Add 1 teaspoon oil to the pan, and sweat the leek for 5 minutes, covered.

5 To prepare the paper parcel, have ready a piece of Bakewell paper about 38cm (15in) square. It should be at least 10cm (4in) larger all round than the piece of lamb. Shape into a *papillote* as described on page 28. Lay the paper flat on the work surface, with the line of the fold lying horizontally. Near the fold, on the half nearest you, place half the apricots, half the leeks and half the remaining sprig of rosemary. Place the lamb fillet on top, and cover with the remaining rosemary, leek and apricots. Pour over the reserved wine marinade.

6 Rub a little of the flour paste on the side of the paper nearest you, and fold the other part over it. Rub a little flour paste over this join and fold the join over again by about 1cm (½in) to seal. The paste will set and seal the *papillote* completely.

7 Lay the paper package on a baking tray and place in the preheated oven. Bake for 10 minutes for pink lamb, 15 minutes for medium, and 20 minutes for well done. Rest in the turned-off oven or in a warm place for 5 minutes before serving.

TO SERVE Meanwhile, steam the carrot, turnip and swede *julienne* for 4-5 minutes. (The *julienne* could also be added to the *papillote*, but expect them to taste of rosemary! Alternatively, cook them in a separate *papillote* with a dessertspoon of white wine or water.) Sauté the spinach *chiffonade* briskly in 1 dessertspoon oil, and season with salt and pepper.

Pour the tomato *coulis* or sauce into a gravy boat. Place the spinach on a warmed serving plate and arrange the vegetable *julienne* around the edges. Bring to the table along with the *papillote* on a carving board, a knife and hot plates. Open the *papillote* at the last moment and discard the sprigs of rosemary. Carve the meat and serve it along with the vegetables and sauce.

RIGHT *Filet d'Agneau en Papillote*

Côtelettes d'Agneau en Cuirasse

LAMB CUTLETS

This is an Haute Cuisine classic. Prepare it well in advance, which will give you more time to attend to the rest of the meal. It keeps very well overnight in the fridge, or for up to 3 months in the freezer.

SERVES 4

PREHEAT THE OVEN TO 450°F/230°C/GAS 8

Pâte Brisée *made with 300g (11oz) flour (see page 44)*
4 lamb cutlets
1dsp grapeseed oil
salt
freshly ground black pepper
1 egg, beaten
4 large thin ham slices, halved
200g (7oz) duxelle *of mushrooms (see page 23)*

SAUCE AU PORTO

25g (1oz) butter
3 shallots, peeled and finely chopped
100ml (3½fl oz) good, old port
600ml (1pt) Fonds de Volaille *(see page 31)*

TO SERVE

150g (6oz) mangetout
200g (7oz) broccoli
150g (6oz) carrot, cut into julienne

1 Rest the pastry for 20 minutes in the fridge.

2 Trim the cutlets well, then heat the oil in a frying pan. Season the cutlets on both sides, then sauté them quickly for 1 minute on each side. Reserve on a cooling rack. When cool, bone them and remove all traces of fat.

3 Roll the pastry out into a rectangle of 40 × 24cm (16 × 9½in) and brush with the beaten egg. Cut the pastry into eight rectangles: cut the shorter sides in half and then divide the longer sides into four rectangles 8cm (3in) wide, leaving a strip at the end for garnish purposes. Layer, on four of the rectangles, a half slice of ham, some *duxelle*, a cutlet, followed by some *duxelle* and another half slice of ham to finish. Bring the pastry up over the sides of the cutlet, and brush with beaten egg. Place another pastry rectangle on top of each cutlet, tucking the excess underneath. Brush all over with beaten egg and garnish with strips of the reserved pastry, so that each looks like a little parcel. Brush again with beaten egg, and rest for at least a few minutes in the fridge. (This can all be prepared a long time in advance.)

4 Brush again with egg just before baking, and put on a baking tray. Place in the preheated oven, turn the heat down to 350°F/180°C/Gas 4, and bake for 20 minutes.

5 Meanwhile, make the sauce. Melt the butter in a saucepan and sweat the shallot over a low heat for 5 minutes. Add most of the port and reduce by half. Add the stock and simmer very gently for 15 minutes. Add the remaining port, then strain the sauce (or leave the shallots in), and pour into a gravy boat.

TO SERVE Meanwhile, steam the vegetables together for 5-10 minutes, depending on size.

If serving traditionally, present the cutlets on a doily-lined serving dish, with the vegetables to the side. Serve the sauce separately.

If serving individually, place each cutlet on a warmed plate, surround with vegetables, and pour the sauce around at the last moment.

LEFT *Côtelettes d'Agneau en Cuirasse*

Pot au Feu

BEEF CASSEROLE

Another very traditional French country dish, this is wonderful when prepared in large quantities for informal family affairs: half of it can be frozen for another occasion; any leftover meat can be made into a Boeuf en Gelée *(see page 122); and the juices are usually served as a soup.*

SERVES 8

4 leeks
2.75 kg (6 lb) beef: 450 g (1 lb) each of chuck steak, shin, leg, flank, oxtail, kept whole and tied like a roast, and lower rib bones
3 onions, unpeeled and washed
1 clove
4 carrots, peeled
4 small turnips, peeled
4 small parsnips, peeled
2 bouquets garnis
1 litre (1¾ pt) strong Fonds de Volaille *(see page 31)*
coarse sea salt
5 each of white peppercorns and coriander seeds, crushed
100 ml (3½ fl oz) white wine
25 g (1 oz) butter
freshly ground black pepper

TO SERVE
1 recipe Choux Rouge Braisé, *using a Savoy cabbage (see page 163), with the leaves whole, not chopped*
450 g (1 lb) baby new potatoes, washed

TWO DAYS BEFORE SERVING

1 Soak the leeks in a large bowl of cold water for 30 minutes. Shake dry, bend in two, and tie together with string.

2 Rinse the meats well and dry on paper towels. Place in a large saucepan with one of the onions, studded with the clove, and the remaining whole vegetables plus the leeks. Add the *bouquets garnis*.

3 Add the stock and as much water as necessary to cover the meat and vegetables completely. Add ½ teaspoon salt, the peppercorns and coriander seeds, and bring slowly to the boil over a medium heat, skimming off the impurities as they rise to the surface. Simmer gently for 2 hours, adding water as it reduces, so that the meat and vegetables are always covered. Allow to cool and reserve in the fridge overnight.

THE DAY BEFORE SERVING

1 Remove all the fat set on top of the stock and bring slowly back to the boil over a medium heat.

2 Meanwhile, peel the remaining onions, cut them in half through the root, and slice across thickly. Place in another saucepan with the white wine, 100 ml (3½ fl oz) of the stock, the butter, a pinch of salt and a little pepper. Simmer gently, letting the liquid reduce completely and allowing the onions to colour well (this can take up to 40 minutes). Add to the meat and vegetables in the other pan, and simmer for 1½ hours. Cool, and reserve again in the fridge overnight.

THE DAY OF SERVING

Preheat the oven to 350°F/180°C/Gas 4.

1 The stock should be firmly set (if not, and you want to use it to make *Boeuf en Gelée*, see page 122). Remove the layer of fat set on the surface. Bring slowly to the boil over a medium heat. Detach the meat from the bones and replace in the stock. Cut the vegetables up into smaller pieces (although they do look good left whole!), and replace them in the stock. When it simmers, the dish is ready to serve.

TO SERVE Meanwhile, steam the potatoes above stock instead of water for 10 minutes (for longer if they are large). Warm the cabbage.

Strain the stock through muslin to remove the impurities and serve with some cut-up vegetables as a soup. For the main course, arrange the meat on a serving dish or individual plates with the vegetables all around. Offer mustard, chutneys, horseradish sauce and pickles to accompany the meat.

If there is any meat and stock left over, prepare *Boeuf en Gelée*.

RIGHT *Pot au Feu*

Sauté de Boeuf Minute

SAUTÉD STEAK WITH TOMATO CREAM SAUCE

True to its name, this dish is prepared at the last minute. It uses rump rather than fillet steak to make a stronger sauce. It is an ideal dish to prepare when entrecôte is on the menu and unexpected guests turn up! The beef steaks for two are cut up into strips which are cooked very quickly, then served with a sauce which combines a traditional cream sauce and a Coulis de Tomates. *Try it, as below, with fresh noodles tossed into the sauce.*

If you are on a gluten-free diet, omit the noodles, and serve the dish with more vegetables.

SERVES 4
PREHEAT THE OVEN TO ITS LOWEST TEMPERATURE

1 recipe Pâte à Nouilles *(see page 45)*
450g (1lb) lean rump or entrecôte steak
freshly ground black pepper
cayenne pepper
grapeseed oil
3 shallots, peeled and finely chopped
1 garlic clove, peeled and crushed
50ml (2floz) Madeira
50ml (2floz) white or red wine
50ml (2floz) whipping cream (optional)
1 recipe Coulis de Tomates *(see page 38)*
salt

TO SERVE
450g (1lb) broccoli or green beans
1dsp fines herbes, *finely chopped*

1 Leave the pasta dough to rest in the fridge for 10 minutes. Cut into noodles, and dry on a floured tray lined with a tea-towel.

2 Cut the meat up into little-finger-sized strips and season with pepper and a pinch of cayenne (do not salt).

3 Heat a skillet well. This is very important as the end result – both meat and sauce – depends on the heat of the pan, and on the way in which the meat will be cooked. Add 1 teaspoon oil to the pan and toss the strips of meat over a high heat for 2 minutes only. Reserve, covered on a plate, in the preheated oven.

4 Let the skillet cool for a moment, then add the shallots with a drop more oil. Sweat slowly until soft, about 5 minutes. Add the garlic and sweat for 1 minute. Deglaze with the Madeira, wine and the juices that have run from the meat. Reduce almost completely, then add the cream (if using), and reduce by half. Add the tomato *coulis*, and simmer for 2 minutes.

5 Take off the heat and add the meat and a pinch of salt. Do not boil again but leave to marinate for 2 minutes before serving.

TO SERVE Steam the vegetables until tender. Meanwhile, boil the fresh noodles until *al dente* (about 2 minutes), then pour a little cold water over them to stop the cooking. Drain and place on a warmed serving dish or individual plates, and pour over a little of the sauce. Using a slotted spoon, put the meat on the bed of noodles, and sprinkle with the fresh herbs. Serve immediately with the vegetables. Serve the remaining sauce in a gravy boat.

Boeuf Bourguignon

BEEF STEW

This is a very traditional Cuisine Bourgeoise dish. Start preparing it 2 or even 3 days in advance; the meat will be more flavourful and the sauce free of fat. You can present it in a timbale *to impress your guests even more, but the dish will no longer be gluten free.*

SERVES 4

450g (1lb) chuck steak, cubed
1 bottle Côtes du Rhône
mirepoix *(1 onion, 1 carrot and 1 celery stick)*
salt
freshly ground black pepper
1 bayleaf
1 thyme sprig
ground allspice
2dsp grapeseed oil
200g (7oz) smoked pork belly, trimmed and diced
3dsp cognac
1 heaped dsp tomato concentrate
4 each of the following turned vegetables: carrot, turnip, potato and courgette
12 pickling onions, peeled
1 clove
1 muslin 'spice bag' containing 1 allspice berry, 1/4 cinnamon stick, 1 slice fresh root ginger and a strip each of lemon, orange and lime rind
1 bouquet garni
grated nutmeg
150g (5oz) frozen petits pois

TO SERVE
450g (1lb) broccoli
1 large or 4 small timbales *(see page 44)*
1dsp parsley, finely chopped

TWO DAYS BEFORE SERVING
Marinate the beef overnight with half the wine, the roughly chopped *mirepoix*, a pinch of salt, some pepper, the herbs and a pinch of ground allspice.

THE DAY BEFORE SERVING
1 Drain the meat and dry it on paper towels. Discard the *mirepoix* and marinade.
2 Heat half the oil in a skillet and sweat the pork dice to render the fat. Remove the pork, drain off the fat, and add the remaining oil to the skillet.
3 Quickly sauté the beef cubes over a very high heat in two batches, so that the meat is sealed well.
4 Put the pork dice back in the skillet with the meat, add the cognac and set alight. Add the tomato concentrate, stir well, and add enough of the remaining red wine to cover well.
5 Add the turned vegetables, the baby onions (one of them studded with the clove), the muslin 'spice bag', *bouquet garni* and a little nutmeg.
6 Cover and bring to the boil, skimming off the impurities as they rise to the surface. Simmer very gently for 15 minutes. The vegetables should now be tender, so lift them out and reserve on a plate.
7 Continue cooking the meat for another 20 minutes until done. Replace the vegetables, cover, and leave to cool. Place in the fridge overnight.

THE DAY OF SERVING
1 Remove the layer of fat set on the surface of the meat, bring back to the boil, and simmer for 5-10 minutes.
2 Cook the peas in salted, boiling water and add to the casserole.
TO SERVE Meanwhile, steam the broccoli.
Remove the 'spice bag' and *bouquet garni*. Reduce the sauce if necessary, adjust the seasoning and serve in the *timbale* or *timbales*, topped with the parsley.

Boeuf en Gelée

BEEF IN ASPIC

This is a delicious potted meat, which use the meat's natural gelatinous protein to set it, and is a very good way of using the leftover meat and vegetables from a Pot au Feu.

SERVES 4

450g (1lb) leftover Pot au Feu *meat (see page 118)*
1.5 litres (2½pt) leftover Pot au Feu *stock*
2 medium carrots, peeled, scored and sliced
2 turnips, peeled, scored and sliced
2 parsnips, peeled, scored and sliced
1 leek, washed, sliced, and leaves reserved
1-2 leaves gelatine (optional)

1 Lift the meat from the stock and cube it.

2 Strain the stock well and cook the sliced vegetables and leek leaves in it until just tender. Reserve them on a plate to cool, then reduce the stock until there is about 350ml (12fl oz) left.

3 If the stock had not set hard (see the recipe for *Pot au Feu*), soak the gelatine leaves and add them to the hot stock after it has been reduced. (If the stock had set, omit the gelatine.) Reserve 100ml (3½fl oz) of this aspic to garnish the terrine.

4 Mix the meat cubes with the remaining aspic or gelatinous stock.

5 Pour half the reserved aspic into the bottom of the terrine, and leave to set in the fridge. When set, garnish with some vegetable slices and leek leaves dipped in the remaining aspic. Put in the fridge to set. Pour the remaining reserved aspic into the terrine through a sieve, and leave in the fridge to set again.

6 When the meat and its aspic start to set, place it in layers in the terrine, interspersing with vegetable slices and leek leaves.

7 Leave it overnight in the fridge to set firmly and then serve the next day with a salad. It can also be frozen for up to 6 months.

Boeuf en Gelée

Escalope de Veau Woronoff

VEAL WORONOFF

The traditional Beurre Café de Paris *uses a lot of butter and is finished off with double and soured cream. This version eliminates the butter and marinates the meat in the* Marinade Café de Paris *which gives it an exceptional taste. Pork, chicken, turkey and even fish – strips of monkfish, for instance – could be prepared in the same way as the veal.*

An ideal accompaniment is fresh noodles, but if you use these, the dish is no longer gluten free.

SERVES 4

1 recipe Marinade Café de Paris *(see page 37)*
4 × 100 g (4 oz) escalopes of veal
2 dsp grapeseed oil
½ tsp potato flour
100 g (4 oz) Greek yoghurt
50 ml (2 fl oz) whipping cream
50 ml (2 fl oz) milk

TO SERVE
1 cucumber
Pâte à Nouilles *made with 350 g (12 oz) flour (see page 45)*
1 dsp parsley, finely chopped

THE DAY BEFORE SERVING
Prepare the ingredients for the marinade. Place in a bowl, cover, and leave overnight (or for 12 hours at least) at room temperature.

THE DAY OF SERVING
1 Trim the escalopes well. Mix the grapeseed oil into the marinade and liquidize it all in the blender. Marinate the escalopes in it for 30 minutes at room temperature.

2 Scrape the marinade off the meat and put into a skillet.

3 Mix the potato flour with the yoghurt, cream and milk, pour into the marinade and heat gently. Do not boil.

4 Place the meat in this mixture and gently poach for 3 minutes on either side.

TO SERVE Meanwhile, prepare the cucumber garnish. Peel, halve and seed the cucumber and cut into chunks. Blanch in lightly salted boiling water for 2 minutes. Drain and refresh immediately under cold running water. Cook the noodles. Remove the meat from the sauce and keep in a warm place. Reheat the cucumber in the sauce gently, but do not let the sauce boil.

On a heated serving dish, make a bed of noodles, and place the escalopes on top. Arrange the pieces of cucumber around the dish and spoon the sauce over the meat. Sprinkle the parsley over the top.

Escalope de Veau Jurassienne en Croûte

VEAL EN CROÛTE

These little pastry parcels can be made the day before you wish to serve them. The original recipe used double the cheese, a slice of ham, and a béchamel *made with flour and butter. The red pepper addition – tasty and colourful – is a new idea!*

SERVES 4
PREHEAT THE OVEN TO 350°F/180°C/GAS 4

Pâte Feuilletée *made with 300g (11oz) flour (see page 42)*
4 × 100g (4oz) thin veal escalopes
salt
freshly ground black pepper
1tsp grapeseed oil
8 × 15g (½oz) slices Emmenthal cheese
300g (11oz) duxelle *of mushrooms (see page 23)*
4 red peppers, skinned (see page 23) and diced
egg wash

SAUCE
500ml (18floz) Fonds de Volaille *(see page 31)*
2 shallots, peeled and finely chopped
1 garlic clove, peeled and crushed
25ml (1floz) white wine vinegar
25ml (1floz) water
100ml (3½floz) white wine
1 tomato, skinned, seeded and diced
1 thyme sprig
1 bayleaf
parsley sprigs

TO SERVE
1 recipe Ratatouille Provençale *(see page 156)*

1 Rest the pastry in the fridge for 20 minutes.

2 Season the escalopes lightly with salt and pepper. Heat 1 teaspoon oil in a skillet and flash-fry both sides of the escalopes. Reserve to cool.

3 To make the sauce, simmer to reduce the stock by half. Sweat the shallots in 1 teaspoon oil for 5 minutes, then add the garlic and sweat for 1 minute. Add the vinegar, water and white wine and reduce until nearly dry. Add the reduced stock, half the pepper dice and the tomato. Season with a little salt and pepper, add the thyme, bayleaf and some parsley sprigs, and leave to simmer for 30 minutes, skimming off the impurities as they rise to the surface.

4 Meanwhile, roll the dough out and cut into eight 12cm (4½in) squares. Have ready the cheese slices, the escalopes, the *duxelle* and the remaining red pepper dice. Divide the *duxelle* and pepper dice into four piles, one pile for each pastry 'parcel'.

5 On to each of four pastry squares lay a slice of cheese, then half the *duxelle*, half the red pepper dice, the slice of veal, the remaining red pepper and *duxelle*, and top with another slice of cheese. Brush the edges of the dough with egg wash, then fold the excess dough up around the layers. Brush the edges of the remaining squares of dough with egg wash and place over the top, making sure the first layer of dough is completely covered. Press to seal. Brush with egg wash and cut a criss-cross pattern on top with the edge of a knife. Chill again if you like for 20 minutes (or overnight, well brushed with egg wash).

6 Bake in the preheated oven for 20 minutes. Brush with egg wash again halfway through the cooking time to obtain a shiny finish.

7 Reduce the sauce until it lightly coats the back of a spoon. Remove the thyme, bayleaf and parsley sprigs, and put the sauce through a liquidizer. Place over the heat and adjust the seasoning.

TO SERVE Pour the sauce into a warm gravy boat, and arrange the little veal parcels on a heated serving dish on top of doilies or a folded napkin.

Serve with the ratatouille.

RIGHT *Escalope de Veau Jurassienne en Croûte* with *Ratatouille Provençale*

Blanquette de Veau ou Lapin

BLANQUETTE *OF VEAL OR RABBIT*

A blanquette *can be made with either veal or rabbit. Here, it has been adapted to make it healthier by eliminating the flour and butter* roux, *most of the cream, and the fat.*

Preparation should cover 2 days, but each day requires only a few minutes of actual work, and the flavour is considerably enhanced by the overnight marinating.

The blanquette *could be further garnished by a green vegetable such as steamed broccoli, by some croûtons or by a* timbale *(see page 44). (If either of the latter is used, however, the dish is no longer gluten free.)*

GLUTEN FREE
SERVES 4

750g (a good 1½lb) shoulder of veal, trimmed, or 1 × 1kg (2¼lb) rabbit and mirepoix *(1 onion, 1 carrot and 1 celery stick)*
salt
2 litres (3½pt) water
mirepoix *(1 onion, 1 carrot and 1 celery stick)*
1 bouquet garni
4 parsley sprigs
1 litre (1¾pt) Fonds de Volaille *(see page 31)*
8 pieces each of the following turned vegetables: carrots, turnips, swedes and potatoes
4 pickling onions
1 dsp potato flour
50ml (2fl oz) whipping cream
150g (5oz) button mushrooms
3 tsp lemon juice
1 tsp grapeseed oil
freshly ground black pepper
100ml (3½fl oz) white wine
100g (4oz) frozen petits pois

TO SERVE
3 dsp fines herbes, *finely chopped*
50g (2oz) Greek yoghurt

TWO DAYS BEFORE SERVING

This applies to the rabbit *blanquette* only. Joint the rabbit as described on page 21, place the pieces in a large saucepan, and add some salt, the *mirepoix*, and the water. Bring to the boil, turn off the heat, and leave to cool. When cold, marinate overnight in the fridge.

ONE DAY BEFORE SERVING

1 For the veal *blanquette*, bring the water with ½ teaspoon of salt added to the boil. Cut the veal into 2.5cm (1in) cubes, and wash in cold running water to remove any impurities. Put the cubes in the boiling water, bring back to the boil, and blanch for 2 minutes.

2 From now on the instructions are the same for both veal and rabbit. Drain the meat, rinse under cold running water, and drain again. Put into a large, clean saucepan or heatproof casserole with the roughly chopped *mirepoix, bouquet garni* and parsley sprigs. Add the cold stock, and bring to the boil slowly, skimming off the impurities as they rise to the surface.

3 Add the carrots, turnips and swede (the potatoes will go in later), along with the pickling onions, and cover. Simmer until the vegetables are done (about 5-10 minutes for the turned vegetables, a little longer for the onions). Turn the heat off, cover, and leave to cool. When cold, place in the fridge overnight.

THE DAY OF SERVING

1 Remove the fat which has set on the surface overnight and place the pan or dish over a low heat. Remove the turned vegetables and onions and reserve in a bowl with a little of the stock so that they do not dry up. Bring the stock in the pan back to the boil, adding the potatoes. Remove when tender, and reserve with the other vegetables. When the meat is done (about 10-15 minutes), remove it and reserve in a warm place with a little of the stock, well covered.

2 For the sauce, strain the stock and discard the *mirepoix, bouquet garni* and parsley sprigs. Place the stock in a large, clean saucepan and reduce by simmering until about 250ml (10fl oz) remain. Mix the potato flour and cream in a bowl, and pour in a little of the hot stock. Mix well, then pour back into the stock. Stir while it returns to the boil, then simmer very gently for about 5 minutes, or until the sauce lightly coats the back of a spoon.

Blanquette de Veau ou Lapin

3 Wash the mushrooms and leave them for 1 minute in a bowl of water with 1 teaspoon of the lemon juice. Heat the oil in a frying pan, and add the mushrooms, some salt and pepper, and another teaspoon of the lemon juice. Sauté briskly and leave over a medium heat for about 2-3 minutes until the juices run. Add the white wine, cover, and simmer until the mushrooms are done, about 5 minutes. Remove the lid and reduce the juices by half (about 2 minutes).

4 Pour the mushrooms and their juices into the pan holding the *blanquette* sauce. Add the meats and all the reserved vegetables, including the peas. (If you wish to freeze the *blanquette*, now is the time to do so.)

5 Reheat the *blanquette* slowly over a low heat, and simmer for 3-4 minutes.

TO SERVE Reserve a dessertspoon of the herbs for garnish, mix the rest with the yoghurt, and stir into the warm sauce. Add the remaining lemon juice and adjust the seasoning if necessary.

Serve the meat and sauce on a large warm platter, arrange the vegetables around, and sprinkle the centre with the remaining herbs.

Timbale de Veau aux Petits Pois

VEAL TIMBALE *WITH PEAS*

This recipe originally used lamb or another red meat, but when we were searching for ways to cut down on red meat, this veal alternative proved delicious. No flour is used in the sauce: its body comes from the onions and tomato concentrate, and reducing the sauce. The addition of the peas gives an attractive colour to the dish as well as providing vitamins and fibre. Use frozen baby onions if you can't find fresh – they're just as good.

If you are on a gluten-free diet, do not serve the pastry timbale.

SERVES 4

- Pâte Brisée *made with 300g (11oz) flour (see page 44)*
- *1 onion, peeled and finely chopped*
- *salt*
- *freshly ground black pepper*
- *500g (a scant 1¼lb) lean pie veal (leg or shoulder), trimmed and cubed*
- *1dsp grapeseed oil*
- *100ml (3½fl oz) white wine*
- *2dsp tomato concentrate*
- *200ml (7fl oz)* Fonds de Volaille *(see page 31)*
- *12 pickling onions, topped, tailed, blanched and peeled*
- *1* bouquet garni
- *2 parsley sprigs*
- *10 coriander seeds*
- *450g (1lb) frozen* petits pois, *blanched*
- *450g (1lb) turnips, cut into* julienne, *blanched*

1 Rest the pastry in the fridge for 20 minutes. Roll out and make a *timbale* (see page 44), and bake it.

2 Sweat the onion in a casserole, covered, for 10 minutes.

3 Salt and pepper the meat, then heat the oil in the onion casserole, and sauté the meat quickly over a high heat. Remove the meat and onions from the pan and leave on a plate to cool.

4 Remove the fat from the casserole, deglaze with the white wine, and reduce until nearly dry. Add the tomato concentrate and let it cook and stick to the pan, without burning. Replace the meat and onions, add the chicken stock and baby onions, and bring to the boil slowly, removing the impurities as they rise to the surface. Simmer, covered, for 15 minutes.

5 Add the *bouquet garni*, parsley sprigs and coriander seeds, then simmer for 20 minutes more.

6 Add the peas and turnip *julienne*. Simmer for 5 minutes, uncovered.

7 Test the meat to see if it is cooked – it should be soft – and when done, remove it and the vegetables, except for the chopped onion. Keep on one side with a little of the stock to moisten.

8 Reduce the juices left in the casserole by half. Put these, plus the onion, through the liquidizer, then pour back into the casserole with the meat and vegetables. Let it boil once, and check the seasoning. (At this stage the meat and vegetables could be left to cool to be served the next day, or to be frozen.)

TO SERVE Meanwhile, warm the *timbale* and its lid in a low oven. Pour the stew into it and cover with the lid. Present on a serving dish lined with a doily or napkin.

RIGHT *Timbale de Veau aux Petits Pois*

Poulet Farci Fendu au Four

BAKED CHICKEN WITH COURGETTE STUFFING

This dish is a challenge for any cook, but see pages 18-19 for full details on how to bone a bird. Roasting is the favoured method here as it drains out all the fat, which is later discarded. The stuffing contains much less fat than the original recipe, and much more vegetable. Serve with an assortment of vegetable purées.

SERVES 6

PREHEAT THE OVEN TO 450°F/230°C/GAS 8

1 × 1.5 kg (3½ lb) chicken
salt
freshly ground black pepper

STUFFING

450 g (1 lb) courgettes, washed, topped and tailed
½ tsp olive oil
1 onion, peeled and chopped
1 garlic clove, peeled and crushed
100 g (4 oz) Ricotta (or other low-fat soft cheese)
1 tsp fines herbes, *finely chopped*
herbes de Provence
25 g (1 oz) Parmesan cheese, grated
1 egg white
50 g (2 oz) dry wholemeal breadcrumbs

TO SERVE

Coulis de Tomates *(see page 38)*
Purées de Légumes *(see page 151)*
spring onion flowers (see page 25)
salad leaves

1 Bone the chicken as described on pages 18-19, then sprinkle with salt and pepper.

2 For the stuffing, grate the courgettes, or cut them into thin *julienne* strips, sprinkle with a little salt and leave for 10-15 minutes. Rinse well, then squeeze dry to eliminate the salt and juices. Heat the oil and sweat the onion and garlic until soft, then add the courgettes. Sweat for 2 minutes. Remove and spread out on a large serving dish and leave to cool.

3 In a bowl, soften the Ricotta, and add the cooled vegetable mixture, the fresh herbs and a pinch of *herbes de Provence*. Mix well, then add the Parmesan, egg white and breadcrumbs. Season well.

4 Lay the chicken flat, skin side up and, with your fingers, separate the skin from the flesh. Lay the stuffing between the flesh and the skin of the leg, then the breast, one side at a time. Be sure not to break the skin between the two breasts.

5 Rub the whole chicken with a little oil and some salt and pepper. Roast in the preheated oven in a roasting tin lined with foil for 10 minutes, then turn the oven down to 350°F/180°C/Gas 4 and roast for a further 40-50 minutes until golden brown.

TO SERVE Lift the chicken out carefully, on the foil, and allow the fat and juices to run back into the tin. Strain the juices through a chinois sieve into a fat-separator, then mix the fat-free juices with the *coulis*. Heat through quickly, carve the chicken as described on page 134, and serve immediately with the vegetable purées and salad leaves.

LEFT *Poulet Farci Fendu au Four*

Chaud-Froid de Volaille

CHICKEN CHAUD-FROID

A traditional chaud-froid *is not very much liked in France, but now that we all recognize the healthiness of plainly boiled poultry, it should become more popular. The classic recipe had a butter and flour* roux *to thicken the white sauce with a lot of cream added, more cream plus tomato concentrate for the pink sauce, and yet more cream and a purée of spinach for the green sauce. We have also replaced the cream with low-fat soft cheese. The base of the sauces is the stock in which the chicken cooks, but no* roux *is added, and it is reduced to concentrate the natural gelatine it contains.*

If you select brands of curry powder and paprika which contain no gluten, this dish is gluten-free.

This dish is best made over two days.

SERVES 6

1 × 1.5 kg (3¼ lb) chicken
1 thyme sprig
1 bayleaf
salt
15 peppercorns, crushed
juice of ½ lemon
1 extra chicken carcass
mirepoix *(3 carrots, 2 onions and 2 celery sticks)*
1 bouquet garni *plus remainder of the leek*
3 garlic cloves, peeled

SAUCES
200 g (7 oz) carrots, peeled and sliced
200 g (7 oz) spinach, cut into chiffonade
1 garlic clove, peeled
1 tsp mild curry powder
5 pinches each of paprika and cayenne pepper
50 g (2 oz) Petit-Suisse or Greek yoghurt
50 g (2 oz) Ricotta (or other low-fat soft cheese)

GARNISH
parsley sprigs

THE DAY BEFORE SERVING

1 Clean the chicken and rinse it under the tap. Dry it well, inside and out, and place the sprig of thyme, bayleaf, ¼ teaspoon salt, a third of the peppercorns and half the lemon juice in the cavity. Put in a large saucepan with the chicken carcass, the *mirepoix, bouquet garni*, leek, garlic, ½ teaspoon salt and the remaining peppercorns.

2 Cover with water and place over a medium heat. Bring to the boil, skimming off the impurities as they rise to the surface. This can take up to 20 minutes. Turn the heat down and simmer for 1 hour from boiling. The liquid should barely move. Turn off the heat and leave to cool at room temperature, then place the saucepan in the fridge overnight.

THE DAY OF SERVING

1 Start by removing all the fat set on the surface of the liquid. Remove the chicken and strain the stock first through a sieve and then through muslin into another pan. Portion the chicken, keeping the skin and smaller bits to put into the stock for extra gelatine. Remove the fillet from the breast and cut the breast in half. Separate the thighs from the drumsticks and cut the thighs in half lengthwise, to remove the bones. You should obtain twelve pieces. Lay the pieces on a cooling tray in the fridge. Keep all the meat trimmings from the carcass for later use.

2 Put the bones and skin into the stock and bring to the boil. Remove the pieces of skin and the bones immediately, as the natural gelatine will have been extracted. Reduce the stock to obtain 600 ml (1 pt), which will take approximately 30-40 minutes.

3 Steam the carrots until soft. Purée them with 200 ml (7 fl oz) reduced stock and a little salt and pepper if necessary. Sauté the spinach with a little water, salt and pepper, then purée it. Drain well in a fine sieve, and blot with paper towels to remove the excess moisture. Add 200 ml (7 fl oz) reduced stock to this purée as well. Put both purées in the freezer to thicken, stirring both occasionally until they are of a good coating consistency.

4 For the third sauce – with a Colombo flavour – work the garlic clove, curry powder, paprika and cayenne pepper together using a pestle and mortar. Add the Petit-Suisse and the soft cheese a little at a time. Thin down the mixture with the remaining reduced stock. Adjust the seasoning, if necessary, and thicken in the freezer as for the other two sauces.

5 When all three sauces can coat the back of a spoon, bring the chicken out of the fridge on its cooling tray and place over a baking tray to retain any of the sauces that fall through. Spoon the carrot sauce over four of the chicken pieces and the spinach sauce over another four. Spoon the Colombo-type sauce over the final four chicken pieces. Coat each piece about three times to obtain a good build-up of sauce. Reserve the remaining sauces.

6 Mix the remaining carrot sauce with the remaining Colombo sauce and pour on to a large, flat dish, at least 40 cm (16 in) in diameter. Make a piping bag from a triangle of paper and pour into it 2 dessertspoons of the remaining green sauce. Pipe small dots of green all around the sauce-lined dish at 1 cm (½ in) intervals. Run a sharp knife from the centre of these dots in towards the centre of the dish in a 'comma'-shaped movement. Place in the fridge to set. Pour the remaining green sauce into a dinner plate to line the bottom. Place in the fridge to set.

7 Chop the small bits of chicken left over from carving and those attached to the carcasses, and mix with the sauces left in the baking tray from the coating. Pack into a ramekin dish or large terrine and place in the fridge. (This will make a delicious terrine, which can be served the next day. Serve with salad leaves for a light summer lunch, or as part of a buffet.)

TO SERVE Take everything out of the fridge. Arrange the chicken pieces on the platter, combining the colours well, and garnish with parsley. Cut the jellied green sauce into shapes to garnish the chicken pieces. Serve immediately.

Chaud-Froid de Volaille

Poulet Grillé au Citron Vert

GRILLED CHICKEN WITH LIME

Start preparing this dish the day before you want to serve it so that it can marinate overnight in the fridge. The lime dissolves the fat completely, and gives the chicken a wonderfully exotic taste. It's a perfect dish for the barbecue too!

GLUTEN FREE
SERVES 4

1 × 1kg (2¼lb) chicken
salt
freshly ground black pepper
½ tsp ground ginger (preferably fresh)
1 small bunch spring onions, washed
2 limes, washed
½ tsp golden granulated sugar
75ml (3fl oz) water

TO SERVE
1 recipe Riz Complet aux Poireaux *(see page 162)*
2 cutlet frills (see page 28)
Coulis de Tomates *(see page 38)*
parsley sprigs

THE DAY BEFORE SERVING

1 Bone the chicken as described on pages 18-19, reserving the carcass for chicken stock. Salt the chicken lightly and sprinkle pepper generously all over it, along with the ginger.

2 Remove most of the green from the spring onions, chop them finely and lay on a plate large enough to fit the flattened chicken. Lay the chicken over the onions, skin side down, pressing down well. Using a zester, cut the lime rind into *julienne*. Sprinkle over the chicken. Squeeze the lime juice over the chicken and rub it in well. Cover with cling film and keep in the fridge overnight. (If you really do not have time to leave overnight, leave for 2 hours at room temperature.)

THE DAY OF SERVING

1 Drain the chicken of all its juices and dry it well with paper towels. Remove the onion.

2 Meanwhile, gather up all the lime rind and blanch it for 1 minute in boiling water. Strain, then put in a saucepan with the sugar and water and leave to simmer until there are about 2 dessertspoons of liquid left in the pan.

3 Heat the grill to maximum. Lay the chicken on a rack flesh side up, and put under the grill. After 2 minutes, turn the grill down by half (if there is no control, leave the chicken for 2 minutes directly under the grill, then place it on a lower shelf). Grill for 12 minutes on each side. Turn off the grill and leave for 5 more minutes.

TO SERVE Carve the chicken. Cut the bird in half lengthwise through the skin holding the breasts together. Cut each breast in half again on the diagonal (to make four pieces) and cut the legs in half through the joints.

Make a bed of rice on a warm serving platter, and reassemble the chicken in its original shape. Put cutlet frills on the drumsticks. Pour the tomato *coulis* all around and serve any remaining in a gravy boat. Garnish with parsley and the drained lime *julienne*.

Poulet Sauté à l'Estragon

CHICKEN WITH TARRAGON

The traditional recipe roasts chicken pieces in their own fat plus some butter. Here the method is more of a braise, and the chicken fat runs into the braising liquid, which will be separated later. The vast amount of cream normally used is reduced drastically, although a little is still used along with some Greek yoghurt, in order to preserve the original creamy taste of the tarragon sauce. Do not chop the tarragon ahead of time, or it will lose its aroma.

GLUTEN FREE
SERVES 4
PREHEAT THE OVEN TO 375°F/190°C/GAS 5

1 × 1 kg (2¼ lb) chicken
salt
freshly ground black pepper
3 tsp grapeseed oil
2 shallots, peeled and finely chopped
2 garlic cloves, peeled and crushed
mirepoix *(1 onion, 1 carrot and 1 celery stick)*
lots of fresh tarragon
100 ml (3½ fl oz) dry white wine
450 ml (15 fl oz) Fonds de Volaille *(see page 31)*
100 ml (3½ fl oz) whipping cream

TO SERVE
brown rice
Lichettes de Légumes *(see page 24)*
50 g (2 oz) Greek yoghurt

1 Cut the chicken into ten portions (see page 20). Remove the fillets and cut the wings in half. Separate the thighs and drumsticks.

2 Remove the wing tips and the ends of the drumsticks and either use with the carcass (discard the parson's nose, fat and skin) to make stock, or freeze to use another time.

3 Discard the excess skin and fat from the chicken. Salt the portions lightly and pepper generously. Heat 2 teaspoons of the oil in a skillet or oven- and heatproof pan and, when hot, sauté the chicken pieces very quickly to seal them. Reserve on a plate.

4 Dab the pan with paper towels to remove the oil, taking care not to take any of the pan juices. Replace over a low heat, add the remaining teaspoon of oil, and sweat the shallots and garlic until soft, about 2-3 minutes. Add the finely chopped *mirepoix* and sweat for about 5 minutes or until soft. Add the chicken thighs and drumsticks, putting a tiny sprig of tarragon underneath each piece, plus the white wine. Bring to the boil, and place in the preheated oven.

5 After 7 minutes, turn the oven down to 350°F/180°C/Gas 4, and add the breast pieces with bones. After 7 more minutes add the other pieces of breast and check that there is still enough moisture. If not, add a little water. Tuck a tiny sprig of tarragon underneath each chicken piece as you put it into the pan.

6 After another 7 minutes, remove the boneless breast pieces and reserve on a plate. Remove all the pieces after another 7 minutes and keep warm. Place the pan over a high heat.

7 Add the chicken stock and let it simmer for 5 minutes. Push it through a chinois sieve into a fat-separator, extracting as much flavour as possible from the *mirepoix*. Rinse the pan of all its fat and impurities and pour the fat-free stock back into it. Add the cream and 2 dessertspoons of chopped tarragon, and reduce the sauce by three-quarters until it becomes syrupy, about 10 minutes.

TO SERVE Meanwhile, prepare the brown rice.

Remove the sauce from the heat to cool it a little, and arrange the rice on a heated platter. Place the chicken on top and surround with the vegetables. Add a quarter of the sauce to a bowl containing the yoghurt. Stir well and pour back into the remaining sauce, mixing well. *Do not heat again.* Spoon a little sauce over the chicken and place the rest in a gravy boat. Just before serving, sprinkle about 1 teaspoon of chopped tarragon over the chicken.

Fricassée de Volaille au Concombre

FRICASSÉE OF CHICKEN WITH CUCUMBER

As with many of our recipes, no flour is used here to thicken the sauce – that is done by reducing. And, again, we use just a small amount of whipping cream, in place of the traditional larger amount of double cream. This makes this dish ideal for those on a gluten-free diet.

GLUTEN FREE
SERVES 4
PREHEAT THE OVEN TO 375°F/190°C/GAS 5

1 × 1 kg (2¼ lb) chicken
salt
freshly ground black pepper
3 tsp grapeseed oil
1 leek, halved lengthwise, washed and cut into 2.5 cm (1 in) julienne
2 shallots, peeled, halved and thinly sliced
100 ml (3½ fl oz) Madeira
mirepoix *(1 onion, 1 carrot and 1 celery stick)*
100 ml (3½ fl oz) white wine
300 ml (10 fl oz) Fonds de Volaille *(see page 31)*
100 ml (3½ fl oz) whipping cream
2 tomatoes, skinned, seeded and cut into thin strips

TO SERVE
1 cucumber
400 g (14 oz) potatoes, peeled and turned
parsley or chervil sprigs

1 Cut the chicken into 10 portions as described on page 20. Keep the carcass for stock. Season the chicken portions with salt and pepper.

2 Heat 2 teaspoons of the oil in a skillet or oven- and heatproof casserole and sauté the pieces of chicken very quickly, starting with the skin side. Reserve on a plate.

3 Dab the pan with paper towels to remove the oil, taking care not to remove any of the pan juices. Sweat the leek and shallot, covered, in the pan juices. After 5 minutes, when the vegetables are soft, deglaze the pan with half the Madeira. Leave to reduce for 5 minutes, and reserve.

4 Heat the remaining oil in the same skillet or casserole and add the finely chopped *mirepoix*. Cover and sweat for 5 minutes. Place the chicken pieces on top of the *mirepoix* and add the wine. Bring to the boil on top of the stove, then place in the preheated oven.

5 After 7 minutes, remove the chicken wings and breasts and reserve in a warm place. If necessary add more water to the casserole so that the vegetables do not burn. After a further 7 minutes, remove the remaining chicken, but check first to see that it is thoroughly cooked; when a skewer is inserted into the thickest part of the thigh, the juices should be clear. (If the juice is pink, leave the chicken for 3 more minutes.) Turn off the oven and put all the chicken pieces into a covered dish in the still warm oven.

6 Make the sauce in the same skillet. Add the chicken stock, bring to the boil, then pour through a chinois sieve into a fat-separator. Meanwhile, reheat the leek, shallot and Madeira mixture in the same pan, covered. Deglaze with the remaining Madeira, reduce for a further minute, then add the fat-free stock and juices. Reduce for 5 minutes over a low heat, then add the cream. Leave to reduce for 2 minutes more by which time it should coat the back of a spoon lightly. Add the tomato strips and heat through gently for 1 minute.

TO SERVE Score the cucumber, keeping the trimmings for garnish. Cut the cucumber in half lengthwise, seed and drain, then cut across the width thickly. Alternatively, you could cut the cucumber halves into 2.5 cm (1 in) sections and turn them like the potatoes. Steam the cucumber pieces and peel for 5 minutes and reserve. Steam the potatoes until tender (about 5 minutes).

While the vegetables are steaming, skin the chicken pieces. Lay them on a heated serving dish or individual plates and spoon over the sauce. Arrange the potatoes all around the dish or plates. Garnish with parsley or chervil sprigs.

LEFT *Fricassée de Volaille au Concombre*

Poulet Sauté Stanley

CHICKEN STANLEY

This very traditional recipe has a mild curry taste. Instead of the usual roux *of flour and butter, we have used onions to thicken the sauce. If you select a brand of curry powder which contains no gluten, this dish is gluten-free.*

SERVES 4

PREHEAT THE OVEN TO 375°F/190°C/GAS 5

1 × 1kg (2¼lb) chicken
salt
freshly ground black pepper
3 tsp grapeseed oil
2 medium onions, peeled, cut in half through the root and thinly sliced
2 garlic cloves, peeled and crushed
1 dsp mild Madras curry powder
100ml (3½fl oz) dry white wine
300ml (10fl oz) Fonds de Volaille *(see page 31)*
200g (7oz) button mushrooms, washed and rinsed with 1 tsp lemon juice
50ml (2fl oz) whipping cream
50g (2oz) Greek yoghurt

TO SERVE

Purée de Légumes *(swede or potato, see page 151)*
parsley sprigs or chervil leaves

1 Cut the chicken into 10 portions as described on page 20. Lightly salt and generously pepper the portions.

2 Heat a casserole, add the oil, and seal the chicken pieces on all sides very quickly over a high heat. Remove from the pan and reserve. Dab the pan with paper towels to remove the oil, taking care not to take any of the pan juices. Add the onions to the pan, cover, and sweat over a low heat for about 10 minutes, tossing frequently so that they do not burn. Add the garlic and sweat for 1 minute. Add the curry powder, and sweat for another minute, tossing well.

3 Add the white wine and reduce for 3 minutes, then add the stock. Bring to the boil and put in the chicken thighs and the drumsticks. Cover, and place in the oven for a total cooking time of 30 minutes. After 10 minutes, add the wings and turn the oven down to 350°F/180°C/ Gas 4. After 15 minutes, add the breasts. With every addition, turn all the other chicken pieces in the liquid. After 20 minutes, add the mushrooms, and cook for a final 10 minutes.

4 Remove the pieces of chicken and wrap them in foil to keep warm. Remove the mushrooms and keep warm. Strain the juices through a chinois sieve into a fat-separator. Put the fat-free juices in a saucepan with the cream to reduce for 5 minutes over a low heat, stirring often so that the sauce does not stick.

5 Place half the onion left in the sieve in a liquidizer, food processor or hand food mill, and liquidize thoroughly with the reduced sauce. Mix the yoghurt with a little of the hot sauce, and pour back into the remaining sauce and add the remaining onions. Adjust the seasoning if necessary. Reserve in a warm place.

TO SERVE Warm the vegetable purée. Skin all the chicken pieces and reserve, well covered, in a warm place.

To serve traditionally, arrange the chicken pieces along the middle of a warmed serving dish, cover with a little sauce, and place a small parsley sprig or chervil leaf on each piece of chicken. Arrange the mushrooms around the dish, and serve the purée in a vegetable bowl, and the remaining sauce in a gravy boat.

To serve individually, arrange a piece of chicken on the front of the plate, and cover with the sauce. Pour more sauce over the rest of the plate. Arrange vegetable purée *quenelles* (see page 26) towards the back of the plate, along with the mushrooms. Serve immediately.

Ballotine de Faisan

BALLOTINE OF PHEASANT

This recipe requires a modicum of boning skill, but follow the instructions for boning chicken (see pages 18-19). Choose a pheasant which has not been hung for too long – 2 days' maximum. Rather than consisting of the usual rich foie gras *and pork, this stuffing uses a little pork and veal, more of the latter as it is leaner. The mushrooms will moisten the mixture in the same way as the fat from the* foie gras *would have done – but with no fat at all. And another moistening tip is to add a Petit-Suisse to the stuffing; it contains slightly more fat than Greek yoghurt but makes the stuffing a little more succulent. It can be served hot or cold.*

GLUTEN FREE
SERVES 4

1 × 750g (a good 1½lb) pheasant
salt
freshly ground black pepper
1½ tsp grapeseed oil
250ml (8fl oz) Madeira
mirepoix *(½ onion, 1 carrot and 1 celery stick)*
1 thyme sprig
1 bayleaf
parsley sprigs
200ml (7fl oz) Fonds de Volaille *(see page 31)*

STUFFING
2 shallots, peeled and chopped
pheasant or chicken liver (see method), roughly chopped
100g (4oz) mushrooms, chopped
150ml (5oz) lean veal, minced
100g (4oz) pork tenderloin, minced
1 egg
50g (2oz) Greek yoghurt or Petit-Suisse
ground allspice
pheasant fillets (see method)

TO SERVE
450g (1lb) turned vegetables

1 Clean the pheasant, reserving the liver. Cut down the backbone and bone completely, including the legs and wings. Remove the breast fillets, taking care not to split the skin, and season the bird well with salt and pepper.

2 For the stuffing, heat ½ teaspoon of oil in a skillet, and sweat half the shallots for a minute or so before adding the pheasant liver. Set alight with 50ml (2fl oz) of the Madeira, then reserve on a plate. Sweat the remaining shallot in ½ teaspoon oil in the same pan, then add the mushrooms. Season with salt and pepper immediately and cook over a high heat until the juices have evaporated. Add another 50m (2fl oz) of the Madeira, and boil to reduce. Mix in the reserved shallot and liver, and put the mixture on a dish to cool.

3 Mix the veal and pork with the egg. Add the yoghurt or Petit-Suisse and season with salt, pepper and a pinch of allspice.

4 Lay the pheasant out on a work surface, skin side down, and place the meat stuffing over the pheasant flesh. Cover this with a layer of the mushroom and the liver mixture, and place the reserved pheasant fillets in the middle.

5 Roll the pheasant up carefully, completely enclosing the filling, and sew the edges together with string and a trussing needle. Tie with string at intervals along the bird to keep the oblong shape.

6 Sweat the *mirepoix* gently in a large pan with the remaining oil until the vegetables exude their liquids, then add the ballotine. Increase the heat slightly and seal the outside of the ballotine well.

7 Add the remaining Madeira and other ingredients and bring to the boil. Simmer, covered with a tight-fitting lid, for 40 minutes. Take the pan off the heat and leave for 10 more minutes to rest.

8 Remove the ballotine from the cooking liquid and keep warm. Strain the sauce or use a fat-separator to remove the fat. If the sauce is too thin, reduce until it coats the back of a spoon. Taste and correct the seasoning, if necessary.

TO SERVE Steam the vegetables for about 5 minutes.

Carve the ballotine, place the slices in the middle of a warmed serving dish, and surround with the vegetables. Hand the sauce separately in a gravy boat.

Perdreaux Vignerons

BRAISED PARTRIDGES

Some people cannot eat game because they find it hard to digest, but the use of sage, a digestive herb, will help.

Beginners might find it a little tricky to bone partridges, in which case leave the bones in to be tackled by your guests. This is quite usual, but it does mean that you will have to use chicken bones and the partridge giblets to make the stock.

Use fresh vine leaves if you are lucky enough to have a nearby grape vine – as we do, growing in our conservatory at the School – but if not, omit them. Never *use the ones preserved in brine, they are full of additives and give a bitter taste to the partridge.*

If you are on a gluten-free diet, omit the breadcrumbs and toast, and use the chopped liver mixture to replace the breadcrumbs in the stuffing.

SERVES 4

PREHEAT THE OVEN TO 450°F/230°C/GAS 8

2 partridges with giblets
salt
freshly ground black pepper
mirepoix *(2 onions, 2 carrots and 2 celery sticks)*
5 tsp grapeseed oil
100 g (4 oz) black grapes, halved and seeded
100 g (4 oz) stale wholemeal breadcrumbs
3 fresh sage leaves, or ½ tsp dried sage
50 g (2 oz) Petit-Suisse or Greek yoghurt
1 tsp tomato concentrate
200 ml (7 fl oz) dry white wine
200 g (7 oz) fresh tomatoes, halved and seeded
750 ml (1¼ pt) cold Fonds de Volaille *(see page 31)*
1 bouquet garni
2 fresh vine leaves
2 rashers unsmoked streaky bacon, halved
2 shallots, peeled and sliced
2 dsp cognac
25 ml (1 fl oz) Madeira
4 slices wholemeal bread

1 Bone the partridges as described on pages 18–19 (but leave the thigh bones and drumsticks to give shape to the bird). Season well on all sides. Divide the finely chopped *mirepoix* between three bowls.

2 To prepare the stuffing, heat up 1 teaspoon of the oil over a low heat, and add the contents of one bowl of *mirepoix*. Sweat for 5 minutes, covered. Add the grapes and sauté for 1 minute over a medium heat. Add the breadcrumbs and 2 of the sage leaves. Stir well so that the bread absorbs the juices and the sage flavour. Reserve to cool. When cold, add the Petit-Suisse or yoghurt and mix well.

3 Heat 1 teaspoon of the oil in a saucepan and briskly colour the partridge bones and giblets (excluding the liver, which is reserved for later). Lower the heat, add the second bowl of *mirepoix*, and sweat for 3-5 minutes or until soft. Add the tomato concentrate, let it sweat for 1 minute, and then deglaze with half the white wine. Reduce for 1 minute, then add the tomatoes and sweat, covered, for 5 minutes. Add the cold chicken stock, the *bouquet garni* and the remaining sage leaf. Add a pinch of salt and bring to the boil slowly, skimming off the impurities as they rise to the surface. Simmer, and reduce, uncovered, for at least 1 hour.

4 Rub the partridges with paper towels inside and out, and season again. Divide the stuffing in half, and stuff the inside of each bird. Using string and a trussing needle, re-shape the partridges to look as if they were not boned. Place a vine leaf on each breast and a rasher of bacon on top. Secure with string.

5 Heat 2 teaspoons of the oil in a skillet large enough to hold both birds, and seal on all sides. Add the remaining *mirepoix* and white wine, and bring to the boil. Place the partridges on top of the *mirepoix*, one leg side down, and place in the preheated oven. Braise for 5 minutes, then for another 5 minutes on the other leg side. Remove the vine leaves and the bacon, and braise the birds, breasts up, for a final 10 minutes; add a little water if necessary and baste frequently to colour. Turn the oven off and leave the birds, wrapped in foil, to rest for at least 15 minutes.

6 Pour the stock into the braising juices, and strain through a chinois sieve into a fat-separator. Pour the fat-free juices back into the skillet. Reduce if too thin – it should lightly cover the back of a spoon. Check the seasoning.

7 Remove the strings and cut the partridges in half through the breast, making sure you divide the stuffing equally. Place a cutlet frill around each drumstick.

8 Just before serving, sweat the shallots in the remaining teaspoon of heated oil. Add the partridge livers and sauté for 1 minute. Add the cognac and set alight. Add the Madeira and remove the pan from the heat. Leave covered for 5 minutes for the flavours to blend and, in the meantime, toast the slices of bread. Trim them to the size of a half partridge. Chop the livers and shallots together, and spread the mixture on the toasts. Arrange the half partridges on the toast.

TO SERVE Warm the vegetable and apple purées.

To serve traditionally, arrange the partridge toasts around a warm serving dish and serve the purées separately. Garnish the dish with extra grapes, arranged like a bunch. Serve the sauce separately.

To serve individually, place the partridge on its toast at the bottom of the plate and, using two spoons, shape the different purées into *quenelles* (see page 26) and arrange them at the top of the plate. Garnish with a small bunch of grapes. Pour a little sauce over the partridge just before serving, and the remainder into a gravy boat.

TO SERVE

Purées de Légumes *(celeriac, swede, and apple, see page 151)*

grapes, seeded and halved, or 4 small bunches

4 cutlet frills (see page 28)

Perdreaux Vignerons

Gigot de Dinde Farcie

STUFFED TURKEY THIGH

This recipe requires some considerable skill as the boning is delicate. This is a case when a good relationship with your butcher could be an advantage! Once again, a predominantly vegetable stuffing is healthier and contains less fat than a more traditional meat one. The gigot *can be prepared ahead of time and reheated. It can also be served cold, sliced more thinly, on a bed of shredded lettuce or young spinach leaves – but if you choose to do this, you must prepare it at least 24 hours before serving.*

If you are on a gluten-free diet, omit the breadcrumbs. Double the quantity of cheese and sauté the courgettes for 5 minutes longer.

SERVES 4
PREHEAT THE OVEN TO 450°F/230°C/GAS 8

1 large turkey thigh, about 1.25 kg (2½ lb) in weight
grapeseed oil
mirepoix *(1 onion, 1 carrot and 1 celery stick)*
100 ml (3½ fl oz) white wine
1 garlic clove, peeled and crushed
1 thyme sprig
500 ml (18 fl oz) Fonds de Volaille *(see page 31)*

STUFFING
75 g (3 oz) courgettes, washed, topped and tailed
salt
1 small onion, peeled and finely chopped
1 garlic clove, peeled and crushed
freshly ground black pepper
25 g (1 oz) low-fat soft curd cheese
1 egg, beaten
25 g (1 oz) fines herbes, *finely chopped*
25 g (1 oz) fresh wholemeal breadcrumbs
25 g (1 oz) each of Parmesan and Emmenthal cheeses, grated
herbes de Provence

TO SERVE
450 g (1 lb) spinach, washed, chopped and sautéd in a little oil
Carottes Vichy *(see page 160)*

1 For the stuffing, grate the courgettes and sprinkle with a little salt. Drain in a colander for 30 minutes, rinse and squeeze dry.

2 Bone the turkey thigh (see page 20) and carefully remove the meat from around the bone cavity, to leave a flat piece of meat ready to be stuffed. Mince the meat from around the cavity – there should be about 250-275 g (9-10 oz).

3 Heat ½ teaspoon of oil and sweat the onion in it for 5 minutes. Add the garlic, sweat for a minute longer, add the courgettes and sweat for another 5 minutes. Leave on a plate to cool.

4 In a bowl, work together the curd cheese and three-quarters of the beaten egg. Add the fresh herbs, the minced turkey meat, the onion and garlic and mix well by hand. Season well with salt and pepper. Add the courgettes, along with the breadcrumbs, cheeses and a pinch of *herbes de Provence* to the meat mixture. Mix well to obtain a firm stuffing.

5 Brush the remainder of the egg over the flattened turkey, season it well, and place the stuffing in the middle. Bring the two ends together and seal tightly, either by tying with string or sewing with string and a trussing needle. (If there is too much stuffing, pack it into small ramekins and bake in a bain-marie in the reduced oven later for 30 minutes. Leave to cool in the oven, then weight it down in the fridge overnight. The result will be lovely little pâtés!) Weigh the turkey and allow 15 minutes braising per 450 g (1 lb), plus 15 minutes resting before carving.

6 Heat about 1 dessertspoon of oil in a skillet or oven- and heatproof dish, and seal the turkey gently on all sides. Add the finely chopped *mirepoix* and sweat until just softened. This can all take up to 20 minutes.

7 Add the white wine and bring to the boil. Add the garlic and thyme. Place in the preheated oven, and cook for the calculated time.

8 Reduce the temperature to 350°F/180°C/Gas 4 after about 15 minutes, and keep adding a little water. The liquid will evaporate and this prevents the vegetables burning.

9 When the turkey is cooked – the juices should run clear when it is pierced with a skewer – place it on an ovenproof plate. Put it back in the turned-off oven to rest for another 15 minutes.

10 Put the roasting dish along with the vegetables and juices from the meat on the top of the stove, add the stock and reduce by boiling to a good sauce consistency, about 10 minutes. Push through a chinois sieve into a fat-separator, and discard the remaining *mirepoix*. Pour the fat-free sauce into a gravy boat.

TO SERVE Remove the strings from the turkey and carve. Arrange the slices on a bed of the spinach and surround with the carrots. Pour a little of the sauce over the meat so that it does not dry up. Serve the remaining sauce separately.

Gigot de Dinde Farcie

Paupiettes de Dinde Verveine Menthe

BRAISED TURKEY ROLLS WITH MINT

This is a wonderful dish, and looks like the best of Nouvelle Cuisine. Once again, the mirepoix *vegetables and the shallots are sieved to give the sauce its smooth consistency and, to make the sauce lighter, a little Greek yoghurt is added at the last moment to replace the large amount of cream in the original recipe.*

GLUTEN FREE
SERVES 4
PREHEAT THE OVEN TO 350°F/180°C/GAS 4

3 turkey escalopes
¼ tsp dried lemon verbena
¼ tsp dried mint
salt
freshly ground black pepper
1 egg, beaten
6 rashers unsmoked back bacon, rind and fat removed
1 tsp grapeseed oil
mirepoix *(½ onion, 1 small carrot and ½ celery stick)*
2 shallots, peeled and finely chopped
300 ml (10 fl oz) Fonds de Volaille *(see page 31)*
25 ml (1 fl oz) Madeira
100 ml (3½ fl oz) white wine
50 ml (2 fl oz) whipping cream
50 g (2 oz) Greek yoghurt

TO SERVE
450 g (1 lb) turned carrots, parsnips and turnips
450 g (1 lb) broccoli
butter

1 Flatten each escalope with a meat cleaver. Rub the verbena and mint well together to mix the flavours, then sprinkle each escalope lightly with salt and pepper and the mixed herbs, pressing them well into the meat.

2 Brush the escalopes with the beaten egg. Place two bacon rashers on top of each escalope and brush with more egg. Roll up the escalopes and secure loosely with string.

3 Heat the oil in an ovenproof casserole or large skillet, and seal the *paupiettes* quickly. Remove them, discard any fat, then sweat the *mirepoix* and the shallots until soft, about 2 minutes. Add half of the chicken stock and the *paupiettes*, bring to the boil, then braise in the preheated oven for 10 minutes.

4 Keep the *paupiettes* warm in between two plates in the turned-off oven, and return the casserole or skillet to the heat on top of the stove. Deglaze with the Madeira, then add the wine and remaining stock. Bring to the boil and allow to simmer for 1 minute.

5 Push the sauce through a chinois sieve into a fat-separator, allow the fat to come to the surface and discard. In the meantime, rinse the pan quickly. Return the fat-free sauce to the pan, add the cream and reduce for 2 minutes. Off the heat, add the yoghurt. Keep in a warm place.

TO SERVE Meanwhile, steam the carrots, parsnips and turnips and the broccoli florets. Glaze in a little butter just before arranging on the dish or plates.

Remove the string from the *paupiettes* and slice them thinly.

If serving traditionally, place the slices in the middle of a warm serving dish and surround with the vegetables. Pour the sauce into a gravy boat.

If serving individually, pour a little sauce on to each plate and arrange the sliced *paupiettes* among the vegetables.

LEFT *Paupiettes de Dinde Verveine Menthe*

Ballotine de Lapin au Thym

POACHED STUFFED SADDLE OF RABBIT WITH THYME

The dish can be prepared ahead of time and reheated, or it can also be served cold on a buffet table; set the sauce with a soaked gelatine leaf added when the sauce is hot. Carve at the last moment so that the meat stays as moist as possible.

The aubergine chunks puréed into the stock thicken it as effectively as flour would, and also add vitamins and fibre. The braising makes the dish very moist, but do not overcook or the meat will become tough.

GLUTEN FREE
SERVES 4
PREHEAT THE OVEN TO ITS LOWEST TEMPERATURE

- *1 × 1 kg (2¼ lb) rabbit, fresh or frozen*
- *4 fresh thyme sprigs*
- herbes de Provence
- *salt*
- *freshly ground black pepper*
- *50 ml (2 fl oz) cognac*
- *4 tsp grapeseed oil*
- *200 g (7 oz)* duxelle *of mushrooms (see page 23)*
- mirepoix *(1 onion, 1 carrot and 1 celery stick)*
- *1 dsp tomato concentrate*
- *100 ml (3½ fl oz) dry white wine*
- *500 ml (18 fl oz)* Fonds de Volaille *(see page 31)*
- *450 g (1 lb) tomatoes, washed and quartered*
- *1* bouquet garni
- *75 g (3 oz) chicken breast, skinned*
- *100 g (4 oz) lean veal shoulder or leg meat*
- *1 egg*
- *50 g (2 oz) Greek yoghurt*
- *1 pinch each of ground cloves, allspice and nutmeg*
- *1 dsp* fines herbes, *finely chopped*
- *1 small aubergine*
- *½ lemon*
- *2 shallots, peeled and finely chopped*
- *50 ml (2 fl oz) Madeira*

TO SERVE

- Purées de Légumes *(swede and/or celeriac, see page 151)*
- *450 g (1 lb) dwarf beans, topped and tailed*

1 Portion the rabbit, but keep the saddle whole and then bone it (see page 21), being sure not to pierce the skin or the presentation will be less effective. Bone the remaining portions, reserving the bones for the stock. The meat will be minced later.

2 Using a pestle and mortar, work together 2 of the thyme sprigs, a pinch of *herbes de Provence*, a pinch of salt and a little pepper, and 1 teaspoon each of the cognac and oil. Spread this paste over the saddle and leave to marinate while the forcemeat is being prepared.

3 To start the stock, crush the bones into small pieces along with any meat left on them, and colour in a saucepan with 1 teaspoon of the oil, about 10-15 minutes.

4 Meanwhile, prepare the *duxelle* of mushrooms, retaining the stalks for later use. Reserve on a plate to cool.

5 Add the roughly chopped *mirepoix* to the bones in the saucepan. Cover and sweat for 5 minutes until soft. Add the tomato concentrate and leave to sweat, uncovered, for 2 minutes, tossing well. Add the wine and simmer to reduce until nearly dry. Add the remaining cognac and set it alight, stirring well until the flames die down. Pour in the chicken stock, and add the tomatoes, the mushroom stalks, 1 thyme sprig, a pinch of *herbes de Provence* and the *bouquet garni*. Bring slowly to the boil, skimming off the impurities as they rise, and simmer for at least 30 minutes.

6 Meanwhile, prepare the stuffing. Mince the reserved rabbit meat (except for the fillets and saddle) along with the chicken and veal. Mix all the meats together well by hand to remove the sinews. Beat the egg with the yoghurt in a bowl, and add it gradually to the meat, working well in between each addition. Add the mushroom *duxelle*, spices, fresh herbs, and remaining thyme and mix together well. (Alternatively, roll the meat mixture into a sausage, divide in two, put the *duxelle* in the middle, and re-form the sausage.)

7 Cut a sheet of foil which is 5 cm (2 in) larger all round than the saddle, and rub with 1 teaspoon of the oil. Lay the saddle on it, fillet sides up. Put the stuffing in a sausage shape in the middle of the saddle and fold up the sides to overlap each other. (If the two sides do not overlap, remove some of the stuffing and bake this separately in a well-covered dish in a bain-marie in an oven preheated to 350°F/180°C/Gas 4 for 30 minutes.) Close the foil carefully over the stuffed saddle, and twist the ends together.

8 Strain the bone stock through a chinois sieve and return to the same saucepan. Peel, seed and cube the aubergine, rub it with the ½ lemon, and add the cubes to the stock. Lower the foil-wrapped saddle into the pan, add a little water if necessary to cover the saddle, then cover with a lid and bring to the boil over a low heat. Leave to simmer for 40 minutes, turning it around halfway through, then turn the heat off and leave to rest for 10 minutes. Remove the foil parcel and keep warm in a low oven. Purée the aubergine into the stock in a food processor or liquidizer to form the sauce.

9 Heat a skillet over a low heat, then heat the remaining oil. Add the shallot and sweat, covered, for 5 minutes until soft. Deglaze with the Madeira, set it alight, and toss the shallots until the flames die down. Add half of the aubergine sauce, mix well and return to the sauce. Leave to reduce for 5 minutes over a low heat. The sauce should coat the back of a spoon; if not, reduce it until it does.

TO SERVE Meanwhile, prepare the purée(s) and steam the beans (for 3 minutes with a lid, then 3 minutes without).

Unwrap the ballotine. Using a very sharp knife, carefully cut four 1 cm (½ in) slices from one end.

To serve traditionally, arrange the beans around the sides of a warm serving dish, and lay the ballotine in the centre. Place the slices along the cut face just as if they had been sliced on the dish. Serve the sauce in a gravy boat and the purée(s) in vegetable dishes.

To serve individually, pour some sauce over the base of the warm plates, lay two slices of meat on each plate, and arrange the beans all around. Shape *quenelles* of purée (see page 26) and arrange towards the back of the plates. Serve the remaining sauce in a gravy boat.

Ballotine de Lapin au Thym

Lapin aux Pruneaux

BRAISED RABBIT WITH PRUNES

Another traditional French country dish, prepared over 2 days, this combines poaching and braising. The only difference between the original recipe and this one is that here the sauce is reduced to thicken, instead of flour being added.

The prunes give fibre and a certain sweetness to the sauce. Served with the vegetables and rice indicated below, the dish contains a high proportion of vitamins, protein and fibre, and very little fat.

GLUTEN FREE
SERVES 4

1 × 1 kg (2¼ lb) rabbit, fresh or frozen
200 g (7 oz) prunes
mirepoix *(2 onions, 2 carrots, and 2 celery sticks)*
2 garlic cloves, peeled and crushed
300 ml (10 fl oz) red wine (Côtes du Rhône type)
300 ml (10 fl oz) Fonds de Volaille *(see page 31)*
1 bouquet garni
ground allspice
salt
freshly ground black pepper
1 dsp redcurrant jelly
2 tsp grapeseed oil
100 g (4 oz) pork belly
100 g (4 oz) pickling onions, blanched and peeled
25 ml (1 fl oz) cognac
1 dsp tomato concentrate
1 slice each of orange and lemon peel (peeled off with a potato peeler)
100 g (4 oz) tomatoes, washed and quartered

TO SERVE
100 g (4 oz) each of carrot and celeriac, cut into julienne
450 g (1 lb) French beans, topped and tailed
brown rice
2 cutlet frills (see page 28)
parsley or chervil sprigs

THE DAY BEFORE SERVING

1 Joint the rabbit as described on page 21.

2 Wash the prunes well. Soak them in warm water for 2 minutes to eliminate the chemicals in their skins, then rinse well in two changes of water.

3 Place the rabbit in a large saucepan with the prunes, half the roughly chopped *mirepoix*, one of the garlic cloves, the red wine, chicken stock, *bouquet garni* and a pinch of allspice. Add a pinch of salt, some pepper and the redcurrant jelly. The meat should be covered with liquid: if not, add a little more stock. Bring slowly to the boil over a medium heat, skimming off the impurities as they rise.

4 Simmer for 1 minute, stirring occasionally, then take off the heat. Cover the surface of the liquid with a circle of paper, and the pan with a lid. Leave to cool at room temperature, and when cold, store in the fridge overnight.

THE DAY OF SERVING

1 Take the pan out of the fridge, remove the fat set on the top, and lift out the meat, prunes and *bouquet garni*. Leave the meat on a cooling rack to drain, and keep the *bouquet garni* and prunes to one side. Reheat the stock and strain through a chinois sieve. Discard the *mirepoix*.

2 Heat a large skillet over a medium heat, then add half the oil. Cut the pork belly into small rectangles across the width of the belly, then sauté slowly so that the fat runs, and the meat colours.

3 Add the onions to the pork belly to colour.

4 When all the fat is rendered and the pork and baby onions are golden brown, remove from the pan with a slotted spoon and reserve them both on paper towels on a plate. Discard the fat in the pan and wipe clean with paper towels. Add the remaining oil, sauté the pieces of rabbit over a medium-high heat very quickly, letting them brown well. Pour the cognac over the rabbit, and set it alight. Let the flames die down, and reserve the rabbit pieces on a plate.

5 Add the remaining *mirepoix* and 50 ml (2 fl oz) of the rabbit stock to the pan over a low heat and cover. Toss once in a while until soft, about 5 minutes. Add the remaining garlic clove, and let it sweat for 1 minute, then add the tomato concentrate, and let it sweat for a minute more. Add 100 ml (3½ fl oz) of the stock, mix well and reduce until nearly dry. Add the remaining stock, a little at a time, to dissolve the tomato concentrate.

Lapin aux Pruneaux

6 Add the pieces of rabbit, pork belly cubes, whole onions, prunes, *bouquet garni*, the orange and lemon peel and the tomatoes. Bring to the boil slowly, skimming off the impurities as they rise, and simmer, covered, for 1 hour. Check to see if the rabbit is well cooked: the meat should be very tender when pressed with a finger, and it should detach easily from the bones.

7 Separate the rabbit, prunes, belly pork and onions from the rest of the ingredients. Cut the meat carefully off the forequarters and the saddle. Reserve all together wrapped in foil to keep warm and moist.

8 Strain the stock through a chinois sieve (discarding everything in the sieve) into another saucepan and reduce over a medium heat for about 10 minutes to obtain the right flavour and consistency (it should coat the back of a spoon). Replace the reserved ingredients in the sauce and keep warm.

TO SERVE Meanwhile, steam the carrot and celeriac *julienne*, and French beans, and cook the rice. Add the *julienne* to the rabbit. Prepare two cutlet frills for the rabbit thighs.

To serve traditionally, arrange a mound of rice in the centre of a large warmed serving dish, with the rabbit pieces on top and down the sides. Arrange some of the vegetables around the meat and pour some sauce over the top. Serve the remaining sauce and vegetables separately.

To serve individually, pour on enough sauce to cover the base of a warmed plate. Lay a piece of rabbit on top, centrally, and garnish it with one or two pieces of vegetable *julienne*. Surround the meat with a few beans and place *quenelles* of rice (see page 26) on the top part of the plate. Place a parsley or chervil sprig on top of the rice. Serve the remaining vegetables and sauce separately.

VEGETABLES AND SALADS

Vegetables are important in Cuisine Santé, but we have not included a lot of specific recipes as the best way to serve them is generally as fresh and as close to uncooked as possible (see Ingredients). There are, however, serving suggestions throughout the book, most of which are based on a quick steaming. Steam vegetables only until *al dente*, or leave them still crunchy. This method keeps in all their nutritional value. Vegetables can also be eaten raw in salads. Try to have a salad at least once a day, as the French do, either before dessert, or before the main course, as a starter.

Purées de Légumes

VEGETABLE PURÉES

The following recipe can be adapted to most root vegetables – such as potato, celeriac, carrot, parsnip, turnip or swede. For vegetables like spinach, broccoli, cauliflower and Brussels sprouts, which already contain a lot of water, omit the milk but keep the Greek yoghurt to give the creamy texture and slightly bitter taste, reminiscent of the traditional crème fraîche. *Be careful if you use a food processor to make the purées, as the machine tends to over-develop the gluten, in potatoes especially, making them gluey.*

These purées can be prepared a few hours in advance and reheated in a bain-marie. Stir occasionally.

SERVES 4

450g (1lb) prepared vegetables
½ lemon (for celeriac only)
salt
150ml (5fl oz) milk
freshly ground black pepper
grated nutmeg
50g (2oz) Greek yoghurt

1 Trim and peel the vegetable as appropriate. After peeling celeriac, rub it with lemon juice to prevent discoloration. Cut the vegetables into large pieces, put into a saucepan of lightly salted boiling water and cook until tender, about 10-15 minutes. Alternatively, steam them until very tender.

2 Drain, keeping the water to make a soup or consommé, and place the vegetable chunks back into the saucepan over the heat to dry.

3 Put the milk into a saucepan and bring to the boil. Season with pepper and nutmeg.

4 Purée the vegetable in a food processor, hand food mill, or with a potato masher, adding the hot milk. Mix well, then add the yoghurt and keep warm, covered.

TO SERVE Season the purée with a little more pepper and salt, beat well to obtain a smooth consistency, and serve either in a heated vegetable dish, or shape into *quenelles* on plates (see page 26).

Salade Niçoise

Like most of our salads, this one is almost a meal in itself, containing protein, carbohydrate, fat, vitamins, minerals and fibre. It differs from the traditional recipe only in that it uses a very much lighter dressing, and very much less dressing. It can be served in small quantities as a starter, but is best as a main course in the summer, or as part of a buffet presentation. It's also very pleasant in the winter when it will remind you of those distant hot, summer days!

The decorative arrangement of the different vegetables in the bowl is very important. Arrange them basically as we describe, but use your own creativity and imagination as well – this is one of the major pleasures of cooking!

GLUTEN FREE
SERVES 4

¼ round lettuce
50 g (2 oz) thin dwarf beans or mangetout, topped and tailed
100 g (4 oz) tuna fish in olive oil
2 large anchovy fillets
1 egg
1 celery stick, topped and tailed
1 red pepper, washed, halved and seeded
2 tomatoes, washed
1 head of chicory
juice of ½ lemon
85 ml (3 fl oz) Sauce Moutarde *(see page 39) made with half olive oil, half grapeseed oil*
4-8 black olives marinated in olive oil and herbes de Provence

1 Separate the lettuce into leaves and wash carefully. Spin them dry, then break the largest leaves in half.

2 Steam the beans or mangetout for 3 minutes, then rinse under cold water. Cut the beans into 1 cm (½ in) lengths.

3 Drain the tuna and anchovies well, and leave on paper towels to soak up the remaining oil. Break the tuna into large chunks and halve the anchovies lengthwise.

4 Put the egg in a pan of cold water, bring to the boil, and simmer for 5 minutes.

5 Remove as many strings as possible from the celery. Cut it into tiny *julienne*. Cut the pepper into thin *julienne*, skin side down. Cut out the stalk end of the tomatoes, and cut the flesh of each into six segments.

6 When ready to assemble the salad, cut the chicory in half lengthwise, then across thinly. Sprinkle with the lemon juice to prevent discoloration.

7 Place the dressing at the bottom of a large salad bowl, and cover with the lettuce leaves. Arrange the tomato segments around the sides of the bowl with a ring of beans or mangetout inside, followed by rings of the celery *julienne*, red pepper, tuna and chicory. Push the hard-boiled egg through a sieve into the remaining circle, and arrange the anchovies in a star shape on top. Place the olives in the middle.

TO SERVE Show your guests the beauty of your salad before you toss it, mixing carefully but thoroughly.

RIGHT *Salade Niçoise*

Fenouil à la Provençale

BRAISED FENNEL

Considered medicinal in the ancient civilizations of the Mediterranean, fennel was used in infusions and concoctions for all sorts of ailments. It is still a characteristically Mediterranean vegetable. Although low in vitamins and minerals, fennel is high in fibre and low in calories. An initial steaming therefore (instead of blanching in water), followed by braising keeps in all the goodness. Both vegetable and juices should be served.

GLUTEN FREE
SERVES 4
PREHEAT THE OVEN TO 350°F/ 180°C/GAS 4

4 small fennel bulbs, washed and quartered
salt
2 tsp olive oil
mirepoix *(1 onion, 1 carrot, 1 celery stick)*
1 recipe Coulis de Tomates *(see page 38)*
200 ml (7 fl oz) Fonds de Volaille *(see page 31)*
1 thyme sprig
1 bayleaf
2 parsley sprigs
herbes de Provence
freshly ground black pepper

1 Steam the fennel for 10 minutes above boiling salted water. Reserve on a cooling rack.

2 Heat half the olive oil and sweat the roughly chopped *mirepoix*, covered, until tender, about 5 minutes. Add the tomato *coulis*, chicken stock, thyme, bayleaf, parsley sprigs and a pinch of *herbes de Provence*. Season with a pinch of salt and a little pepper. Simmer for 10 minutes, covered. Remove the lid and reduce for 5 minutes, removing the impurities and the fat as they rise.

3 Scoop out the *mirepoix* vegetables with a slotted spoon and place in the bottom of a gratin dish. Arrange the fennel on top and coat with the tomato *coulis*. Sprinkle with the remaining olive oil and bake in the preheated oven for 20 minutes, covered with foil. Remove the foil and leave to colour lightly, approximately 10 minutes.

TO SERVE Take the fennel out of the gratin dish. Arrange the vegetables as a base in a hot serving dish, and spoon over a little of the sauce. Arrange the fennel quarters on top in a star shape, topped with more sauce. More traditionally, serve straight from the gratin dish, on a liner plate with a doily or napkin in between.

Salade d'Endives

CHICORY SALAD

GLUTEN FREE
SERVES 4

3 heads of chicory, washed
lemon juice
1 red dessert apple, washed
50g (2oz) Emmenthal cheese, cut into small cubes
25g (1oz) walnuts
4dsp Sauce Vinaigrette *(see page 35)*

This is a delicious way of eating chicory. It is naturally high in fibre, but the addition of walnuts and apple gives a lot more goodness.

1 Reserving some whole leaves for garnish, cut the chicory in half lengthwise and slice across thickly. Sprinkle with lemon juice to prevent discoloration, and place in a mixing bowl.
2 Core the apple and cut the flesh into cubes. Add to the chicory.
3 Add the Emmenthal to the chicory and apple.
4 Chop half the walnuts roughly and add to the salad.
5 Pour the vinaigrette over the salad, toss well, then place in a salad bowl lined with the whole chicory leaves. Garnish with the walnuts and marinate for at least 10 minutes before serving.

Poireaux Vinaigrette

LEEKS VINAIGRETTE

GLUTEN FREE
SERVES 4

4 leeks
100ml (3½fl oz) Sauce Vinaigrette *(see page 35)*
25g (1oz) fines herbes, *finely chopped*
1tsp capers, drained and finely chopped
2 cocktail gherkins, drained and finely chopped

GARNISH
½ hard-boiled egg

RIGHT *Salade d'Endives* and *Poireaux Vinaigrette*

Not long ago every corner café in France used to serve food at lunchtime for their regulars: now the regulars grab fast food and hurry back to the office.... This dish was once part of the standard menu offered by the patron *along with something like* Côte de Porc Charcutière *or* Cervelas Vinaigrette.

The leeks can be prepared a few hours ahead of time – the important stage is the cooling down in the vinaigrette, so that they absorb its flavour. The dish is best served either tepid or ice cold, when it makes a very refreshing summer evening starter.

1 Remove the upper green part of the leeks, leaving the pale green and white parts. Cut through the centre, leaving the root attached, and clean very carefully to remove any sand or grit. Leave to soak in cold water for 5-10 minutes.
2 Cut the leeks to fit inside a steamer, and steam for approximately 10 minutes until tender but still crunchy. Take the upper part of the steamer off and leave the leeks to cool for 2 minutes. Take the leeks out and cut in half across the width. Place on a flat dish and cover with vinaigrette. Leave to marinate and cool.
3 Drain the leeks and arrange on a serving dish. Mix the vinaigrette with the herbs, capers and gherkins. If the mixture is too thick, add a little more vinaigrette. Spoon the dressing over the leeks. Chop the yolk and white of egg separately and push through a sieve. Sprinkle over the top.

Ratatouille Provençale

BRAISED RATATOUILLE

Traditionally, all the vegetables in ratatouille are first separately fried in olive oil, which results in a very rich and heavy stew. Our version is much lighter because we sweat the vegetables, then reduce, rather than frying.

At the last moment, if available, add a few chopped basil leaves to the ratatouille. Serve it as a garnish for a meat or fish dish, or with scrambled eggs as a main course for a brunch or evening meal.

GLUTEN FREE
SERVES 4

2 dsp olive oil
1 onion, peeled and thickly sliced
2 garlic cloves, peeled and crushed
1 green pepper and 1 red pepper washed, halved and seeded
1 small aubergine, washed
juice of ½ lemon
salt
freshly ground black pepper
2 courgettes, washed, topped and tailed
300 g (11 oz) tomatoes, skinned and seeded
1 thyme sprig
1 bayleaf
herbes de Provence

1 Heat half the olive oil in a large saucepan and sweat the onion, covered, for 5 minutes. Add the garlic and sweat for a minute longer.

2 Slice the peppers, add to the onion and garlic, and sweat for 5 minutes, covered.

3 Cut the aubergine into quarters, and sprinkle with lemon juice. Cut across into small chunks, and sprinkle with lemon juice again. Add to the saucepan, sprinkle lightly with salt and pepper, and sweat, covered, for a further 10 minutes.

4 Cut the courgettes in half lengthwise and slice thickly. Add to the saucepan, sprinkle lightly with salt, and sweat, covered, for 10 minutes.

5 Remove the lid and continue cooking to let the juices evaporate and the vegetables brown slightly.

6 Add the tomatoes, the thyme, bayleaf and a pinch of *herbes de Provence*. Simmer, covered, for a further 15 minutes.

7 Remove the lid and let the juices reduce well, but make sure the vegetables do not burn. Try not to stir too often, or the vegetables will break up.

TO SERVE Remove the thyme sprig and bayleaf, let the mixture cool slightly, then add the remaining olive oil. Serve either as a garnish with a meat or fish dish (see page 125), or in a heated vegetable dish.

Navets Glacés

GLAZED TURNIPS

A classic French cuisine garnish, this is revamped here with honey rather than granulated sugar, which gives a very special taste to the turnips.

In spring, use the baby new turnips with their flavourful skin; in the winter, use the old ones turned, or cut into the various shapes – julienne, lichettes, *etc. – mentioned throughout the book.*

GLUTEN FREE
SERVES 4

1.5 kg (3 lb) turnips
1 tsp grapeseed oil
1 tsp honey
salt
freshly ground black pepper
1 dsp fines herbes, *finely chopped*

1 Place the turnips in a saucepan and barely cover with water. Add the oil, honey, a pinch of salt and pepper.

2 Cover with a lid and bring to the boil over a high heat. Simmer for 2 minutes, then remove the lid and boil, again over a high heat, so that the water evaporates, a maximum of 10 minutes (the timing will depend on how the turnips are cut).

3 Just before serving add the herbs and toss lightly.

Salade de Choux aux Lardons

CABBAGE AND BACON SALAD

This salad, normally prepared with a vast amount of streaky bacon, has been rendered a little healthier by the use of back bacon which is slowly cooked so that all the fat is removed. In the traditional recipe, both the bacon and fat are added to the salad: here we throw away the fat. The croûtons are healthier if prepared as described on page 25, and can be omitted for a gluten-free dish.

SERVES 4
PREHEAT THE OVEN TO 350°F/180°C/GAS 4

1 small white cabbage
4 dsp white wine or tarragon vinegar
3 garlic cloves, peeled
salt
freshly ground black pepper
10 dsp grapeseed oil
3 dsp fines herbes, *finely chopped*
4 thick slices wholemeal bread
4 rashers back bacon, fat and rind removed

1 Quarter the cabbage and shred it. Leave to marinate in cold water and 1 dessertspoon of the vinegar for 15-20 minutes (to tenderize it a little).

2 To prepare the dressing, crush 1 garlic clove into a bowl, and add 2 pinches salt, a little pepper, and 1 dessertspoon of the vinegar. Mix thoroughly and whisk in 5 dessertspoons of the oil. Keep to one side.

3 To prepare the croûtons, heat ½ dessertspoon of the oil, crush the remaining garlic into it, and sweat for 2 minutes. Place on one side to cool. Add 3½ dessertspoons of the oil and the herbs. Mix well and brush this herbed oil on to the slices of bread. Stack the slices on top of each other and leave to marinate for 10 minutes. Cut into 2.5 × 1 cm (1 × ½ in) rectangles, arrange on a baking tray, and toast in the preheated oven until golden brown. Keep in a warm place.

4 To prepare the bacon, blanch the rashers for 1 minute in boiling water, putting them in a slice at a time so they do not stick together. Rinse well, place on paper towels to dry, then cut up into small pieces. Heat the remaining oil in a skillet over a medium heat, add the bacon and sweat over a low heat (to remove the fat) for approximately 7-10 minutes.

5 Drain off all the fat, leaving the bacon in the pan, and increase the heat (to make the essential pan juices needed to finish the dressing).

6 Drain and dry the cabbage, toss in the dressing, and leave for 5 minutes to marinate. Toss again.

7 Just before serving, drain the bacon and the fat on kitchen towels. Add the bacon to the salad, and toss again.

8 Deglaze the pan with the remaining vinegar, and pour over the salad. Toss, and serve immediately.

Salade Gribiche

MIXED SALAD

This salad, full of vitamins, protein and fibre, is quite filling and nourishing, and therefore can be served as a meal. Be careful when blanching the green vegetables: this should be done in a steamer over a very high heat so that none of the goodness is lost.

The gribiche *dressing can also be used on a simple lettuce salad, giving it a fuller flavour.*

GLUTEN FREE
SERVES 4

½ round lettuce
salt
100g (4oz) broccoli florets, washed
50g (2oz) mangetout, washed, topped and tailed
1 egg
1 celery stick, washed, topped and tailed
2 tomatoes, washed
1 cucumber, washed
50g (2oz) Gruyère or Emmenthal cheese
1 shallot, peeled and finely chopped
1 tsp capers, drained and finely chopped, and a few cut into flowers (see page 25)
1 cocktail gherkin, drained and finely chopped
85ml (3fl oz) Sauce Moutarde *(see page 39), made with 1 extra tsp Dijon mustard*

1 Separate the lettuce leaves and wash them. Spin dry, then break the largest leaves in half.

2 Prepare a steamer with 1 litre (1¾pt) water and 1 teaspoon salt, and bring to the boil. Steam the broccoli and mangetout for 3 minutes each, then rinse in cold water to stop the cooking and fix the colour. Drain in a sieve or colander, and set aside to cool.

3 Put the egg in a pan of cold water, bring to the boil, and simmer for 5 minutes.

4 Peel all the strings from the celery. Cut into thin *julienne*. Cut out the stalk end of the tomatoes and cut each into six segments.

5 If the cucumber is large, cut it in half and remove the seeds before slicing thinly. If it is small, simply halve lengthwise and cut across in thin slices.

6 Cut the cheese into small cubes.

7 Add the shallot, capers and gherkin to the mustard sauce. Shell the egg, and push through a sieve into the dressing. Mix well, and adjust the seasoning if necessary.

8 Place the dressing at the bottom of a large salad bowl and cover with the lettuce leaves. Arrange the cucumber slices around the side of the bowl, in a ring. Arrange a ring of tomatoes inside the cucumber ring, and a ring of cheese cubes inside that. Arrange the mangetout in a star shape in the middle with the celery *julienne* between each point. To finish, place the broccoli florets in the middle of the mangetout star.

TO SERVE Bring the bowl to the table and let your guests enjoy your artistry before, alas, you ruin it all by tossing the salad!

Alternatively, arrange all the ingredients separately round the edge of a plate, and spoon the dressing into the centre. Garnish with caper flowers.

RIGHT *Salade Gribiche*

Carottes Vichy

VICHY CARROTS

Originally, this recipe contained 50g (2oz) butter and 25g (1oz) sugar, and also used Vichy water which has a very high salt content. We have omitted all three of these ingredients.

These carrots can be served as a garnish for a meat or fish dish, or on their own accompanied perhaps by a poached egg for the main course of a light supper.

GLUTEN FREE
SERVES 4

450g (1lb) carrots, scrubbed
200ml (7fl oz) Fonds de Volaille *(see page 31)*
salt
freshly ground black pepper
½tsp honey
1 small slice fresh ginger root, peeled
1tsp parsley, finely chopped, or chop up and mix with the carrots

1 Score the carrots along their length using a decorator or scorer, then slice them thickly.

2 Place the carrot slices in a saucepan, barely cover with the chicken stock, and add some salt and pepper, the honey and ginger. Cover, bring to the boil, and simmer for 1 minute. Remove the lid and continue simmering until the saucepan is nearly dry. Discard the ginger.

TO SERVE Toss the carrots well in the remaining juice, and sprinkle with the parsley. Place in a heated vegetable dish or use as a garnish.

Salade de Champignons de Sabine

MUSHROOM SALAD

This is a very quick and simple salad, which Mme Brassart prepares for us for a quick working lunch. It is always well appreciated as it is nourishing – full of vitamins, minerals and fibre – as well as being refreshing and light.

In the summer, basil adds its distinctive flavour, in the winter, parsley and chervil.

GLUTEN FREE
SERVES 4

200g (7oz) button mushrooms, washed
1 lemon
200g (7oz) ripe tomatoes, washed
salt
freshly ground black pepper
4dsp olive oil
2dsp basil and/or fines herbes*, finely chopped*

1 Leave the mushrooms to soak for 3 minutes in cold water with the juice of half the lemon.

2 Cut the tomatoes into thin slices, and place in overlapping circles in the centre of a round serving dish.

3 To prepare the dressing, place a pinch of salt, a little pepper and the remaining lemon juice in a bowl. Mix well, then whisk in the olive oil. Spoon 2 dessertspoons of this dressing over the tomatoes.

4 Drain the mushrooms well, then slice them thinly and arrange around the tomatoes. Spoon the remaining dressing over them.

5 Sprinkle the herbs all over the tomato and mushrooms, and marinate for 5 minutes before serving.

Salade Waldorf

WALDORF SALAD

This salad, made famous by a French chef at the Waldorf-Astoria in New York, was dressed originally with a Sauce Rémoulade. *This contained a minimum of three egg yolks and a lot of mustard. Although we keep the mustard, we use no egg, thus reducing the amount of cholesterol, and the traditional raw ingredients are packed with vitamins, minerals and fibre.*

GLUTEN FREE
SERVES 4

1 small head celeriac, washed
1 lemon, cut in half
1 Granny Smith apple, washed
1/2 recipe Sauce Moutarde *(see page 39) made with double the given quantity of mustard*
100g (4oz) button mushrooms, washed
50g (2oz) walnut halves

GARNISH
parsley sprigs
4 small tomato roses (see page 26)

1 Peel the celeriac, and rub with the lemon. Cut into pieces small enough to pass through the funnel of a food processor (fitted with a thin grating blade). Rub these with lemon juice as well, then grate in the machine. Sprinkle with more lemon juice.

2 Core the apple, and cut it in half. Grate in the machine and mix in with the celeriac. Mix in enough mustard sauce – about 3 dessertspoons – to bind the celeriac and apple together. Reserve.

3 Cut half the mushrooms into slices and the remainder into dice, and sprinkle both with lemon juice. Mix the dice with the celeriac and apple. Wrap the slices in cling film, and reserve for later.

4 Chop half the walnuts, reserving the best ones for garnishing later. Mix the chopped nuts into the salad.

5 Press the salad mixture into four ramekins, cover, and place in the fridge to set for at least 20 minutes before serving.

TO SERVE Lay the mushroom slices and parsley sprigs round the edge of a serving dish or individual plates, and turn the salads out into the middle. Spoon any remaining sauce over the top. Lay the walnut halves on top. Garnish with tomato roses, and serve immediately.

Riz Complet aux Poireaux

BROWN RICE WITH LEEKS

This delicious dish, combining brown rice and leeks, is packed full of vitamins, minerals and fibre. It can be served on its own, served in a feuilleté *or butterfly case (see page 14) with vegetable* julienne, *or as a garnish for a main course dish.*

SERVES 4
PREHEAT THE OVEN TO 350°F/180°C/GAS 4

250g (9oz) brown Basmati *rice, washed*
600ml (1pt) Fonds de Volaille *or* Bouillon de Légumes *(see pages 31 and 32)*
1 bouquet garni
salt
freshly ground black pepper
1dsp grapeseed oil
450g (1lb) leeks, cut in half lengthwise, washed and sliced

TO SERVE
1dsp olive oil
2tbsp fines herbes, *finely chopped*

1 Wash the rice well to remove the impurities and some of the starch.

2 Bring the stock to the boil with the *bouquet garni* and seasoning. Leave to infuse, covered, for 5 minutes.

3 Heat the oil in a heavy casserole. Sweat the leek, covered, for 10 minutes, until soft.

4 Add the well-drained rice and sweat with the leek for 5 minutes, without colouring, over a low heat.

5 Reserve 50ml (2fl oz) of the stock and leave to cool, and add the remainder, with the *bouquet garni*, to the casserole. Stir well, and cover with a piece of Bakewell paper and a lid. Place in the preheated oven for 50-70 minutes. Take out of the oven, pour in the reserved cold stock, and keep warm.

TO SERVE Pour in the olive oil and add the herbs. Mix well and taste for seasoning. Transfer to a heated dish and serve.

Choux Rouge Braisé

BRAISED RED CABBAGE

Cabbage is rich in vitamins, minerals, calcium, magnesium and sulphur; it is also low in calories and high in fibre. The only trouble is that it has been so misused over the years that no-one now dares to produce it at a dinner table, because of its undeserved bad reputation! This very traditional sweet and sour recipe is perfect as an accompaniment for a chicken or fish dish.

You could also braise a Savoy cabbage in the same way, keeping the leaves whole, which is very good with Pot au Feu *(see page 118).*

GLUTEN FREE
SERVES 4
PREHEAT THE OVEN TO 350°F/180°C/GAS 4

450g (1lb) red cabbage, quartered
100g (4oz) sultanas
150ml (5floz) lager beer
salt
freshly ground black pepper
1 bayleaf
1tsp grapeseed oil
2 onions, peeled and sliced
2 Golden Delicious apples, washed and cored
1tsp honey
1tsp tarragon vinegar
1 garlic clove, peeled

1 Shred each cabbage quarter. Place in the top of a steamer and steam for 5 minutes, tossing occasionally.

2 Wash the sultanas very carefully. Place them in a small saucepan with the beer, salt, pepper and the bayleaf. Bring to the boil and leave on one side to cool.

3 Heat the oil in a large ovenproof pan or cast-iron casserole, and sweat the onion covered, for 5 minutes. Uncover, and let the onion colour slightly. Add the cabbage and toss for 5 minutes over a low heat.

4 Cut the apples in small cubes and toss in with the cabbage.

5 Add the vinegar and honey to the beer and sultana mixture, and pour into the apples and cabbage. Mix well. Add the whole garlic clove. Lay a sheet of Bakewell or greaseproof paper on top of the cabbage, cover and braise in the preheated oven for 40 minutes or until tender, tossing every 15 minutes.

TO SERVE Remove the bayleaf and garlic. Using a slotted spoon carefully transfer the cabbage and sultanas to a warmed vegetable dish, or if serving with meat, arrange around the prepared meat. If serving individually, arrange a nest of cabbage surrounded by the sultanas, with the meat or fish on top.

LEFT *Riz Complet aux Poireaux* and *Choux Rouge Braisé*

DESSERTS AND CAKES

The French, probably even more than other people, love to eat a sweet dish before leaving the table, in spite of all the warnings about sugar. In our dessert recipes, however, sugar is either partially (in some cases entirely) eliminated, or it is replaced by another ingredient which will bring out the natural sweetness of the dish's principal element. Most fruits, in fact, are quite high in natural sugars. In addition, the sorbets here are much less sweet than traditional ones, and are therefore far more refreshing. They can, in fact, be served as a middle course (*entremet*) on formal occasions, to cleanse the palate. The soufflés, made without butter, are very light. Do not only attempt the ones given here, but use your imagination to vary the flavours. The cakes and tarts use wholemeal flour, and again the contents are low in fat and high in fibre, and use fresh fruit where possible.

Soufflé de Passion

PASSION FRUIT SOUFFLÉ

This wonderful soufflé is a prime example of the success of this new soufflé method. With its very delicate flavour, it should be served at the end of a meal, after cheese, as in France – the best way to finish a meal!

GLUTEN FREE
SERVES 4
PREHEAT THE OVEN TO 350°F/180°C/GAS 4

250 ml (8 fl oz) skimmed milk
1 dsp honey
1 tsp butter
4 passion fruit, halved
2 eggs, separated
25 g (1 oz) potato flour
2 egg whites
2 tsp golden granulated sugar

TO SERVE
icing sugar, to dust

1 Place the milk, less 2 dessertspoons, in a saucepan with the honey and bring to the boil. Butter a 900 ml (1½ pt) soufflé dish and put in the fridge for the butter to set.

2 Scoop the passion fruit flesh and seeds into a bowl, and mix with the egg yolks. Put the potato flour into another bowl with the reserved cold milk, and mix well. Add the scalded milk, whisking well, then return to the heat and boil for a minute. Pour into the bowl with the passion fruit and leave to infuse for 5 minutes.

3 Whisk all the egg whites until they form soft peaks, adding 1 teaspoon of the sugar. Fold one-quarter of this into the passion fruit.

4 Push through a chinois sieve (to eliminate the seeds) on to the remaining egg whites, and fold together carefully.

5 Dust the soufflé dish with the remaining sugar and pour in the soufflé batter. Bake in the preheated oven for 20 minutes.

TO SERVE Dust the top with icing sugar. Place the dish on a plate lined with a napkin or a doily and serve *immediately*.

Gratin d'Oranges à la Maltaise

GRATIN OF ORANGES

This is an ideal winter dessert as it is warming and oranges are at their best in winter, when the vitamin C of the fruit and the calcium and vitamin B of the nuts are needed most. If available, use blood oranges which will give an even nicer flavour.

GLUTEN FREE
SERVES 4

4 oranges
25g (1oz) honey
50ml (2floz) water
1 slice fresh root ginger, peeled and cut into thin julienne
1tsp Grand Marnier
1 fresh pomegranate, halved, or 1tsp grenadine (pomegranate syrup)
¼tsp ground allspice
5 pistachio nuts
1 egg yolk
50g (2oz) Greek yoghurt
50ml (2floz) whipping cream

THE DAY BEFORE SERVING

1 Wash the oranges carefully, and brush with a vegetable or clean nailbrush to get rid of any residual chemicals. Peel, then segment them carefully (see page 27) and reserve the segments and juice in a china bowl. Keep the peel of two of the oranges, cut it into *julienne*, and blanch for 1 minute in boiling water.

2 Put the honey and water in a saucepan, bring to the boil and add the orange peel and ginger *julienne*. Simmer very gently for 2-3 minutes until tender, then remove from the liquid. Continue reducing the liquid until it caramelizes, then pour in the orange juice from the bowl and the Grand Marnier. Mix well and add the pomegranate seeds and juice (or the grenadine).

3 Leave to stand for 15 minutes until cold and then strain through a chinois sieve over the orange segments. Add the allspice, orange peel and ginger. Cover with cling film and keep in the fridge overnight.

4 To prepare the pistachios, shell them, plunge into a saucepan of boiling water, then simmer for 1 minute. Drain and refresh under the cold tap. Wrap in a tea-towel and rub them; most of the skin will come off, but finish by hand. Chop roughly on a board, then dry in a warm oven for 3 minutes. Reserve in a cool dry place.

THE DAY OF SERVICE

Preheat the grill to its maximum.

1 Mix the egg yolk and the yoghurt together in a bowl. Thin down with some of the juice strained from the segments to form a light sauce that can coat the back of a spoon. Whip the cream, fold in and mix in the nuts.

2 Drain the orange segments and arrange them on individual heatproof plates or a round heatproof serving dish. Cover the segments and the bottom of the plate(s) with the sauce. Place under the preheated grill for 2 minutes or until brown, and serve immediately. Decorate with the peel and ginger *julienne*. Serve the remaining sauce separately.

LEFT *Gratin d'Oranges à la Maltaise*

Oranges Soufflées

ORANGE SOUFFLÉS

This recipe originally contained a large amount of cream and flour, neither of which are really necessary. Our much lighter version is served in the orange shells – but do make sure you serve them immediately after they come out of the oven: like any soufflé, these deflate very quickly.

GLUTEN FREE
SERVES 4
PREHEAT THE OVEN TO 350°F/180°C/GAS 4

4 oranges
2 dsp muscovado sugar
1 dsp potato flour
100 ml (3½ fl oz) skimmed milk
1 vanilla pod
1 dsp Grand Marnier
2 egg whites

TO SERVE
icing sugar, to dust

1 Cut the oranges in half and segment them as you would a breakfast grapefruit. Put the segments and juice into a bowl, and with a teaspoon remove the core and all pith from the peel.

2 Take the segments out of the juice with a slotted spoon and place on a sheet of greaseproof paper on a tray and dry out for 2 minutes in the oven.

3 Mix half the sugar with the potato flour in a bowl and make a well in the centre. Bring the milk with the vanilla pod to the boil, and, mixing well slowly pour into the well. Return to the heat and boil for 1 minute, beating well to remove any lumps, before adding the Grand Marnier. Remove the vanilla pod.

4 Whisk the egg whites until they form soft peaks, then add the remaining sugar. Mix one-quarter of the egg white into the hot sauce, then fold the sauce gently into the bulk of the whites. Transfer into a piping bag with a fluted nozzle.

5 Place the half oranges in a roasting tin lined with a sheet of paper and with just enough hot water to cover the paper. Pipe a small amount of the soufflé mixture into the bottom of the orange cups. Divide the orange segments equally between the cups, and pipe the remaining mixture over the oranges. Bake for 10-15 minutes.

TO SERVE Remove from the oven, dust with icing sugar, and serve immediately on a doily-lined plate.

Sorbet aux Pommes

APPLE SORBET

A wonderful palate cleanser in the middle of a meal or a much appreciated end to a meal, this so-called sorbet is in fact a compromise between a sorbet and a granité, *using a little more sugar than a* granité, *but much less than a traditional sorbet. Other varieties of apple could also be used, but adjust the sugar level accordingly.*

GLUTEN FREE, EXCEPT FOR THE PANIERS
SERVES 4

450 g (1 lb) very green Bramleys, washed, or ¾ litre (1½ pt) pure apple juice

1 Cut the apples into large cubes, core and peel included.

2 Place in a saucepan with the water and sugar, bring to the boil and simmer until the apples are tender and the sugar has melted.

3 Mash the apples roughly, then strain through a chinois sieve to separate the juice and pulp from the peel and cores.

4 Add the Calvados to the juice and pulp when it is cool.

5 Either put the mixture into an ice-cream machine or *sorbetière* – follow the manufacturer's instructions – or make it 'by hand'. Set the freezer to its coldest temperature several hours beforehand, and put a shallow tray, a bowl and a fork into the freezer to chill. Pour the apple juice and pulp into the tray and freeze.

6 When the mixture is almost solid, scrape it out into the chilled bowl and mash with the fork until the largest lumps have been beaten out. Return to the tray and to the freezer. Repeat this beating and freezing several times more for a smooth-textured sorbet.

TO SERVE Use two spoons to make *quenelle* shapes from the sorbet (see page 26) and place in the *Paniers*. Serve immediately.

550 ml (a scant pt) water
150 g (5 oz) caster sugar
25 ml (1 fl oz) Calvados

TO SERVE
4 Paniers *(see page 170)*

Sorbet de l'Été

SUMMER FRUIT SORBET

This delicious sorbet is a perfect combination of the Continental sorbet and the delicious taste of the British summer pudding. In fact we could call it 'Summer Pudding Sorbet'. Compared with a traditional recipe, the sugar has been cut down considerably, and an egg white added to give volume and the smooth consistency.

GLUTEN FREE
SERVES 4

50 g (2 oz) each of raspberries and strawberries, washed and hulled
50 g (2 oz) each of redcurrants and blackcurrants, washed, topped and tailed
25 g (1 oz) sugar
250 ml (2 pt) water
1 egg white

TO SERVE
1 recipe Paniers *(see page 170)*

1 Bring the sugar and water to the boil and add the redcurrants. Simmer for 1 minute (timing from when the syrup starts to boil again), then remove the redcurrants using a slotted spoon. Reserve in a bowl.

2 Add the blackcurrants to the still simmering syrup, and simmer for 2 minutes. Reserve with the redcurrants.

3 Add the strawberries and raspberries to the simmering syrup and take off the heat immediately. Add the redcurrants and blackcurrants and leave for 5 minutes to infuse. Transfer into the bowl to cool.

4 Reserve some of the fruit for decoration, covered with a little juice. Push the rest through a sieve or hand food mill to eliminate any pips.

5 When cold, either put into an ice-cream machine or *sorbetière* – follow the manufacturer's instructions – or make it 'by hand' (see the recipe above).

6 While the mixture is still soft, add the beaten egg white and churn in the machine, or beat well by hand. Place in the freezer, in a bowl covered with cling film.

TO SERVE Half an hour before serving, transfer the sorbet from the freezer to the fridge. When it is soft, make into *quenelle* shapes (see page 26) and place in the *Paniers* (see page 171). Decorate with the reserved fruit and juice.

Paniers

FEATHERLIGHT BASKETS

You may find making these a little difficult at first, but do persevere – once you have the hang of it, they'll take you no time to prepare and they will make your presentation of ice-cream, sorbets and fresh fruit salads so much more successful.

The little trick of warming up the egg white helps a lot in the preparation of the batter, but it does need time to rest. The batter will keep 3-4 days in the fridge, but remove it a few minutes before using so that it spreads more easily. It freezes perfectly too.

MAKES 8

PREHEAT THE OVEN TO 350°F/180°C/GAS 4

75 g (3 oz) egg whites (about 2 × size 3 eggs)
75 g (3 oz) unsalted butter
90 g (3½ oz) caster sugar
75 g (3 oz) plain flour

1 Pour the egg whites into a bowl and place the bowl over a saucepan of hot water (122°F/50°C maximum). Prepare a baking tray, greasing it well.

2 Soften the butter thoroughly, add the sugar and work well to a white and creamy consistency. Add the warmed egg whites a little at a time.

3 Add the flour quickly, and mix together, but do not overwork. Rest the batter for 20 minutes in the fridge.

4 Place approximately 1 heaped dessertspoon of the batter on the sheet, and shape it into a 15 cm (6 in) round with the back of the spoon. Bake for 5-10 minutes in the preheated oven until the edges start to brown.

5 Remove from the oven immediately, and quickly turn over an inverted bowl. Use a palette knife if necessary to detach it from the baking tray. Place a larger bowl on top – or shape it with the fingers – and leave to cool.

6 Once you have mastered the method for this first basket – and grasped the speed at which you have to work once it is out of the oven – bake and cool the remainder in the same way.

7 Keep the baskets in a cool and dry place until ready to serve; they should be made no longer than 5-6 hours in advance. Fill at the last moment.

RIGHT *Paniers* with *Sorbet de l'Été*

Tarte aux Fraises

STRAWBERRY AND CUSTARD TART

A very traditional strawberry tart, this is made a little healthier by using our pâte brisée, *much less sugar and egg yolks, and no butter in the* crème pâtissière *(custard). Only make this dish while strawberries are in season as the recipe is not suitable for frozen strawberries. Frozen redcurrants may be used for glazing, and if they are not available, use redcurrant jelly instead.*

Do not assemble more than 1 hour ahead of time as the juice of the strawberries runs.

SERVES 6

PREHEAT THE OVEN TO 350°F/180°C/GAS 4

1 recipe Pâte Brisée *(see page 44)*
450 g (1 lb) fresh strawberries, washed, drained and hulled
200 g (7 oz) redcurrants
100 g (4 oz) golden granulated sugar

CRÈME PÂTISSIÈRE
250 ml (8 fl oz) skimmed milk
1 vanilla pod
1 dsp wholemeal flour
1 dsp potato flour
25 g (1 oz) golden granulated sugar
1 egg
icing sugar, to dust

1 Rest the pastry in the fridge for 20 minutes. Roll out thinly and line a 25 cm (10 in) tart tin. Bake blind in the oven until completely cooked. Remove from the tin and leave to cool down so that the base becomes firm.

2 To make the *crème pâtissière*, reserve 50 ml (2 fl oz) of the milk and bring the remainder to the boil with the vanilla pod in a saucepan. In another saucepan mix together the two flours and the golden granulated sugar. Beat the egg lightly in a bowl with the reserved milk, then pour it slowly into the flour mixture, mixing well with a small whisk until smooth. When the vanilla milk is boiling, pour it into the egg and flour mixture a little at a time, stirring well with a whisk. Place the saucepan immediately over a medium heat and, stirring and whisking constantly, return to the boil. Boil, stirring vigorously for 1 minute, then remove the vanilla pod (rinse it and place in a jar with sugar to use again another time).

3 Pour the *crème pâtissière* into the tart case to cool, and dust the top with icing sugar to prevent a skin forming.

4 When the custard is cool, arrange the strawberries very closely together on top.

5 To make the redcurrant jelly, wash the fresh redcurrants (or leave frozen to defrost inside a bowl and use both fruit and juice). Detach the currants from the stalks with a fork.

6 Place the redcurrants in a saucepan with 2 dessertspoons water, cover, and place over a high heat to make them pop, about 2 minutes. Add the sugar, stir well, then return to the high heat and bring to the boil. After 3 minutes, remove from the heat. Remove any froth, strain, and leave to cool for 5 minutes.

7 Pour slowly or brush over the strawberries. Leave the tart to set in the fridge for a minimum of 10 minutes.

TO SERVE Serve on a round serving dish lined with a doily.

Sorbet à l'Ananas

PINEAPPLE SORBET

This sorbet proves that little or no sugar is needed in a sorbet if the combination of fruits is right. The teaspoon of sugar used here is only to stabilize the egg whites which give the right consistency. Both fruits contain good amounts of vitamins as well as fibre; pineapple is also reputed to contain an enzyme which absorbs excess fat in the body.

GLUTEN FREE
SERVES 4

1 medium pineapple
1 orange
2 egg whites
1 tsp muscovado sugar
2 dsp Grand Marnier
50 ml (2 fl oz) water

1 Quarter the pineapple as described on page 27. Insert the blade between flesh and skin and remove the flesh. Cut into cubes and place in a liquidizer or food processor. Keep the pineapple skin.

2 Score the orange rind with a zester or scorer and reserve. Segment the orange (see page 27) and put the segments into a liquidizer or processor with the pineapple flesh.

3 Liquidize together thoroughly, then place in an ice-cream maker or *sorbetière*, or in a tray in the freezer, and whisk vigorously with a fork every 15 minutes until the mixture is almost solid.

4 Beat the egg whites until stiff, adding a couple of pinches of the sugar, and fold into the sorbet, while the *sorbetière* is running, or by hand. Add half the Grand Marnier and return to the freezer.

5 Meanwhile, prepare the orange rind zest for the decoration. Blanch for 1 minute in boiling water, then drain and replace in the saucepan with the water and remaining sugar and Grand Marnier. Simmer very slowly until 1 dessertspoon of liquid is left in the pan. Lay the zest on a piece of Bakewell paper, and leave to dry in a warm, dry place (a low oven, for instance).

TO SERVE Just before serving, put the sorbet in a piping bag with a fluted nozzle, and pipe over each pineapple skin quarter. Decorate with the orange zest.

Sorbet à l'Ananas

Cygnes au Citron

CHOUX SWANS WITH LEMON MOUSSE

These choux pastry swans,. filled with a lemon mousse, are delicious and impressive. Although the choux pastry contains butter, when it is divided between six people it means less than 10g or ½oz per person! The swans could also be filled with sorbets.

The mousse contains very much less sugar, cream and egg yolk than the original recipe. The mixture could also be shaped into quenelles *(see page 26), and, along with orange and lime mousses made in the same way, served in a* panier *or basket (see page 170).*

SERVES 6
PREHEAT THE OVEN TO 450°F/230°C/GAS 8

1 recipe Pâte à Choux *(see page 42)*
egg wash (optional)
icing sugar, to dust

LEMON MOUSSE
1 gelatine leaf
1 lemon, washed well
25g (1oz) sugar lumps
25g (1oz) golden granulated sugar
2 eggs, separated
2 egg whites
50g (2oz) Greek yoghurt

1 Place the choux pastry in a piping bag with a 1cm (½in) plain nozzle. Place a 6mm (¼in) nozzle *over* the existing nozzle, and pipe six figure 2s on to a baking tray, covered with Bakewell paper. These will be the heads and necks of the swans. Remove the smaller nozzle and pipe six oval shapes for the swan bodies. Dab the shapes with a wet finger to smooth them and, for a better shine, brush with egg wash.

2 Bake in the preheated oven for 5 minutes, then turn the oven down to 350°F/180°C/Gas 4. Bake for a further 20 minutes, but remove the necks after 5-10 minutes or when brown. If using a conventional oven keep the choux bodies in the oven for an extra 5 minutes with the door slightly open (keep ajar with the handle of a wooden spoon).

3 Cut the top layer off the bodies. Cut this layer in half lengthwise to form the wings. Spoon any excess dough from the bodies and dry out in the oven if necessary. Leave to cool.

4 To make the mousse, first soak the gelatine in cold water.

5 Dry the lemon and rub the sugar lumps over the skin to extract the oil. Place these lumps, the granulated sugar and the juice of the lemon in a bowl with the egg yolks and beat over a pan of hot water until a light fluffy batter. Remove from the heat and carry on whisking. Put in the drained gelatine while it is still warm.

6 In another bowl beat all the egg whites until stiff. Fold into the mousse mixture, along with the yoghurt.

7 Pour into a piping bag.

TO SERVE Pipe the mousse into the hollowed-out bodies of the swans. Dust the wings with icing sugar and place them at an angle to form the wings. Push each neck into the mousse at one end. Dust with icing sugar and serve immediately on a doily-lined dish.

RIGHT *Cygnes au Citron*

Aumonières Surprise

FRUIT CRÊPES

Inside these little pancake packages are low-fat vanilla ice-cream and delicious fruit salad. The accompanying sauce is a simple coulis of strawberries.

All the preparation can be done ahead of time, but the assembling should be done just before starting dinner, and the packages kept in the freezer until it is time for dessert.

SERVES 4

CRÊPE BATTER
40g (1½oz) plain flour
40g (1½oz) wholemeal flour
1 egg
150ml (5fl oz) skimmed milk
salt
sugar
grapeseed oil

VANILLA ICE-CREAM
250ml (8fl oz) skimmed milk
1 vanilla pod
25g (1oz) golden granulated sugar
2 egg yolks
50ml (2fl oz) whipping cream
200g (7oz) Greek yoghurt

FRUIT SALAD
1 orange
½ lemon
1dsp golden granulated sugar
100ml (3½fl oz) water
¼ pineapple, peeled
4 strawberries, hulled
1tsp Grand Marnier

COULIS DE FRAISES
200g (7oz) strawberries
juice of ½ lemon
1dsp icing sugar

DECORATION
4 strips angelica, 12.5cm (5in) long or 2 lengths of thin liquorice (to tie the parcels together)

1 To prepare the crêpe batter, sieve the flours together into a bowl, add the bran from the sieve, and make a well in the centre. Put the egg, milk, and a pinch each of salt and sugar into the well and mix these wet ingredients together. Using a light whisk, gradually take in a little flour at a time until it has all been worked in. The batter should be light and cover the back of a spoon thickly. If too thick, thin down with a little more milk. Rest in the fridge for 20 minutes.

2 To prepare the vanilla ice-cream, bring the milk and vanilla pod to the boil. Meanwhile whisk the sugar and the egg yolks until white and fluffy. When the milk boils, add a third of it to the egg and sugar mixture, then return the milk to the heat. Mix the egg mixture well and add to the boiling milk. Take off the heat immediately and stir. Replace the saucepan over a low heat for 2 minutes, stirring slowly, then remove from the heat. Cover and leave to infuse for 5 minutes so that the vanilla pod gives its flavour. Transfer to a bowl, add the cream and place in the freezer to cool quickly, stirring occasionally. When cold, remove the vanilla pod.

3 Place the mixture in an ice-cream machine, or in a container in the freezer and leave. When semi-hard, add the yoghurt, a spoonful at a time, then finish churning. Alternatively, make the ice-cream by hand (follow the directions given in the recipe for *Ananas Princesse* on page 180).

4 To prepare the fruit salad, remove the zest of the orange and the half lemon with a scorer or zester. Place the shreds in a saucepan with the sugar and water, and simmer to reduce until only 1 dessertspoon of liquid is left. Reserve to one side. Segment the oranges (see page 27) and place in a bowl with the zest and the juice of the half lemon. Cut the pineapple into very small chunks (see page 27), and the strawberries in quarters, and add both to the bowl, with the Grand Marnier. Cover the bowl and leave in the fridge to marinate for at least 20 minutes.

5 To prepare the *coulis*, reserve 4 strawberries for decoration, and place the remainder in a food processor or liquidizer (or use a sieve or hand food mill). Add the lemon juice and icing sugar. Liquidize well for 3 minutes and reserve. If the purée is too thick, thin it down with a little of the juice from the fruit salad. Reserve in a bowl and cover well with cling film.

6 To cook the crêpes, add a dessertspoon of oil to the batter, stirring it in very gently. Heat a 20cm (8in) skillet or non-stick frying pan over a low heat. Add a drop of oil and wipe it around the

Aumonières Surprise

pan with a paper towel. Add a small ladleful of batter, and spread it evenly around, turning the pan in a circular motion. Cook over a low heat for 2 minutes, then toss it to cook the other side (use a fork and spoon if you can't toss!). Cook for 2 minutes, then reserve on a plate. Cover the plate with a lid (another plate, for example). Repeat until all the batter has been used. No more oil should be necessary, but you should wipe the pan with the greased paper towel between every pancake.

7 For the decoration, bring a saucepan of water to the boil and blanch the angelica (*not* the liquorice) for 2 minutes. Leave to soak and soften in the water for 15 minutes, then cut into long strips. Leave in the water until ready to use.

8 Drain the juices from the fruit salad and add to the *coulis*. Lay the pancakes on a board and place a spoonful of the fruit salad in the middle. Add a spoonful of the ice-cream. Bring the sides up and tie with a strip of angelica (or liquorice) to form a little purse. Place in the freezer to keep the ice-cream solid, but for no more than 10 minutes or the fruit salad will be frozen too! (Keep in the fridge thereafter.) Make eight purses. Reserve the remaining ice-cream and fruit salad in bowls to serve separately.

TO SERVE To serve traditionally, shape the remaining ice-cream into a mound on a large round serving plate and place the purses all around. Pour some of the *coulis* over the mound, with the remainder in a sauceboat. Halve the reserved strawberries, and use to decorate. Serve the remaining fruit salad separately.

To serve individually, line the base of each plate with *coulis*. Place the remainder in a sauceboat to serve separately. Place two purses on each plate, and decorate with the reserved halved strawberries. Serve with the remaining ice-cream and fruit salad.

Soufflé au Chocolat

CHOCOLATE SOUFFLÉ

Our selection of desserts would not be complete without a traditional chocolate soufflé. Chocolate is very rich, as we all know, which is why we have removed the butter from the recipe; this also makes the soufflé lighter.

Adding the orange zest oil gives a very special flavour which is similar to the Reine de Saba *on page 186. For a different flavour try adding a teaspoon of instant coffee powder to the milk or, better still, replace some of the milk with 2 dessertspoons strong fresh coffee and a dash of Tia Maria or Kahlua.*

GLUTEN FREE
SERVES 4
PREHEAT THE OVEN TO 350°F/180°C/GAS 4

1 tsp butter
white flour, to dust
25 g (1 oz) potato flour
25 g (1 oz) ground almonds
200 ml (7 fl oz) milk
1 vanilla pod
75 g (3 oz) dark chocolate, broken into pieces
2 sugar lumps
1 orange, washed
2 eggs, separated
1 tsp Grand Marnier
2 egg whites
1 dsp golden granulated sugar

1 Grease a 600 ml (1 pt) soufflé dish (or four individual ramekin dishes if to be served individually) with the butter, and place in the fridge for the butter to set. When set, dust with a little white flour and tap upside-down on the work surface to remove the excess.

2 Sieve the potato flour and almonds together into a bowl, and make a well in the centre.

3 Bring the milk and vanilla pod to the boil in a saucepan, then remove from the heat. Pour slowly into the well in the flour, working the flour and almonds in slowly with a whisk. Beat vigorously to get rid of any lumps. Return to the heat, bring just to the boil, then remove from the heat. Remove the vanilla pod.

4 Add the pieces of chocolate and cover the pan. Rub the sugar lumps against the orange peel to obtain the oil, then add the sugar to the saucepan and stir well to dissolve it.

5 Add the egg yolks and Grand Marnier and mix well. Cover and reserve in a warm place.

6 Whisk all 4 egg whites until they form soft peaks, then add the granulated sugar. Whisk in well, then stir a third into the chocolate mixture. Fold in the remaining egg whites carefully.

7 Pour the soufflé mixture into the dish or dishes to come three-quarters up the sides.

8 Bake the soufflés in the preheated oven – 20 minutes for a big one, 10-15 minutes for individual ramekins.

TO SERVE Serve immediately. A soufflé does not wait for guests, they wait for the soufflé!

Tarte au Fromage Blanc

CHEESECAKE

How can a cheesecake be healthy, you may well ask! Well, it took a long time to figure it out...but as we love the taste, we experimented and experimented. The cream cheese was replaced by low-fat soft cheese and Greek yoghurt, the vast amount of double cream by a small amount of whipping cream, and the refined sugar by muscovado sugar with its delicious liquorice flavour.

SERVES 6

PREHEAT THE OVEN TO 350°F/180°C/GAS 4

Pâte Brisée *made with 300g (11oz) flour (see page 44)*
100g (4oz) sultanas
2dsp cognac
1 egg yolk
50g (2oz) muscovado sugar
zest and juice of 1 lemon
2 eggs
25g (1oz) potato flour
200g (7oz) Ricotta (or other low-fat soft cheese)
50g (2oz) low-fat cream cheese
100ml (3½floz) skimmed milk
100ml (3½floz) whipping cream
100g (4oz) Greek yoghurt
egg wash

TO SERVE
icing sugar, to dust

1 Rest the pastry in the fridge for 20 minutes.

2 Wash the sultanas, then dry on paper towels. Place them in a saucepan with the cognac, heat for 1 minute, and set alight. Wait for the flames to die, then cover the saucepan and reserve for later.

3 Whisk the egg yolk, sugar, and lemon zest and juice together very well. Add the whole eggs and mix well. Add the potato flour and mix in without overworking the mixture.

4 Sieve the cheeses, add the egg mixture and whisk to a smooth paste. Mix in the milk, cream and yoghurt.

5 Roll out the dough, and use to line a 23cm (9in) loose-bottomed tart tin. Push the dough well into the edges, and cut off the excess. Prick the base with a fork and line with Bakewell paper and baking beans. Bake blind for 5 minutes in the preheated oven, then turn the tin around in the oven. Leave for 5 minutes. Remove the paper and baking beans, and bake for 5 minutes more. Glaze with egg wash, and cook for 1 minute. Coat again and cook for another minute.

6 Scatter the sultanas evenly over the pastry case. Add the cheese mixture and bake in the oven for 15 minutes. Don't be alarmed by the wobbly texture: it will set as it cools. Remove the base and sides of the tin, place the tart on a cooling rack, and leave.

TO SERVE Serve cold, sprinkled with some icing sugar.

Tarte au Fromage Blanc

Ananas Princesse

PINEAPPLE WITH STRAWBERRY ICE-CREAM

This dessert is a combination of light strawberry ice-cream and pineapple slices served in the pineapple shell. Double cream has been replaced by half whipping cream and half Greek yoghurt which makes the ice-cream lighter and healthier; very little sugar is added (less will be needed if the strawberries are very ripe); the lemon juice both adds vitamin C and helps bring out the flavour of the strawberries.

Frozen strawberries could be used instead of fresh. Defrost in a bowl and use both the fruit and the juice in the recipe.

Never freeze the pineapple and ice-cream together, the result is not good at all.

GLUTEN FREE
SERVES 4

1 gelatine leaf
300g (11oz) ripe strawberries, rinsed, drained and hulled
50g (2oz) icing sugar (plus extra, to dust)
1tsp lemon juice
50ml (2floz) cold water
100ml (3½floz) whipping cream
100g (4oz) Greek yoghurt
1 small ripe pineapple
1dsp Grand Marnier

TO SERVE
dusted mint leaves (see page 25)

1 Place the gelatine in a bowl of cold water to soften it.

2 Reserve a few strawberries for decoration, and place the rest in a food processor with the sugar, and the lemon juice. Process well, and reserve 50ml (2oz) for decoration.

3 Drain the gelatine, then place with the measured water in a bowl over a pan of simmering water. Stir, and leave over a low heat long enough to melt the gelatine. Pour into the strawberry purée and mix well. Strain through a nylon sieve. Place in an ice-cream machine and leave to chill and churn. If you don't have a machine, put the ice-cream in a cake tin in the freezer and whisk vigorously every 10 minutes until thick.

4 Whip the cream lightly, then add the yoghurt, spoonful by spoonful. Reserve a dessertspoon in a piping bag for decoration. When the ice-cream is the consistency of a thick purée, fold in the cream and yoghurt mixture. Leave to churn until well frozen, then put into a piping bag fitted with a fluted nozzle, and return to the freezer.

5 Prepare the pineapple as explained on page 27, leaving a good shell. Cut the pineapple flesh into thin slices, sprinkle with the Grand Marnier, cover and reserve.

TO SERVE No earlier than 20-30 minutes before serving, pipe a layer of ice-cream into the pineapple shell, and lay a slice of pineapple on top. Repeat until the shell is full, and decorate with more ice-cream to mound over the top. Dust the leafy head of the pineapple lightly with icing sugar and place on top. Pour the reserved *coulis* on to a serving plate, and pipe a thin circle of the reserved cream and yoghurt mixture 1cm (½in) inside the edge of the *coulis*. Feather with the tip of a knife. Place the pineapple in the centre of the *coulis* and serve immediately with the remaining pineapple slices and ice-cream in separate dishes.

RIGHT *Ananas Princesse*

Marquise à la Passion

PASSION FRUIT MERINGUE CAKE

This is a delicious dessert to prepare for a buffet party or a special dinner party. It originally contained a lot of cream and sugar, but in reducing these we have, happily, increased the flavour of passion fruit. If no passion fruit juice is available, use a tropical fruit juice, in which the flavour of passion fruit is always predominant.

As it is such a lengthy recipe, prepare it the day before so that you're not too exhausted to prepare the main course and starter on the day itself.

SERVES 12

PREHEAT THE OVEN TO 350°F/180°C/GAS 4

8 gelatine leaves
8 passion fruit
550 ml (a scant pt) passion fruit or tropical fruit juice
100 g (4 oz) golden granulated sugar
oil
2 dsp rum, preferably white
200 ml (7 fl oz) whipping cream
100 g (4 oz) Greek yoghurt

GÉNOISE

1 tsp grapeseed oil
65 g (2½ oz) wholemeal flour
65 g (2½ oz) muscovado sugar
2 large eggs

MERINGUE ITALIENNE

100 g (4 oz) golden granulated sugar
25 ml (1 fl oz) cold water
4 egg whites

TO SERVE

450 g (1 lb) strawberries, washed and hulled
2 kiwi fruit, peeled and sliced
½ tsp lemon juice

THE DAY BEFORE SERVING

1 First prepare the *génoise*, using the ingredients listed here, and following the method outlined on page 185. Bake in a 20 × 30 cm (8 × 12 in) cake tin lined with Bakewell paper for 10-15 minutes. Turn out on to a cooling rack and leave to cool. When cool, split in half horizontally.

2 Soak the gelatine in cold water until soft, about 5 minutes. Cut all the passion fruit in half like grapefruit, and scoop the flesh out of 8 of the halves into a saucepan. Add 150 ml (5 fl oz) of the juice and the sugar, and bring to the boil. Simmer for 1 minute, then remove the impurities and add 3 leaves of the gelatine. Leave to cool down in a bowl, stirring occasionally, until cool.

3 Wash the cake tin used for the *génoise*, rub with a little oil, and line with cling film (the oil helps the film cling to the sides of the tin). When the jelly is cool, pour it into the prepared tin and place in the fridge to set hard. If you don't want the seeds (although they are quite decorative), strain the jelly through a chinois sieve before pouring into the tin.

4 Scoop out the flesh of the remaining 4 fruit into a bowl, and add 350 ml (12 fl oz) of the juice. Place the remaining gelatine in a saucepan and add a little of the juice from the bowl. Place over a low heat until the gelatine melts. Pour into the juice in the bowl. Strain the pips through a chinois sieve. Stir occasionally.

5 Place the small remaining amount of juice in a ramekin dish with the rum. Cover, and reserve for later.

6 To prepare the *meringue italienne*, reserve 2 dessertspoons of the sugar and place the remainder in a saucepan with the water. Bring to the boil, cleaning the sides of the pan well with a brush dipped in a bowl of cold water. Boil for approximately 3 minutes over a medium heat, then take the pan off the heat and dip, for 1 second, into the bowl of cold water to stop the cooking. Take a small amount of the sugar syrup out with a teaspoon and place in the bowl of cold water. It should form a soft ball; if too runny, replace the pan over the heat and boil again until the right consistency is reached. Every time you take it off the heat, dip the bowl into cold water to stop the cooking.

7 Whisk the egg whites until they form stiff peaks, then add the reserved sugar and beat for another minute. Still beating, add the sugar syrup in a steady flow, and beat until cool. Reserve for later.

Marquise à la Passion

8 Whip the cream, then add the yoghurt a little at a time. If the juice in the bowl has not thickened yet, place the bowl over some ice-cubes and water to thicken more quickly, stirring gently all the time. Both the cream and yoghurt mixture and the juice in the bowl should have the same consistency to mix properly. When ready, fold the cream, jellied juices and the meringue together using a lifting motion with a whisk.

TO ASSEMBLE

1 Pour half of the cream/jelly/meringue triple mixture on to the set jelly in the cake tin. Place the bottom half of the *génoise* on top and soak with the juice and rum mixture. Cover with the remaining mixture, then soak the remaining half of the *génoise* with the remaining juice and rum. Cover with the top of the *génoise*, crust side up.

2 Place in the fridge for at least 3 hours to set – it is best left overnight.

TO SERVE Dip the cake tin in a basin containing hot water for 10 seconds, and turn out on to a large serving board. Remove the cling film carefully, and cut the *marquise* in half lengthwise, and then across at 5 cm (2 in) intervals widthwise to obtain twelve portions.

Decorate each portion with a strawberry half, and a slice of kiwi fruit, fanned out. Purée the remaining strawberries with the lemon juice. If served on individual plates, pour a little purée over the plate and place the decorated portion on top.

Compôte de Pommes aux Oranges Confites

APPLE COMPÔTE WITH ORANGES

This stewed apple recipe was only created to use up leftover Oranges Confites, *but it became so popular that often it was prepared regardless! So whenever you are making a dish which uses these cooked orange slices, prepare a few more than you need, and make this deliciously simple sweet the next day.*

GLUTEN FREE
SERVES 4

4 Golden Delicious apples, washed
100 ml (3½ fl oz) cold water
1 vanilla pod
1 star anise
1 slice fresh root ginger, peeled and cut into thin julienne

ORANGES CONFITES
4 oranges, washed
50 g (2 oz) golden granulated sugar
1 dsp muscovado sugar
300 ml (10 fl oz) cold water

THE DAY BEFORE SERVING

1 Prepare the *Oranges Confites*. Slice the oranges carefully. Put both sugars and the water into a pan and bring to the boil, making sure the sugars have dissolved first. Add the orange slices and cover with a circle of Bakewell paper and a lid. Simmer for an hour. Remove from the heat and leave to cool. Keep in the fridge overnight.

THE DAY OF SERVING

1 Prick the skin of the apples all over with the tip of a sharp knife, then core and quarter them. Cut each quarter in half again. Place in a saucepan with the water, the juice from the *Oranges Confites*, the vanilla pod, star anise and ginger *julienne*.

2 Place over a low heat and bring very slowly to the boil, covered with a lid. Stir very gently once in a while, making sure not to break up the pieces of apple. Simmer for 5 minutes, then take off the heat.

3 Leave to cool, still covered, for 30 minutes.

TO SERVE Remove the vanilla pod and the star anise. (Keep the pod, discard the star anise.) Chop half the orange slices finely and add to the apples. Cut the remaining orange slices in half and reserve.

Lift the apples out on to a serving dish or individual plates, using a slotted spoon, and decorate with the remaining halved orange slices. Serve the juices separately in a sauceboat.

Compôte de Pommes aux Oranges Confites

Génoise aux Pommes

APPLE SPONGE CAKE

This génoise *or sponge is made with half wholemeal flour to add fibre. The finished cake is hollowed out and the hollow filled with lightly baked apples.*

SERVES 6
PREHEAT THE OVEN TO 350°F/180°C/GAS 4

1 kg (2¼ lb) dessert apples, washed
butter
1 dsp Calvados
water
25 g (1 oz) muscovado sugar
icing sugar, to dust

GÉNOISE
1 tsp grapeseed oil
50 g (2 oz) plain white flour (plus extra, to dust)
50 g (2 oz) 100% wholemeal flour
3 large eggs
25 g (1 oz) golden granulated sugar
25 g (1 oz) muscovado sugar

1 Prepare the *génoise*. Use the oil to grease a 25 cm (10 in) cake tin, then cut a circle of Bakewell paper to line the bottom. Place in the fridge to set the oil, about 2 minutes. When set, dust the inside of the tin with extra flour, then bang the tin upside-down on the work surface to remove the excess.

2 Mix the flours together and sieve on to a piece of Bakewell paper. Mix in the bran left in the sieve.

3 Bring a saucepan of water to the boil and place the eggs and the sugars in a heatproof bowl. Whisk the eggs and sugar together until they start changing colour, about 1-2 minutes. Take the saucepan of boiling water off the heat and place the bowl over it (the bowl must touch the water). Beat well until the batter thickens or when lifted with the whisk it falls in 'ribbons'. This will take up to 5 minutes. Take the bowl out of the pan and continue beating for 1 minute to cool. Fold the flour into the cooled batter, pouring quickly from the paper so that the batter does not collapse.

4 Pour into the middle of the tin, being careful not to splash the sides, and bake for 20-30 minutes in the preheated oven. The cake is cooked when it is golden brown and, when pressed lightly with a finger, the top springs back. Turn out immediately and cool on a cooling rack.

5 Prepare the apples. Turn the oven down to 325°F/160°C/Gas 3. Core the apples, then cut in half through the core. Slice across the core 'bridge', keeping the half apple shape together, and place on a buttered roasting tin or tray with a tiny knob of butter and a dash of Calvados on top of each half. Pour 2 dessertspoons water into the base of the tin or tray, cover with buttered foil, and bake for 15-20 minutes. Remove from the oven, and leave to cool.

6 Put the sugar and 100 ml (3½ fl oz) water into a small saucepan and heat to make a syrup. Add the remaining Calvados.

TO ASSEMBLE

1 Using a small knife, cut a circle around the cake, 1.5 cm (¾ in) in from the outside edge. Do not cut right through to the bottom. To separate the bottom, insert the knife horizontally 1.5 cm (¾ in) from the base of the cake on one side and swing it from side to side. Do this again at the opposite side of the cake, making sure not to enlarge the openings on the outside too much. Using a fork, ease up all round the cut circle on top of the cake, and remove the whole circular section. Cut this in half horizontally.

2 Dab the syrup all round the insides of the hollowed-out cake. Place the cake on a serving plate and arrange the apple slices in the hollow in layers. Place the crusty half of the cake circle on top of the apples and dust with icing sugar.

Reine de Saba aux Oranges Confites

CHOCOLATE CAKES WITH ORANGES

Do indulge once in a while in these delicious little chocolate 'mushroom' cakes. The recipe has, as usual, been modified; the butter has been reduced considerably, and the flour has also been reduced to a minimum – but never forget the richness of the chocolate! The oranges make a very good decoration and are at their best cooked slowly and left overnight to marinate.

SERVES 4
PREHEAT THE OVEN TO 350°F/180°C/GAS 4

½ recipe Oranges Confites *(see page 184)*
25 g (1 oz) potato flour
25 g (1 oz) ground almonds
200 ml (7 fl oz) skimmed milk
100 g (4 oz) dark chocolate, grated
25 g (1 oz) butter
2 sugar lumps
1 orange, washed
3 eggs, separated
white flour, to dust
1 vanilla pod
25 g (1 oz) golden granulated sugar
1 tsp Grand Marnier

TO SERVE
½ tsp icing sugar, to dust

1 Sieve together the potato flour and almonds.

2 Bring 50 ml (2 fl oz) of the milk to the boil, then remove from the heat and add the chocolate and half the butter. Rub the sugar lumps against the skin of the orange to take up the oil, then add the sugar lumps to the saucepan. Cover, let it all melt together, and stir well. Meanwhile, use the remaining butter to grease four ramekin dishes. Place them in the fridge for the butter to set.

3 Away from the heat, add two of the egg yolks, one at a time, to the chocolate mixture. Add the sifted flour and almonds while mixing. Whisk the egg whites until they form soft peaks. Add 1 tablespoon of the sugar and whisk well. Fold the egg whites into the chocolate mixture.

4 Dust the ramekin dishes with a little extra white flour and tap them lightly upside-down on the work surface to remove the excess. Divide the mixture between the ramekins, and bake for 10-15 minutes in the preheated oven. Unmould the cakes as soon as they come out of the oven, and cool on a rack.

5 To prepare the *crème anglaise* sauce, bring the remaining milk and the vanilla pod to the boil. Meanwhile whisk the remaining golden granulated sugar and egg yolk together until white and fluffy. Pour a quarter of the scalded milk on to this, mix well and return it to the remaining milk. Keep over a low heat, stirring constantly, until it thickens. Do not boil or it will curdle (if that happens, liquidize it).

6 Remove the slices of *Oranges Confites* carefully from their syrup, reserving twelve slices for decoration. Reduce the orange syrup by half (or until 100 ml or 3½ fl oz is left) and mix into the *crème anglaise*. Purée the remaining orange slices (by hand or in a food processor) and add to the *crème anglaise* with the Grand Marnier. Marinate for at least 20 minutes before serving.

TO SERVE Put four dessert plates into the fridge to chill. Cut the reserved orange slices in half.

Dust each little cake with icing sugar (through a sieve) and place one in the centre of each plate, surrounded with a circle of overlapping orange slices. Strain the *crème anglaise* through a chinois sieve, discarding the chopped oranges (but keep the vanilla to use later). Pour a little sauce on to the plate. Serve the remaining sauce in a sauceboat.

RIGHT *Reine de Saba aux Oranges Confites*

Rosace à l'Orange

ORANGE GÂTEAU

Another delicious cake, from which a lot of the sugar, butter and cream have been removed. Start preparing it 2 days in advance, by making the Oranges Confites, *the* crème pâtissière *and the* génoise. *It will not take long to assemble the cake, but make sure to leave it in the fridge for at least 12 hours to set.*

SERVES 6

1 recipe Oranges Confites *(see page 184)*
1 recipe Génoise *(see the recipe for* Génoise aux Pommes *on page 185)*

CRÈME PÂTISSIÈRE
250ml (8floz) milk
1 vanilla pod
1dsp potato flour
1dsp cornflour
1dsp golden granulated sugar
1 egg
icing sugar, to dust

ORANGE FILLING
2 gelatine leaves
2dsp Grand Marnier
1tsp grapeseed oil
50g (2oz) Greek yoghurt
150ml (5floz) whipping cream, whipped

TWO DAYS BEFORE SERVING

1 Prepare the *crème pâtissière*. Use the ingredients listed here, but follow the method described in *Tarte aux Fraises* (see page 172). Reserve on a plate to cool, and dust with icing sugar to prevent a skin forming. When cold, cover with cling film and refrigerate.

THE DAY BEFORE SERVING

1 To prepare the orange filling, soak the gelatine leaves in cold water for 5 minutes.

2 Drain the slices of *Oranges Confites* carefully, and reserve 150ml (5floz) of the juice. Add half of the Grand Marnier to it, and add the other half to the remainder of the juice. Reserve.

3 Use the oil to grease the tin in which the *génoise* was cooked. Line the inside with cling film (the oil will help the film to cling).

4 Choose the best orange slices and use them to line the base and sides of the tin. Chop the remaining oranges and reserve.

5 Place the gelatine in a saucepan with enough of the reserved 150ml (5floz) juice to cover it (keep the remainder to one side). Place over a low heat just long enough for the gelatine to melt, then add to the rest of the juice. Reserve on top of a bowl with water and ice-cubes to help it thicken.

6 Push the *crème pâtissière* through a sieve and add the reserved chopped oranges and thickened juice to it. They should each have the same consistency.

7 Add the yoghurt to the cream, a spoonful at a time, and fold into the *crème pâtissière*.

TO ASSEMBLE

1 Cut the *génoise* in to three layers horizontally.

2 Pour one-third of the orange filling on top of the oranges inside the tin, and cover with the first layer of the cake. Soak the cake with a little of the reserved orange juice. Pour in another third of the filling, cover with the second layer of cake, and soak with juice. Pour in the remainder of the filling, and cover with the last layer of cake, soaked in juice, placed upside-down over the filling. Place a small plate on top of the cake and a heavy weight on top of that. Leave for at least 12 hours to set.

TO SERVE Dip the tin in a bowl of hot water and turn out on to a serving dish carefully. Wipe the oranges on top of the cake free of any surplus cream.

LEFT *Rosace à l'Orange*

Tarte aux Pignons

SPINACH AND PINE NUT TART

SERVES 6
PREHEAT THE OVEN TO 350°F/180°C/GAS 4

Pâte Brisée *made with 200 g (7 oz) flour (see page 44)*
25 g (1 oz) butter
300 g (11 oz) spinach leaves, cut into chiffonade
75 g (3 oz) honey
50 g (2 oz) sultanas
grated nutmeg
ground allspice
juice of 1/2 lemon
2 eggs, beaten
25 g (1 oz) pine nuts
100 ml (3½ fl oz) whipping cream
100 ml (3½ fl oz) milk

SAUCE
150 g (5 oz) Greek yoghurt
2 tsp liquid honey

No, the editor did not put this recipe in the wrong place; it is still a dessert, despite the spinach. Swiss chard in fact is traditional in Provence, where the recipe originates, but as it is not often available, we use young spinach leaves instead.

1 Rest the pastry for 20 minutes in the fridge.

2 Melt the butter in a large saucepan and sauté the well-dried spinach briskly over a high heat. Add the honey (reserving 1 teaspoon), the sultanas, a pinch each of the spices, and the lemon juice. Leave to cool on a large plate, so that the sultanas absorb any remaining liquid.

3 Roll out the pastry and use to line a 25 cm (10 in) quiche tin. Line the pastry with foil or greaseproof paper, and cover with baking beans. Bake blind in the preheated oven. After 10 minutes remove the paper and beans and continue baking blind until the dough is firm but not too coloured, about 10 minutes. Brush with a little beaten egg and return to the oven for 5 minutes. Repeat this once more.

4 While the pastry is cooking, place the pine nuts on a baking tray and roast them in the same oven until golden brown.

5 In a bowl mix the remaining beaten egg, the cream, milk, a little more nutmeg and allspice, and the reserved teaspoon of honey. Add the spinach mixture and mix together well. At the last moment add the pine nuts, then pour this mixture into the pastry case. Bake for 20 minutes.

TO SERVE Remove the tart from the quiche tin and cool briefly on a cooling rack. Serve tepid with a little sauce made from the yoghurt mixed with the honey.

Tarte aux Pignons

INDEX

ACKNOWLEDGEMENTS

I would like to thank the following people without whose cooperation this book would never have seen the light of day.

First my parents and family who always supported me in every circumstance, whatever choices I made, especially 'maman' who researched a lot on my behalf for the herb section.

Very special thanks, too, to Sabine de Mirbeck-Brassart who, like a 'mother', has helped me and always supported me throughout eight years of working closely together. Thank you also for the tedious task of testing the recipes without being able to let your wonderful culinary imagination take over...

Then Patrick Brassart, a very special 'boss' to me, who has always fascinated me throughout my life with his ideas and enthusiasm. He took me like a 'son' into his business venture...

A very big thank you to the team of staff at the school – Bertrand and Nathalie Brassart, Mandy Wagstaff, Sarah Woodbridge and Wayne Edwards. Bertrand made possible the first contacts with Swallow Books, and Nathalie helped Sabine with the testing of the dishes. The delightful presentation of the dishes in the pictures is owed to Mandy, my assistant teacher for many years, now home economist and caterer *extraordinaire*. Her attention to detail is remarkable and her taste exquisite. The ingredients list is due mainly to Wayne, and a lot of typing and the introduction to Sarah, but their main job was to keep the courses running and take away some of my responsibilities so that I could dedicate my time and attention to the book.

Thanks also to the team at Swallow Books, who had to cope with our continental approach (*vive l'entente cordiale!*) Tim Imrie, photographer; Elaine Partington, art director, and her stand-in, Dave Allen, who came to the school every weekend for two months; and Susan Fleming, who adapted my continental English!

More privately, special thanks to all my friends, whom I have neglected since I started on this book, and Betty, in particular, who had to put up with a *ménage à trois* – with a book!

The School would like to thank the following establishments for the loan of props: Ateliers de Ségrières, Paris; David Hicks, Paris; Faiencerie de Giens, Paris; Cristalleries Daum, Paris; Nappes Porthault, Paris; Alfriston Antiques, Alfriston, Sussex; Steamer Trading, Alfriston, Sussex.